The Anxious

In the western world, cities have, arguably, never been more anxious: realistic anxieties about personal safety, and metaphorical anxieties about the uncertain place of the city in culture are the small change of journalism and political debate. In this context, the contemporary revival of city centres is remarkable. But in a culture that largely fears the urban, how can the contemporary city be imagined? How is it supposed to be used or inhabited? What should it look like? What should be its purpose? Which existing forms of urban life might serve as models for a new city? Taking England since the Second World War as its principal focus, this provocative and original book considers the western city at a critical moment in its history.

Among the most urbanised of countries, England is an extraordinary urban laboratory. The energy and thoroughness with which its cities have been transformed in the 1990s have lessons for urban development everywhere. *The Anxious City* examines the problem of the contemporary city through a series of detailed case studies: Poundbury, Milton Keynes, Liverpool's Albert Dock redevelopment, Trafalgar Square, Canary Wharf, the Great Court of the British Museum and central Manchester after the 1996 IRA bomb. It deals with some broader cultural phenomena too: the continuing attraction of picturesque aesthetics, and the lure of southern European urbanism and the complex, contradictory relationship between urbanism in England and the US. The experiences of these places, the book argues, show a culture where the idea of the city remains contested: the frantic redevelopment of city centres in the 1990s represented one vision of the city – the city of spectacular consumption, competing in some imaginary urban race with other world cities. But such development took place against continuing suburbanisation and sprawl. In spite of all the building works, the city was still being worked out.

This book is essential reading for anyone interested in the recent history of the urban. It argues that the contemporary city is uniquely anxious, caught between nostalgia for the past and uncertainty about the future. At a crucial moment in the history of the city, it cuts through the urban propaganda spread by architects and politicians. This unique and challenging study will be of interest to students and practitioners alike.

Richard J. Williams is a Lecturer in the Department of History of Art, University of Edinburgh. His publications include *After Modern Sculpture: Art in the United States and Europe 1965–70* (2000).

The Anxious City

English urbanism in the late twentieth century

Richard J. Williams

Routledge
Taylor & Francis Group

LONDON AND NEW YORK

First published 2004
by Routledge
2 Park Square, Milton Park, Abingdon, Oxon OX14 4RN

Simultaneously published in the USA and Canada
by Routledge
270 Madison Ave, New York, NY 10016

Routledge is an imprint of the Taylor & Francis Group

Typeset in Univers by
Florence Production Ltd, Stoodleigh, Devon
Printed and bound in Great Britain by
TJ International, Padstow, Cornwall

British Library Cataloguing in Publication Data
A catalogue record for this book is available from the British Library

Library of Congress Cataloging in Publication Data
A catalog record for this book has been requested

ISBN   0–415–27926–7 (hbk)
          0–415–27927–5 (pbk)

For Stacy and Abigail

Contents

Illustration credits

The authors and publishers gratefully acknowledge the following for permission to reproduce material in the book:

Laurie Abbott/Richard Rogers Partnership 6.5, 6.6

Archigram Archives 3.5, 3.6

Architectural Review 1.7, 2.3, 2.4, 2.5, 4.1

Kenneth Browne, *Architectural Review* 3.7, 3.8

English Partnerships 3.1

Foster and Partners 6.9, 6.10

Dennis Gilbert/ VIEW, copyright Foster and Partners 8.6, 8.7

Louis Hellman, *Architectural Review* 7.5

Andrew Holt/ VIEW, copyright English Partnerships 1.5, 1.6

HRH the Prince of Wales, *A Vision of Britain* (1989) 2.8

Helmut Jacoby English Partnerships 3.2, 3.3, 3.4

Quentin Hughes 5.3, 5.4, 5.5

Léon Krier 2.10

Carl Laubin 2.12

The National Gallery Picture Library, London 1.1

Richard Rogers Partnership 1.4, 6.4 (photograph by Richard Davies), 6.7

The Royal Collection, 2003, Her Majesty Queen Elizabeth II 2.7

Ian Simpson/ Crosby Homes 9.9, 9.10

Tate Gallery, Liverpool 5.1

Tate Gallery, London 5.6

All other images by the author.

Every effort has been made to contact copyright holders for their permission to reprint material in this book. The publishers would be grateful to hear from any copyright holder who is not acknowledged here and will undertake to rectify any errors or omissions in future editions of the book.

Foreword

The London of Virginia Woolf's *Mrs Dalloway* is a London of multiple fears: anxiety of war and destruction; anxiety of post-war reconstruction; the disequilibrium in high society introduced by the unwanted effects of war; the real shell-shock of returning soldiers, unable to speak of the horrors they have witnessed; anxiety of a new generation determined to break free from the social conventions of their elders; anxiety of the professional class whose preconceptions of neurosis and fear have been shaken by their real irruption in war. All these anxieties and more are set in an apparently unchanged London of springtime parks and broad streets; a pre-war London imagined as without anxiety. Woolf's London, if extended to the London of Second World War anxieties; of bombardment and destruction, of wholesale death from aerial attacks, of claustrophobia in the underground and agoraphobia on the roof-tops at night, and if extended still further to post-terrorist London; subject to random attacks from within, once thought safely confined to the late-nineteenth-century anarchism of Joseph Conrad's *The Secret Agent*, this twentieth-century vision of London stands, for all world cities, for the fears of modernity.

First cataloged in the late nineteenth century, and characterized as phobias, neuroses, and neurasthenias that seemed tied to anxieties of place and space, then incorporated into the sexual etiologies of Freud, only to be resurrected in the modern world by war and real terror; these anxieties that haunt the metropoles of the world, equally haunt their plans for redevelopment. The architecture of their reconstruction, apparently so pure and well-intentioned, so modern and postmodern, is similarly shadowed by fear: fear of contamination by an insensitive populace; of decline in value by an uncertain market; of stylistic obsolescence in a rapidly changing taste culture; and now, more urgently, of security from ground and aerial attack.

If New York's attempt to proudly reassert resistance to terror and freedom from fear by means of a triumphalist architecture of height and display following September 11, 2001, remains the most extreme example of an architectural culture determined by fear, nevertheless all cities share the disease to some degree. The fear of the 'laboring and dangerous classes' of the eighteenth and nineteenth centuries, authorized the clearing and re-development of Haussmann's Paris; the anti-city dis-aggregation supported by the Garden City movements in the late nineteenth century and the linear city movements of the early twentieth; the city-center 'renewal' programs of the 1950s and 60s; and the more recent large-scale commercial redevelopment plans for Berlin, London, and almost every city in the US, all attest to the underlying fear of population density, social heterogeneity, and economic instability. The so-called 'New Urbanism' in the US, with its soft-focus nostal-gia for historical small-town community, is only one example of design masking fears of ethnicity, foreignness, and cultural difference. The pre-slavery images of white clapboard houses with their porches overlooking the green, or of the clustered cottages of Poundbury mocking the historical evolution of the English village, are pictures of barely suppressed fear. And when the fear itself is exacerbated by epic disaster movies, sponsored by the same corporation that sells its own version of New Urbanism in Florida, we can be sure that anxiety now sells in real-estate terms.

In this context, the case studies assembled in this book are essential probes into the anxiety complexes of modern urbanism; stories of apparently benign development projects, launched with all the 'best intentions' in the world, that in fact serve to hide our worst fears from ourselves, and, in the end, act to increase the alienation that, from the beginning of the modern period, has been a watchword of our mental disturbances. Anxiety has also been, wittingly or not, our greatest defence against any positive action that might expose the hollow promises of our bourgeois social conscience.

Anthony Vidler, New York, July 2004

Acknowledgements

First, I want to thank the numerous architects, planners, urbanists, property developers and critics who are the subject of this book. In many ways, it stands in critical relation to their work, and there are sections of it with which they will doubtless disagree: in some ways, I hope that they do. But without them there would be no book. My criticisms, such as they are, spring from a profound interest in, and respect for what they, collectively, do. Those of them who participated in the book by granting interviews, answering letters or granting permission to reproduce images did so with enormous courtesy and willingness, even when my project must have seemed obscure. My thanks to them all.

The book would not have happened without the support of the Leverhulme Trust, who provided a research fellowship for the year 2002–3. Nor could it have happened without the support of my colleagues in History of Art at the University of Edinburgh. My particular thanks go to Martin Hammer, Norma Henderson, Tom Tolley and Richard Thomson. I would also like to thank my students at Edinburgh on the 'Contemporary City' course, to whom I subjected my thinking about cities over the past three years: they made perfectly clear which ideas were nonsense and which weren't. The following people provided interviews, or helped arrange them, for which I am extremely grateful: Peter Babb, Howard Bernstein, Sir Alan Bowness, Kevin Carrucan, Jeremy Dixon, Terry Farrell, Tom Forrest, Norman Foster, Spencer de Grey, Baron Isherwood, Edward Jones, Carl Laubin, Oscar Niemeyer, Richard Rogers, John Rouse, Charles Saumarez Smith, Ian Simpson, Sir Crispin Tickell, David Williams and Graham Wiseman. Mark Crinson, Alex Potts and Brandon Taylor wrote in support of the project at crucial moments. My conversations with Stacy Boldrick, Fiona Bradley, Stephen Cairns, Andrew Causey, Deborah Cherry, Viccy Coltman, Penelope Curtis, David Dunster, Brian Edwards, Clive Fenton, Jane M. Jacobs, Tiffany Jenkins, Sylvia LaHav, Jules Lubbock, Rodney Mace, Matthew Rampley, Helen Rees, Norma Rosso, Richard Sennett, Deborah Strickland, Marcus Verhagen, Victoria Walsh and Iain Boyd Whyte, all had a great impact on my thinking, even when they didn't directly concern the book. Lesley Horne broadened my thinking about anxiety,

Acknowledgements

and didn't wince when I proposed using it as the book's theme. The following people and organisations very kindly granted permission to use images: the *Architectural Review*, English Partnerships, Her Majesty Queen Elizabeth II, Foster and Partners, the late Quentin Hughes, Léon Krier, the National Gallery (London), Richard Rogers, Ian Simpson and the Tate Gallery. My thanks go finally to my editor at Taylor and Francis, Caroline Mallinder, for supporting the project all along.

Edinburgh, November 2003

Chapter 1

The anxious city

Introduction

During the last decade of the twentieth century, English cities underwent a series of astonishing, sometimes bizarre transformations. Against a back-drop of public squalor, these long-decayed and inward-looking conurbations became self-consciously spectacular, juxtaposing extraordinary wealth with equally extraordinary poverty, modernity with the ruins of the past, urban sophistication with entropic decay. The means of making these contrasts was architecture, in the form of new museums, public spaces and monuments. Such architectural spectacles provided agreeable settings in which to enjoy coffee, food and shopping, and, superficially at least, seemed of benefit to those with the time and money to enjoy them. These people also discovered the pleasures of urban wandering, and they aspired to live in increasingly vertiginous glass high rises, whose appearance of technical sophistication spoke of new ways of being in the city.

Some of these changes occurred opportunistically. Manchester, in the north west of England, used the consequences of a terrorist bombing to galvanise the development of a somewhat decayed central city.[1] Many changes, there and in other cities, were facilitated by the Heritage Lottery Fund, which began operating in November 1994 and produced a sudden boom in cultural buildings. A fashion for short vacations to European cities, facilitated by budget airlines, may have also contributed to change, as no doubt, did a growing economy.[2] However, I am concerned here not with the reasons for these changes, but with their nature. Everywhere, it seemed, from Hull to South Kensington, got or had plans for some new architectural symbol of modernity and sophistication. A preliminary list of projects might include the following: the Brindleyplace and Bull Ring developments in central

Birmingham; the waterfront in Bristol; the Royal Armouries and Millennium Square in Leeds; the waterfront and Ropewalks in Liverpool; Canary Wharf, the Millennium Dome and Tate Modern in London; the Lowry in Salford; the Imperial War Museum in Trafford; the Millennium Quarter in Manchester; the waterfront of the Tyne including the Baltic Arts Centre in Gateshead and the Wilkinson Eyre 'winking eye' footbridge; and the National Centre for Popular Music and Millennium Galleries in Sheffield. At the time of writing, a clutch of urban projects in the planning stage included a dramatic expansion of London to the east (the 'Thames Gateway'), and a true skyscraper in Manchester.[3]

Now, on the scale of the contemporaneous changes in Berlin, Kuala Lumpur or Chongqing, these transformations were often relatively small.[4] But they took place in a country with a long established anti-urban culture, whose architecture has tended to the domestic and inward looking, contriving where possible, an accord between the urban and the natural, an aesthetic expressed most clearly in the picturesque. English forms of Modernism, although sometimes exported, represented a compromise with tradition and nature, at odds with the unapologetically urban expression it stood for elsewhere (Pevsner 1964). The English city is therefore in some senses oxymoronic. In English architectural criticism, traditionally the city has only grudgingly existed, meeting approval when it least resembles itself, which is to say when it most closely approaches the condition of nature.

What happens when a nation such as England suddenly wants an urban culture is, therefore, a matter of more than local interest, for it calls into question the meaning of the urban itself. What England does in terms of the way it (re-)imagines its cities is not done in isolation but relates to international practice, principally in the US and continental Europe. It acts as both a local interpretation of, and a form of critical commentary on urbanism in these places, and the way we think about these broader urbanisms ought to be regarded in part through the English example. For despite England's economic wealth, the continuity of its political traditions and the apparent security of its place in the world, the way it has sought to re-image itself through the medium of urban architecture has put identity questions into play in the most dramatic way. England's urban changes, when seen against those of China, may be physically small – but *ideologically* they are not, for they suppose nothing less than a revolution in the way the urban is understood.[5]

Now in using the word revolution, I am not, it must be made clear, imagining something complete, finished and beyond contestation: rather, the reverse. The new architecture of urban England does indeed suppose a revolution in the way its cities are consumed and inhabited, but it has been only partially realised, and as is the way with so much of English culture, it divides along class lines. It is a revolution very largely of bourgeois taste, which excludes that of the working class as traditionally defined, and also that of the aristocracy, such as it still exists.[6] It exists in tension with these other kinds of taste, and with the other attitudes to the urban that underpin them. If, for example, one pattern of English urban life in the 1990s has been the boom in central city apartments for the wealthy, this has to be seen against a pattern of continuing population decline, or at best, stagnation. Outside of London, no city has registered significant growth; and what growth there has been in the capital is recent, and not great in historical terms. The English city revolution is visually and architecturally spectacular, but it exists in a state of tension with other existing ways of perceiving, and being in, the city. If the revolution has been supported by capital and by government, it has equally met with resistance. The English city is, it could be said, still contested as an idea. Unlike its counterparts in continental Europe, it is still being worked out.[7]

The word I use to describe the city's ambiguous condition is *anxiety*. Anxiety describes the uncertainty of the English city's current identity, its ambiguity vis-à-vis past and future visions of the city, the lack of resolution about its position vis-à-vis private and public realms, and the competing visions of consumption and residence. Throughout the book, I use the term anxiety in two related, but distinct ways. First, I mean it to describe the realistic experience of being in the city. I mean to suggest that the English city in its current state may often be actually productive of anxiety, for a variety of demonstrable reasons. This is not an architecturally determinist argument, but one based on the notion that the use and inhabitation of cities is *learned*, and culturally specific. The English, in other words, have learned to be anxious in the modern city. The second sense in which I use anxiety is as a metaphor. I argue that the English city may be described as anxious because its cultural position is so uncertain. The imaginative and material investment in the English city in the 1990s needs to be set against a cultural context in which the city was long regarded as an alien phenomenon, from which those who could, fled. Its present position is anything but resolved. Therefore, throughout this book, I describe the city both *as* anxious in this metaphorical way, and *as productive of* anxiety in those who use or inhabit it.

The English problem

England's anxieties about the city are unique. I say England here, rather than Britain or the UK, because in respect of urban questions the English experience is distinct from those of the countries it dominates. Scotland's cities, whatever their material difficulties, have maintained an urban élite, supported by political and cultural institutions, and a distinct body of property law that has helped maintain dense urban habitation (see Gifford *et al.* 1984). The experiences of Wales, and especially Northern Ireland are different again, with the political capitals and biggest cities resembling English colonial outposts, and the urban élites and political centres that such status implies. The urban cultures of the four UK nations are also legally and politically separate, controlled by different legislatures; the Urban Task Force led by Lord Rogers that reported in 1999, referred only to England (HM Government 1999). England's urban culture is distinct, and it needs to be treated as such.

England's distinctness in urban matters is represented by a historic culture of anti-urbanism that has had demographic, as well as artistic, expression. There has been substantial population loss from the biggest cities in the second half of the twentieth century, only partially arrested in recent years. Greater London's decline has been especially marked; it shrank from a peak population of 8,350,000 in 1939, to 6,700,000 in 1991, a decline of about 20 per cent. The populations of the other main conurbations tended to show similar losses, Greater Manchester and Merseyside in the north west of the country both registering substantial declines. More marked still have been the losses from each of the core cities of these conurbations, 725,000 to 439,000 in the case of Manchester, 850,000 to 460,000 in the case of Liverpool.[8] Similar, if less marked, patterns could be shown for Newcastle and Bradford. Nicholas Schoon, writing for the Joseph Rowntree Foundation, a charity that supports sociological research, has claimed that England's metropolitan regions suffered a net loss of 300 people per day to 'smaller towns and the countryside' (Schoon 2001: 6).

Most of these people have gone to suburbs just outside the boundaries of existing cities, and in this respect, England's experience is not unique, as urban population decline is a fact of the developed world. The same phenomenon can be seen in cities such as Washington DC, New York or Berlin.[9] However, what is specific to the English case has been a highly cultivated anti-urban culture, expressed at all levels of society. Despite its condition as the second most urbanised nation in Europe, Prime Minister Stanley Baldwin could declare in the 1920s 'England is the country' (Wiener 1980: 6).[10]

The English city since the nineteenth century has been a place of darkness that is essentially foreign, a site of alienation and estrangement. The industrial novel is perhaps its most familiar cultural expression. In the nineteenth century, Charles Dickens and Elizabeth Gaskell constructed a sense of urbanity that is, in terms of national identity, other, despite the fact that by the time they were writing England was in population terms already predominantly urban. D. H. Lawrence did the same in the twentieth century.[11] This anti-urban cultural tradition was reinforced by late nineteenth- and early twentieth-century fictions by William Morris and H. G. Wells, in which urban life was seen to dissolve. In Morris' *News From Nowhere*, industrialised London vanishes, to be replaced by an enlightened state of pure air, greenery and unalienated labour. The industrial epoch signals its presence by the ruin of the Houses of Parliament, which to the city's new inhabitants is a 'silly old building', mysterious but essentially benign (Morris 1984: 209).

Raymond Williams' *The Country and the City* made clear for the first time in an academic context the weakness of the position that the city occupies in English culture (R. Williams 1973: 1–8). In both Williams' work and the literary texts he discusses, the city is always alien, a place that is both unnatural and unreal. Real life must take place somewhere else, in Williams' own case the Black Mountains of his Welsh childhood. The works he describes in *The Country and the City* are all profoundly anti-urban in which the narrator is always alienated from the city. This position would not matter if it was presented as one aspect of English literary culture, but anti-urbanism is presented as its true condition. The city in English cultural life is the place from which one traditionally escapes. For the political left there is an equal, and complementary anti-urban tradition, that of the city as a symbol of capital, which is fought against. Williams relates a story about H. G. Wells: exiting a radical political meeting in London, Wells looked around and declared that the city was 'a measure of the obstacle, of how much must be moved if there was to be any change' (see R. Williams 1973: 5). Williams' work, now thirty years old, has been widely read and continues to inform academic discussions of English culture including the present one.

A commentary on Williams by the cultural historian James Donald has made clear the extent to which Williams' own position underwrites his thesis. Williams' background in the Black Mountains of Wales is rural, and for him, as Donald demonstrates, the life of that place always has a greater sense of reality about it than the life of the city. It is real specifically because it is there and nowhere else, whereas the city's cosmopolitanism (at least in Williams' understanding of it) means that it has no such deep roots. Cities might as well be anywhere. Donald's study therefore makes clear the extent to which this well known study of cultural anti-urbanism is itself anti-urbanist; the power of anti-urbanism extends to ostensibly even-handed discussion of it as a phenomenon (Donald 1999: 148–9).

Anti-urbanism is not only responsible for the production of litera-ture, but also, as Martin Wiener argued in 1980 and Will Hutton elaborated in 1996, a political phenomenon that literally forms England's cities. In his *English Culture and the Decline of the Industrial Spirit* (1980), Wiener wrote that England's post-1945 industrial weakness resulted from a nineteenth-century failure to modernise socially as well as industrially. Industrialisation, as manifest in Manchester, Birmingham and Leeds, was achieved with relatively little social change, leaving the established class structure more or less intact. In particular, industrialisation failed to weaken the power (both cultural and economic) of inherited wealth. 'The rentier aristocracy', he wrote 'succeeded to a large degree in maintaining a cultural hegemony and [. . .] in reshaping the industrial bourgeoisie in its own image' (Wiener 1980: 6). This had two specific consequences, Wiener argued, first, that the bourgeoisie aspired to the aristocratic cultural model, investing in land and a life of gentlemanly leisure rather than industry and the town, and second, that it provided 'legitimacy to antimodern sentiments'. Both tendencies legislated in favour of the country rather than the city, with the general result that England now lacks an established urban bourgeoisie of the types found in the US, Northern Europe or even, to a lesser extent, in Scotland.[12]

Wiener's thesis of 1980 can be said to have been elaborated and updated by the economic journalist Will Hutton in *The State We're In* (1996).[13] Wiener's analysis ends in 1980, but Hutton has pointed to the continuing attractiveness of the gentlemanly ideal, which made the development of an English civic culture unlikely: 'Educated apart and socially apart', the English establishment

> have no republican sense of civic responsibility. Their world is private. Their manners are cultivated. A studied and amused dis-interestedness is their hallmark [. . .] Long before opting out was exalted to the status of a political philosophy, these were the opted out.
>
> (Hutton 1996: 44–5)

These contemporary aristocrats, or quasi-aristocrats may inhabit parts of urban Britain, typically London, but they have no stake in the public services the city provides, as they can, and do, buy themselves out of it. The gentrification of certain parts of English cities since Wiener's book has not, Hutton would argue, produced a strengthened urban culture, but the reverse. Because so many of the city's new residents have no need of the collective services the city can provide – its schools, its healthcare, its public transportation, its public spaces – they deteriorate as a result.[14]

In summary, the continued existence of the English city is compromised as an idea by a deep anti-urban culture. Materially the city strongly exists, albeit with some population erosion, but positive images of urban identity are rare. Instead, 'deep England' as Patrick Wright has termed what there is of a national culture, is construed in rural terms (see Wright 1985). John Constable's iconic painting of 1821, *Landscape, Noon: The Haywain* (London, National Gallery) is an image of rural labour that contrives the appearance of a settled order in deepest Suffolk. It is this, rather than an image of urban or industrial vitality, that has become a kind of national symbol (Figure 1.1).

Anti-urban culture therefore creates immense difficulty for the imagination of the English city. The establishment in July 2000 of a directly elected London mayor notwithstanding, English city politicians exercise less power over financial and legislative matters than their counterparts in the US and continental Europe (Schoon 2001: 340–5). There has until recently rarely been a political language here to describe the city in terms other than decline. On both the left and right there has been deep scepticism about the existence of cities at all. It represents a view, widespread on the left, of cities as essentially redundant products of historical processes that are now complete. The job of the elected officials was simply to manage that decline (see Peck and Ward 2002: 76–94). In this scenario, the city, in some distant future, ceases to be.

1.1
Landscape, Noon:
The Haywain,
1821
John Constable

The anxious city

The English city therefore exists in a curious state: it is an undeniable, and in some cases, burgeoning, material fact, yet it exists in a culture that still largely wishes to deny or repress it.[15] This ambivalent condition may be described as anxious. Throughout this book, I regard anxiety as manifest in both a realistic response to actual urban conditions, and as a metaphor which informs the wider cultural understanding of urban life. In Freudian terms, anxiety is an affective state, a condition of unpleasurably tense excitation, which one is not able to control by discharging. Its cause, in the main, is a failure by the ego to master the external world, morality or the unconscious. In other words, it may be a quite natural response to external danger; or it may result from (let us say) the restrictions it places on the exercise of the libido; or it may be a failure to master other demands placed on it by the unconscious. In all these forms, anxiety may be quite inexpedient, producing either an inappropriate flight response from a perfectly safe situation, or worse, if the symptoms are extreme, paralysis (Freud 1977: 392–411).

Now in my summary of Freud's thinking, anxiety is suffered by an individual in response to external or internal stimuli. It might not immediately seem to have much to do with the city, or the way we perceive cities, yet as Anthony Vidler has argued, in Freud they were closely connected (see Vidler 1992, 2000). In 'The Uncanny' (1919) Freud reports the disturbing feelings provoked by his being lost in unfamiliar Italian town. Not only is he lost, but he finds himself time after time in the part of the town frequented by prostitutes, where his conspicuousness, as a Viennese bourgeois 'was beginning to excite attention'. His anxiety rises as he repeatedly returns to the place he most wishes to avoid (Freud 1985b: 359). Here architectural space and the experience of anxiety are intimately connected; the former does not necessarily cause the latter but it certainly helps stage it, and it exacerbates its development.

Freud's account of the uncanny has suggested new, non-formalist ways of 'doing' architectural history in which the apprehension of space by the user, and the related histories of its apprehension, are the key terms of analysis. This is a suggestion taken up especially by Vidler, for whom the uncanny is inherently bound up with the apprehension of space (Vidler 1992: 53). In relation to the uncanny therefore, Vidler's reference point is not only Freud, but the contemporaneous work by the philosophers associated with the Frankfurt School of Social Research, specifically Walter Benjamin, Siegfried Kracauer and Georg Simmel, who all marked out the modern city as peculiarly anxiety-inducing. At the same time, as Vidler has described, new kinds of neurotic symptoms were being codifed, which seemed to their observers to be produced by modern life: agoraphobia, for example, a paralysing anxiety produced in urban space, a condition which much interested the Viennese architect Camillo Sitte (Vidler 2000: 26–7). Vidler writes in summary that, 'the metropolitan uncanny was increasingly conflated with metropolitan illness, a pathological condition that potentially afflicted the inhabitants of all great cities' (Vidler 1992: 6).

In the Frankfurt School's writings, the city's new forms, particularly the burgeoning spaces of transit and commerce, the shopping arcades, waiting rooms and hotel lobbies, were productive of new and neurotic forms of behaviour. I will cite two examples of this: first, Simmel's classic essay 'The Metropolis and Mental Life', in which the author argues that the modern city forces the visitor to develop a protective psychological barrier, to contrive a neurosis of non-communication as it were, in order to protect himself from the unprecedented stimulation that it causes him (Leach 1997: 73). The adoption of the willed state of the 'blasé' becomes the only way to survive.[16] Second is Kracauer's now equally well-known essay, 'The Hotel Lobby' which ironically describes how the modern city has effectively replaced the purposeful, moral assembly of the church with the godless, arbitrary gathering of the waiting room (explored further by Tallach in Leach 2002: 139–51). In each of these accounts, the inhabitant of modern space is simultaneously drawn to that space, and alienated by it. In her useful account of these theoretical approaches, the architectural historian Hilde Heynen has written that the modern city is a unique space, in which anxiety is 'inherent' (Heynen 1999: 72).

I would add that the interest in the relationship between anxiety and the city is not restricted to the historical past, but continues to the consideration of present-day phenomena. The representation of Los Angeles, for example, in the differing works of Mike Davis, Fredric Jameson and Charles Jencks has made fear a key term in architectural-historical discussions of that city (Davis 1990, 1999; Jameson in Leach 1997: 238–47; Jencks 1993). We now expect Los Angeles to be represented in academic discourse as a terrifying disciplinary space in which the hapless visitor is imperilled by the city's tactics of surveillance and deterrence. Jameson's well-known essay on the John Portman-designed Westin Bonaventure hotel in downtown LA, 'The Cultural Logic of Late Capitalism', describes an architectural scenario in which the rhetoric of modernity is exacerbated to the extent that the visitor can no longer find his way in or out, or for that matter, around (Jameson in Leach 1997: 238–47). In Jameson's hyperbolic text, the Bonaventure is a space that has evolved beyond the reasonable comprehension of its users, such that (to the author's apparent pleasure) it no longer seems to make commercial sense[17] (Figure 1.2).

1.2
**Westin
Bonaventure
Hotel, Los
Angeles, 1976,
architect:
John Portman**

My use of the term anxiety has a good deal to do with these accounts of the experience of the individual in the modern city. But it has a specifically English character too. I think all of the urban spaces used as case studies in this book are, in one way or another, anxiety-producing because they inadvertently stage peculiarly English uncertainties about city life. Superficially they reiterate the great city forms of the past – the arcades, passages, boulevards, squares, towers and so on – but because they are in England, they unwittingly position the visitor in a situation for which he is ill-prepared.[18] They are idealisations of urban life, which can only be inhabited uneasily. So the refurbished Albert Dock (see Chapter 5) refers picturesquely to urban Italy, yet despite the café tables and neoclassical architecture, it is functionally very different, having much more in common with a suburban shopping mall than central Bologna. Trafalgar Square (see Chapter 6) too has been the subject of a major refurbishment, producing a public space that is now architecturally tidy, but ideologically uneasy, neither acknowledging nor erasing the imperial past, and whose use must be formally programmed. Canary Wharf (see Chapter 7) resurrects the vocabulary of early twentieth-century Chicago to create a vast business district that is *in* London, but somehow not *of* it – its official presentation, as well as criticism of it, is suffused with the language of anxiety. The spectacular Great Court of the British Museum (see Chapter 8), despite its location in one of the greatest symbols of Empire, most closely resembles the non-place of the airport departure lounge (with the attendant sense of panic). Or, finally, the new public spaces of Manchester (see Chapter 9), extraordinary as they are, demonstrate a palpable fear about the libertarian possibilities of the city. There, new spaces for public gathering abound, but it is gathering that has to be kept under surveillance, limited to easily monitored practices of consumption[19] (Figure 1.3).

These are all anxious spaces in that they are generative of anxiety, and I suggest that England 'does' the anxious city very well. However, I want to argue here for an expanded use of the term anxiety to refer not only to the experience of the individual in modern space, but also to a collective

1.3
**Exchange Square,
Manchester,
1997–2000,
architect: Martha
Schwarz and
EDAW**

experience of the city. This makes the term anxiety slide towards metaphor, away from being simply a label for a psychological condition, but as I hope will become clear this usage provides a helpful vocabulary to describe urban experience. It also has a precedent in Freud. Consider, for example, what he says about panic in large institutions, citing the army and the Church, where a negative thought can be quickly transferred from one individual to another, with catastrophic general effect. Freud extrapolates this sense of group panic from his thinking about individuals, and, in so doing, loosens anxiety's ties with a demonstrable psychological state, with a physiological basis. It is, in the following passage, halfway to metaphor: 'A panic', he writes,

> arises if a group of that kind becomes disintegrated. Its character-
> istics are that none of the orders given by superiors are any longer
> listened to, and that each individual is only solicitous on his own
> account, and without any consideration for the rest. The mutual
> ties have ceased to exist, and a gigantic senseless fear is set free.
>
> (Freud 1985a: 125)

Now we have come to understand cities as much more heterogeneous and complex organisms than institutions such as the army, yet often when we speak of the city, or a debate about its identity, we mean the interests of a clearly identifiable social or professional group: architects, for example. This being the case, anxiety is certainly possible as a group psychological state. Throughout this book, the English city is meant in these terms, where a professional group, specifically architects and the allied professions, speak on behalf of the totality.

For an example of how anxiety can be understood in this collective sense, I will refer to the architect Richard Rogers and his 1992 book *A New London*, written with the then Labour spokesman for the arts, Mark Fisher. The book is a manifesto of sorts, its publication coinciding with the 1992 general election campaign, which Labour lost to a fourth Conservative term. It is a critique of existing British urban policy, especially its relative lack of interest in urban design. Britain's cities look bad, they argue, and will perform badly as a result. As one critic of the book put it 'we have become dowdy and depressing and should go out and buy a new hat' (Campbell 1992: 19). The experience of Docklands is a prime negative example for them, a programme that favoured market instruments of city development. The results, Rogers and Fisher argued, were patchy and anti-social, producing a handful of landmarks, but large areas of waste or derelict land in between. The alternatives they offered included the pedestrianisation of the north bank of the Thames, the creation of a new ceremonial route from Soho to Waterloo, via a reconstructed and civilised Trafalgar Square, and a monorail across Hungerford Bridge (Figure 1.4). They argue:

> London is failing to keep up with the progress of its continental counterparts [. . .] Trafalgar Square was once the heart of an empire, Piccadilly Circus the centre of the universe. Today they are just two more jammed roundabouts in a shabby city playing a less and less culturally central role, at least where the vitality of city life is concerned, on the European, and indeed world stage.
>
> (Rogers and Fisher 1992: xiv)

Thwarted by Labour's electoral failure in 1992, Rogers returned to the theme with increased urgency in 1997: 'Rudderless and polluted, this great city's future hangs in the balance' (Rogers 1997: 106). Anxiety is a useful term for analysing statements like these, as it describes an affective state brought on in relation to a possible future, rather than the present. As an expedient state, it facilitates an appropriate reaction to a future possibility, putting one in a state of hypothetical readiness for the unknown. And here in Rogers' statement is an illustration of the anxious process. They articulate a set of fears about the future of the city, specifically that it has lost a world role as the centre of Empire, that its decline is inevitable, and will be increasingly manifest in material terms, and that, London's peer cities, once subservient, now beat it in some imaginary urban competition. At best, London will, they fear, be left behind; at worst, it faces ecological catastrophe.[20] The expedient action Rogers and Fisher propose, the new monuments and linkages and pathways, will ameliorate this otherwise inevitable process. There is much in common between the common affective state of neurotic anxiety in an individual, and this statement of Rogers' in which a group fear is articulated. Both concern fears in the imaginative future rather than the present; both involve a certain amount of catastrophic thinking; both are precipitative of action, in Rogers' case a drastic restructuring of the centre of the capital in which very little remains untouched.

I have already discussed how England's new city spaces might be actually productive of anxiety in the viewer. However, what Rogers' statements exemplify is the broader metaphorical condition of the anxious city, in which the English city is always in terminal decline. In English architectural culture Rogers has become a self-appointed prophet of doom, through books such as *Cities for a Small Planet* (1997) and *Cities for a Small Country* (2000), through his work for the government appointed Urban Task Force, and through his fluent interventions in the professional media about the government's failure to implement its own recommendations (*Building Design* 2002, Hetherington 2002). In all of these public statements, clear anxieties are articulated: the English city is ever more brutal and uncivilised by comparison with its continental rivals; each day it slips further behind them; ever more drastic corrective action is required. However, it is not only Rogers, but the professional culture that makes public these anxieties. Rogers' anxiety about the condition of the English city in relation to the European city is reiterated by the professional journals, especially the *Architectural Review*, and to a lesser extent, the *Architect's Journal* and the *RIBA Journal*. And there have been many books published in which a similar argument is made, contrasting the deregulated, free-market orientated English city with an urbane, ordered, specifically European model (Rowe 1997; Rykwert 2000; Worpole 2000).

And further, these anxieties about the English city have been a constant and developing theme in the popular media, the subject of articles in newspapers, and programming on radio and television.[21]

The Millennium Dome

Let me present an extremely well known example of a building that exemplifies what I mean here by anxiety: the Millennium Dome (Figure 1.5). A remarkable engineering achievement, it defined a new east London quarter, but was the object of the most sustained and brutal criticism in the news media, as if its scale and the poverty of the reception were in direct proportion. Built for the government by the Richard Rogers Partnership on the site of a derelict gasworks on the Greenwich peninsula in east London, opposite the Isle of Dogs, as a building, the Dome was impressive in scale. A huge hemispherical marquee, 364 metres in diameter with the world's largest flexible membrane roof, it was covered in 80,000 square metres of glass fibre, supported by twelve steel masts 90 metres in height, bearing cables anchored at ground level. The 50-metre height of the interior could easily accommodate

1.5
Millennium Dome, 2000, exterior view, architect: Richard Rogers Partnership

existing London monuments such as Nelson's column (*Architectural Review* 2000: 52). In daylight the membrane was more or less opaque; at night it was ghostly and translucent.

It was extraordinarily expensive, costing £758,000,000 overall, a figure which included a Heritage Lottery Fund grant of £509,000,000, making it six times as costly as the next largest cultural project supported by the same fund (*Architectural Review* 2000: 57). Urbanistically, it was highly significant. From Canary Wharf, it completed a long vista from One Canada Square, visually connecting the south and north of the Thames. And it brought a huge transport infrastructure to the area, such as the Jubilee Line underground extension, which included a dramatic and only briefly used station at North Greenwich.

The negative media reception, which lasted the duration of its opening, had much to do with its continuing financial insecurity, but much centred on the persistent lack of clarity of purpose, in particular what it contained. Originally proposed in 1994 by Michael Heseltine, then deputy Prime Minister in the last Conservative government, who thought of it as a kind of exhibition hall, it was revived by the first Labour government in 1997 (in spite of having criticised it whilst in opposition) who adopted it as a symbol of their own political project. Peter Mandelson, the government minister responsible for the Dome, and its chief advocate, said that he wanted the Dome to 'capture the spirit of modern Britain – a nation that is confident, excited, impatient for the future' (Seldon 2001: 548). But from its inception to the opening in the last hours of 1999, its content remained mysterious. On its opening it became clear it was a temporary indoor theme park, with human-istic 'zones' designed by leading architects (Zaha Hadid did the Mind Zone, Nigel Coates the Body Zone, Eva Jiricna the Faith Zone, Imagination the Journey Zone) (Figure 1.6). As well as these areas, organised as discrete stalls using the aesthetic of the garden fête, according to the *Architectural Review*, there was to be a spectacular theatrical show on the hour, with music by the rock musician and producer, Peter Gabriel (*Architectural Review* 2000: 54). The essentially humanistic, multicultural and secular tone of the exhibits were disturbed by a residual sense of obligation to the Christian origins of the cele-bration – so the official guide to the Dome opened with two explicitly Christian messages, from the Queen and the Reverend Richard Burridge, Dean of King's College, respectively.[22]

The Dome's opening, on New Year's Eve 1999, was widely considered a disaster. Ten thousand guests were specially invited to share champagne and mince pies with the Queen and the Prime Minister, but many barely arrived in time: many had to queue for seven hours to collect tickets which ought to have been mailed, while persistent security failures

1.6
Millennium Dome, 2000, interior view, architect: Richard Rogers Partnership

kept thousands marooned at Stratford underground station (see, for example White 2000).

Functionally and symbolically, the Dome had two clear London antecedents, the Great Exhibition of 1851, which produced the extraordinary structure of the Crystal Palace, and the Festival of Britain of 1951, which established the South Bank of the Thames as a cultural zone (Millennium Experience 2000: 5). The latter provided an architectural image too, namely the Dome of Discovery, designed by Ralph Tubbs[23] (Figure 1.7). Like the Millennium Dome, these two festivals were state-contrived celebrations of national identity. Unlike the Millennium Dome, they represented that identity at two periods when it could be said to have been relatively uncontested. The 1851 Exhibition used the engineering triumph of the Crystal Palace to represent a nation secure in its imperial position. The Palace itself demonstrated the nation's technological mastery, while the objects it contained, brought from every part of the Empire, showed off the extent of its political and military conquests (Crinson 1996: 62–70). It was an overt material symbol of imperial power. A century later, the Festival of Britain took place in an impoverished and battered nation, whose cities had been half-ruined by war. But the experience of war created, albeit temporarily, a shared culture which was enshrined in the creation of the Welfare State (see *Architectural*

Review 1951). The Festival represented a post-war and post-imperial identity, very different from that of 1851, but no less secure. In contrast, the Millennium Dome was built in a nation that was affluent, but increasingly ill at ease with its identity. Politically, Britain's existence was called into question by its membership of a growing European Union, and by the ambitions of its own constituent states and regions.[24] And economically, after the convulsions of the 1980s, there was little shared sense of what the nation's distinctive business was.

      The unease about national identity resulted in difficulties in establishing a clear programme for the Dome.[25] Its premise, the celebration of the year 2000, was absurd, for as Peter Davey noted in the Architectural Review,

1.7
**Dome of
Discovery,
1951, architect:
Ralph Tubbs**

Britain was no longer an especially Christian country (Davey 2000b).[26] The positive reception of the Dome, made unlikely by the calamity of the opening night, was made less likely still by the uncertainty of the content, which could neither celebrate and glory in the nation's power (1851), nor look forward to a better and healthier future, free of the immediate threat of war (1951). The Dome therefore occupied an anxious position in English culture; furthermore, it was (as I say of a number of buildings throughout the book) itself productive of anxiety. What was advertised as a pleasurable experience was confusing and expensive, with a variety of conflicting and often negative messages from the news media colouring the experience. A *Guardian* editorial at the end of the year quoted from exasperated visitors, whose experience best resembled a visit to a peculiar shopping centre, for which privilege they paid £20 (see *The Guardian* 2000). Other reviews noted an inclusive-seeming but uncomfortable mixture of high and low culture, a combination that was politically correct but unsettling for the visitor (*Sunday Times* 2000). On the evidence of the newspaper reviews, alienation and disappointment were the key terms of engagement with the Dome.[27]

What does the critical reception of the Dome tell us? On the one hand it is the story of a prolonged financial crisis, with a cast of increasingly desperate characters (see Seldon 2001: 549–50).[28] On the other hand it is a story of prolonged anxiety about identity, in which a new government desires a material symbol of renewal, an English *grand projet*, signifying its commitment to modernity and the metropolis. Such a desire articulates an anxiety that England has been left behind, a fear often expressed by the Dome's designer, Richard Rogers. But the action such desire expedites, the hurried building of the Dome without any clear cultural programme, or content, or symbolism, is itself productive of an anxious experience. I cite the perceived failure of the Dome as one particular instance of England's city problem. It is on the one hand an example of the urban revolution that I say has overtaken English cities in the 1990s – a self-consciously modern architectural spectacle designed by an architect whose tastes have, over two decades since the Pompidou Centre, informed the changing bourgeois perception of the city. Like Rogers' earlier buildings, it speaks of new ways of being in, and of consuming the city. At the same time, the Dome at the time of its building was held in tension by both its surroundings and its contents, both of which represent alternative ideas of the city. Its surroundings, the blasted, post-industrial wastes of the Greenwich peninsula in the mid-1990s, spoke of urban decay, the emptying out of the city, the loss of its purpose and role. And the contents of the Dome, an uncertain mélange of trade fair and circus had little to do with the site.[29] The uncertainty about the Dome's purpose and its contents indicated wider uncertainties about the place of cities in English culture. But as my account of it shows, it is productive of further anxiety on the part of its users. The attempt to make a symbol of contemporary urbanity in a culture inimical to it produces a space that is anxious in both experiential and metaphorical terms.

Methods and sources

This book is not, and does not attempt to be, comprehensive. To begin with, the definition of 'city' that it employs is precisely focused on aesthetic questions. It is essentially an art historical definition of city, in that it is primarily concerned with the city at the level of aesthetic representation. This does not mean that questions of use, or inhabitation, or social demography are excluded, but that they appear in terms of their relation to the city as a form of material representation. Very close to the territory covered here, both methodologically and in terms of context is Nan Ellin's important *Postmodern Urbanism* (1996), which has particular emphases on France and the US, and is cited throughout. But thinking more widely, there are a number of art historical models for the present work, one example being T. J. Clark's widely read *Painting of Modern Life*, a history of late nineteenth-century Paris as represented in the painting of the Impressionists. In Clark's view, the city's new forms both frame and permit new modes of aesthetic representation (Clark 1984). In my argument, the subject is the aesthetic representation embodied in the city's forms themselves: how is an actual, or desired for, change in the social city represented in architecture?

Walter Benjamin's work on Paris is symbolically important here, in the form of the vast but incomplete *Arcades Project* (Benjamin 2000, discussion in Gilloch 2002: 113–39). Benjamin's work focused on the spectacular city of consumption, working towards a history of the experience of modernity through the architectural figures of the modern city. His understanding of the city, like the one deployed here, was of it as a multi-authored, layered phenomenon, whose existence was found as much in its representation in cultural ephemera, as in material objects like buildings. The *Arcades Project* therefore makes use of an astonishing range of ephemeral material.

The present work, needless to say, is no *Arcades Project*. It privileges architectural criticism, but it does make use of a very wide range of other sources on urban experience, from the novel, to advertising, to non-professional journalism, to cartoons. I make good use of material that might seem ephemeral, such as the perspective drawings made for architects before a building is built, the kind of image designed for general dissemination and consumption. Produced mostly but not always in house, sometimes using a professional renderer like Helmut Jacoby, these were traditionally pen-and-wash drawings but have increasingly been made digitally (see, for example, the Foster images in Chapter 6). In seeking public approval, these images are often quietly polemical, emphasising the familiar and traditional elements of scheme, or presenting a spectacular if idealised vision of public life. For me, these kinds of images more than anything else are revelatory of otherwise rather obscure ideological positions, a repository of what Benjamin referred to as the 'optical unconscious' (Benjamin 1979: 240–57; Krauss 1993: 178). Produced for clients, or public dissemination, or both, they exist in a highly compromised condition, attempting to imagine the desire of the other. Yet it is precisely in this air of compromise that something important is revealed, and in paying attention to them we can move away from the urban as a history of great works. The urban is, as we instinctively know, not simply about production, but about the relationship between production and consumption, in which superficially negative or passive processes may be of great import.

Now, in citing Benjamin, it should be clear that my emphasis on the spectacular city is not made from an uncritical, affirmative point of view. Henri Lefebvre has written of the dangers of such an uncritical perspective on the city:

> The section of space assigned to an architect – perhaps by 'devel-opers', perhaps by government agencies – is affected by calculations that he may have some intimation of but with which he is certainly not well acquainted. This space has nothing innocent about it: it answers to particular tactics and strategies; it is, quite simply, the space of the dominant mode of production, and hence the space of capitalism, governed by the bourgoisie.
>
> (Lefebvre in Leach 1997: 144)

This amounts, he writes, to nothing more than the 'reign of the façade over space' (Lefebvre in Leach 1997: 145). I have a good deal of sympathy with this position. Nevertheless, I think that the 'reign of the façade' needs further interrogation rather than dismissal, especially in a country such as England where the façade (both literally, and in the wider metaphorical sense that Lefebvre employs) for much of the twentieth century held little appeal.[30] In this statement of Lefebvre's, which, admittedly, I take out of context, the conceptualisation of the market is a little crude. As Wiener and Hutton have argued, markets are social phenomena, with mutable effects, not least in the field of architecture. England's relative similarity to the rest of northern Europe has not prevented it from producing significantly different city spectacles. Its peculiarity deserves investigation.

In citing Benjamin and Lefebvre, I emphasise that the book stands in critical relation not only to the spectacular city itself, but also to the architectural discourse that affirms it. In particular, it should be regarded as a critical commentary on the vast body of architectural polemic that has lately appeared on the virtues of the compact European city, of which Siena is possibly the prime exemplar. A preliminary list of this literature might include George Baird's *The Space of Appearance* (1995), Richard Rogers' three books on urbanism, Peter G. Rowe's *Civic Realism* (1997), Witold Rybczynski's *City Life* (1996), Joseph Rykwert's *The Seduction of Place* (2000), Ken Worpole's *Here Comes the Sun* (2001), and the publications of such organisations as the Commission for Architecture and Built Environment (CABE). In the same context I would cite Nicholas Schoon's *The Chosen City*. Schoon, an environmental journalist, distrusts the design-led solutions of the architects, but otherwise subscribes to their position (Schoon 2001: 14). Like them, he thinks a better, more just city can be built on an explicitly European model, with more dense forms of habitation, and a more controlled relationship between the public sector and the market. In all of this polemic, the author's principal concern is to imagine a better future. Rowe would like the world to look like Siena; Rykwert wishes England to acquire the dense urbanity of New York; Worpole thinks that urban life will be improved by building parks. All regard the city's model as essentially European rather than American[31]; all to greater or lesser degrees favour the patronage of the state over the market; all regard architecture as having a moral purpose that involves a restraining role on (what is viewed as) a more or less immoral market. Architecture, they argue, requires the market's patronage to a greater or lesser extent, but it should exist in a critical relationship with it. It is the position theorised by Kenneth Frampton as 'Critical Regionalism' in which architecture is a moral preserve, a necessarily marginal culture operating in opposition to the culture of capital (Frampton 1992: 314–27).

My project stands in critical relation to these works, not so much in the sense that I challenge what they say, but in that I use them as evidence of an entrenched ideological position. I am not an architect, I have no professional interest in what gets built, other than as an observer of the built environment, and I offer no design solutions. As a historian, I treat this (mostly architectural) polemic as the evidence of an ideological position, or group of related positions. My task here is to try to explain such ideology, or ideologies, a task that desperately needs to be done. The professional anxiety about the state of the English city, and the rash of spectacular new buildings that have appeared as a result are functionally part of the same culture in which a set of supposedly commonsense values have been advanced about density, mix of uses, monumentality and the nature of public life, values which as I suggest above, derive from explicitly continental European models of architecture and urban governance. Through tourism, aided no doubt by budget airlines' cheap flights to the continent of Europe, such a view of city life has been widely disseminated and absorbed. Yet its meaning has never really been interrogated, despite the myriad of problems it entails. As I argue in Chapters 4 and 10, the desire for vibrant streets and squares of the kind found in Mediterranean countries occludes the fact that, in those countries, such architecture frames pre-existing activities, such as the *paseo* and the *passegiata*. It also occludes the persistence of traditional family life, religious belief and authoritarian traditions of policing, all of which inform a quite different conception of public life. The importation of the architectural setting does not of itself produce the social behaviour.[32] As I wonder in Chapter 6 – does not the return to traditional architectural forms of the city, its streets and squares and pedestrian ways mark a desire for a return to more conservative social order?[33]

I have drawn back from attempting a survey of all English cities. My case studies are drawn from six only – London, Liverpool, Manchester, Milton Keynes, the Dorchester suburb of Poundbury and the imaginary city of Civilia. I would be the first to admit that this is not representative, but it is not meant to be. I have sympathy with readers in the West Midlands or Yorkshire who feel aggrieved that I have not chosen to discuss Birmingham or Leeds, but there is a rationale for the selection. The changes to the representation and consumption of the English city have been remarkable, as I state in the introduction, but my precise interest is in architectural representation. My cases are those in which urban identity has been recast in specifically architectural terms, and the majority of those cases have, England being unusually centralised, been in London, or in the case of Milton Keynes, in London's orbit. I would nevertheless qualify London by saying that, in the terms of the project, it rarely seems like one city. The imaginative gulf between Canary Wharf and Trafalgar Square is vast, despite the involvement in both projects of the same architect, Norman Foster. The two north western cities I discuss have been unusual in their enthusiasm for design solutions. Liverpool's revisiting of the Albert Dock complex was an early example of the desire to remake a city in architecturally spectacular terms. Manchester, a late convert to the idea, has now embraced the spectacular with gusto: there were few occasions in 2002 when the domestic professional journals did not discuss a Manchester project.[34] But these are unusual places. In all of the cases I have chosen, architecture, and not some other method, has been consciously used as a tool for remaking a place: it is this new emphasis on architectural spectacle which is my main concern and drives the selection of case studies. Architectural spectacle is what makes the recent experience of Manchester qualitatively different from Leeds, although in other respects these cities are culturally and economically comparable. Newcastle's architectural renaissance, underwriting its (failed) bid to become European Capital of Culture 2008 would be a potential further case, but occurred too late for inclusion in the book.[35]

The architectural spectacles I have chosen are for the most part familiar. Much has been written about them in the architectural press, and elsewhere in newspapers and magazines of general circulation, and as a result most of them exist in some way as public cultural property. This is certainly true of Trafalgar Square (Chapter 5), Canary Wharf (Chapter 7) and the British Museum Great Court (Chapter 8). In the other cases, there is, it could be said, a general understanding of Barcelona as an ideal city to which English cities might aspire (Chapter 4), an idea much cultivated in the travel supplements of the broadsheet newspapers. At the same time the differing ways in which Liverpool (Chapter 5) and Manchester (Chapter 9) have been lately reconstructed have been widely discussed in professional and non-professional sources, the latter's regeneration for the Commonwealth Games in 2002 being widely praised (see Baillieu 2002). The idea of the picturesque in architecture, an aesthetic which of itself is normally a matter of academic interest, has reached the public domain through the widely reported and controversial remarks of HRH the Prince of Wales (Prince Charles), after the competition to build the Sainsbury extension to the National Gallery (1984), and his subsequent patronage of the new village of Poundbury, a suburb of the Dorset town of Dorchester (covered in Chapter 2). Milton Keynes, finally (Chapter 3) has had a long existence in the wider culture as a kind of joke, notorious for the way its plan allegedly impedes rather than assists navigation, a view that exists alongside the city's evident prosperity and growth. My questions throughout the book have to do with the meaning of these urban spectacles. Erected in the name of an English public, I wonder what they are, precisely who they are for, and to what purpose, and finally, how they negotiate English anxieties about the city.

Chapter 2

The picturesque city

Introduction

Throughout the industrialised world since the 1970s, architecture has manifested its anxiety about the city in a return to traditional, and supposedly reassuring, forms of urbanism. Generally speaking, this has meant the re-emergence of the pre-modern forms of the street and the square, and the privileging (if only in theory) of the pedestrian. In built form, this tendency has been most manifest in Aldo Rossi's architecture and that of the neo-Rationalists in Italy, the Berlin work of Mathias Ungers, the town planning of Léon Krier in the Florida town of Seaside and the closely related 'new urbanism' of Andres Duany at Windsor and Celebration, also in Florida[1] (Figure 2.1). It was theoretically justified by such texts as Rossi's *The Architecture of the City* (1966, translated 1982), Manfredo Tafuri's *Architecture and Utopia* (1976) and Colin Rowe and Fred Koetter's *Collage City* (1978).

England's peculiar anxieties about the city have been marked by a particularly vivid revival of traditional styles. At the level of commercial building, it has been legible in the refusal of builders of speculative housing from the late 1970s onwards to build in anything other than historical styles, or rather pastiches of them; it was legible too in the contemporaneous tendency of supermarkets to appropriate a southern English rural vernacular, albeit grotesquely enlarged.[2] At the level of architecture, the return to tradition is identifiable in the neoclassical designs of such architects as Quinlan Terry, John Simpson and Demetri Porphyirios, and on a grand scale in the new town of Poundbury. An urban extension of the Dorset town of Dorchester, Poundbury was built by the Duchy of Cornwall with the close involvement of HRH Prince Charles, to a design by Krier, with individual buildings by Simpson and other neoclassicists. Poundbury was a philosophical

statement as much as a town, a materialisation of the belief that a site-specific urbanism based on the use of traditional forms would naturally create a happier settlement than that offered by either the big house-builders or the state.[3] Its commercial success now seems assured, but despite the involvement of no less than fifteen architectural practices in its design, its reception by the majority of the architectural press has been marked by hostility and derision.[4] This revival of traditional urbanism in England is nearly always characterised by the picturesque: Poundbury is its most celebrated, and most reviled, expression.

The picturesque is my subject here. It has a long history, and the case of Poundbury is only one of a number of modern revivals. Despite its origins in the tastes and habits of the eighteenth-century élite, it remains, as this chapter argues, a pervasive aesthetic in English urbanism, more so than may be immediately apparent. This is by no means a new argument: see Nikolaus Pevsner's *The Englishness of English Art* for an important statement of the idea of the mid-1950s (Pevsner 1964).[5] But there has been little discussion either of the persistence of the picturesque in contemporary urbanism in general, or of the ways in which it is manifest. Its contrivance of an appearance of naturalness is ideological, though the precise ideology it represents may differ according to the specific case. The picturesque may be deployed in a variety of ways, some of them more socially liberal than others. But in spite if this, its view of history is unavoidably conservative, staging the future in terms of reassuring images of a happy past. This chapter discusses two revivals of the picturesque, namely Poundbury, and as an important historical context, the *Architectural Review*'s ideology of Townscape. It treats them as different manifestations of the same pervasive phenomenon, and it concludes with a discussion of the way the picturesque continues to assert itself in some unlikely places. The persistence of it as a means of imagining the English city has resulted in some unexpected continuities between ostensibly modern and anti-modern positions. It is this strange continuity, more than anything else, that makes the English city so distinctive and at the same time so problematic.

The origins of the picturesque

The etymology of the word 'picturesque' suggests Italian seventeenth-century roots ('pittoresco', or 'picture-like' was current in the middle of that century) but it became widespread in eighteenth-century England as an aesthetic that was, according to David Watkin, no less than 'the universal mode of vision for the educated classes' (Watkin 1982: vii).[6] The key legitimising texts cited by Watkin are Edmund Burke's *Philosophical Inquiry into the Origin of our Ideas of the Sublime and the Beautiful* (1757), William Gilpin's *Observations Chiefly Relative to Picturesque Beauty* (1782–1809) and Uvedale Price's *An Essay on the Picturesque as Compared with the Sublime and the Beautiful* (1794–8). In these texts, the picturesque was an aesthetic mode principally applicable to landscape. It provided two aesthetic innovations: a set of perceptual rules for looking at the land, and a vocabulary to describe the experience. Such things did not previously exist; prior to the invention of the picturesque, landscape could not, in effect, be seen.

There was broad agreement between the theorists of the picturesque on what it meant. First, they were agreed that it was an aesthetic mode, a way of regarding the world. Second, they were agreed that it was exclusive. Not every scene therefore, could be picturesque. As an aesthetic, it was supposed to exist between Burke's categories of the Sublime and the Beautiful, containing elements of both. It was therefore supposed to induce some of the feelings of awe, terror or large size that are provoked by the Sublime, but to check these feelings by means of Beauty. David Watkin, in his study of the early theories of the picturesque, described its principal characteristics as 'Variety, movement, irregularity, roughness and intricacy' (Watkin 1982: ix). Third, the cultivation of the picturesque grew in association with the taste for foreign travel. In the first instance travel for the picturesque meant to Italy, the development of the picturesque as a mode of vision being very closely bound up with the growth in popularity of the Grand Tour.[7] But shortly after that, certain sorts of British landscapes were developed for their picturesque potential, the Lake District and North Wales especially, represented for example in the paintings of Richard Wilson and later, J. M. W. Turner.

Fourth, the picturesque theorists agreed that it was culture, not nature; nature was its subject, but the picturesque per se was a means of making something artificial out of it. It selected and edited, coloured and composed. It required the use of special equipment like the Claude Glass. This pocket-sized, smoked mirror enabled the user to make a picturesque scene out of an actually existing landscape, the mirror selecting, darkening and composing a scene in the manner of a French landscape painting, the term Claude referring to Claude Lorraine. The viewer would stand with his back to the actual scene to create the picturesque representation. In Jane Austen's satirical treatment of the picturesque, the heroine of *Northanger Abbey* can therefore reject 'the whole city of Bath, as unworthy to make part of a land-scape' (Austen in Brewer 1997: 615). To Austen the picturesque was clearly absurd, as it was to the architect A. W. N. Pugin who claimed that his work was based on necessity rather than frivolous ornament; he invoked 'truth to make the picturesque seem absurd' (Forty 2000: 299).

Fifth, it was agreed that the picturesque depended on the *genius loci*, a term which can be translated here as site-specificity. The composition of the picturesque view should, in other words, make use of what was already present in the scene; elements could be added or removed, imaginatively or otherwise, but the composition should respect the character of the place.

Finally, it was clear to the early theorists as much as contemporary historians that the picturesque was a powerful mode of vision. Its looking was, in other words, not value free, but implied domination over what was seen. Hence Uvedale Price's view:

> [I]n our own species, objects merely picturesque are to be found among the wandering tribes of gypsies and beggars, who in all the qualities which give them that character, bear a close analogy to the wild forester and the worn-out cart horse, again to old mills, hovels and other inanimate objects of the same kind.
>
> (Price in Langmuir 1989: 252)

The contemporary historian John Brewer has put a useful gloss on this view. The picturesque tourist, he notes,

> was a spectator rather than a part of the natural world he observed [. . .] when the picturesque tourist looked at peasants on the Welsh hillside or at Highlanders and their cattle, he did not expect or want the natives to look back [. . .] like the sturdy husbandsmen of

Georgic poetry, they were supposed to be self-sufficient, self-contained, inhabiting a world that the tourist might admire, record, collect, but never inhabit.

(Brewer 1997: 654)

Erika Langmuir has described this visual power as a means for the aristocracy to neutralise pressing social problems. Through the picturesque they could 'view distressing or threatening aspects of the country as pictorial themes rather than practical or ethical problems' (Langmuir 1989: 252). The picturesque, to put it another way, turned the poor into aesthetic subjects.[8] In this conception of the world, the viewer remained distant from his subject, and was therefore not threatened by any of the things he sees. The rougher characteristics of the picturesque were thus neutralised as tourist sights. Educated, leisured and well-travelled, the picturesque tourist implied by the aesthetic mode was essentially detached from his subject, and exerted visual power over it (Watkin 1982: vii). The nature of this powerful position is made clear by the picturesque representations, which made their subjects into aesthetic commodities.

Now these aspects of the picturesque – its visuality, its anti-formal character, its relationship to foreign and other travel, its inherent artifice, its concern for the character of the site, its power over its subjects – are all based on the assumption that the ideal picturesque subject is the landscape. Yet as Pevsner made clear in his Reith lectures of 1955, the picturesque was traditionally also acceptable as a mode for perceiving the city. Indeed, in the eighteenth century, Joshua Reynolds had talked of the 'essentially pictorial' nature of the city, and he implored architects to 'regard building not as a form complete in itself, but as the background of a picture' (Reynolds in Hussey 1927: 193). Irregularity, a central concept of the picturesque landscape, could also be important for the city. Uvedale Price, for example, disparaged formal tendencies in planning, arguing that it might be logical to build in straight lines, but 'it is hardly necessary to say that nothing can be more formal or insipid' (here 'formal' was clearly a term of abuse) (Price in Watkin 1982: 181). Gilpin saw the possibility of 'occasional groups of villages' supplying some amusement to a picturesque landscape view (Gilpin in Watkin 1982: 185). Reynolds again, in the thirteenth of his *Discourses*, praised the irregularity of London. Its streets might appear unplanned, he argued, but they were no less pleasant to walk through or see as a result. The regularity of Christopher Wren's plan for the City, had it been realised might, by contrast 'have produced weariness and a slight sense of disgust' (Reynolds 1786 in Watkin 1982: 187).[9] A number of architectural schemes of the early nineteenth century consequently made the picturesque a design principle, among them Nash's designs for Regent's

Park in which formal terraces are contrasted with trees, water and mean-dering paths (Watkin 1982: 187). Likewise the *genius loci*: Price wrote of the need to accept accident, avoid symmetry, to preserve old buildings and trees, to encourage climbing plants and flower gardens, and to make the church the object of special attention (Price in Hussey 1927: 204). Christopher Hussey's classic book on the subject ends with an image of contemporary London which suggests to him that picturesque city planning had continued to the then present day:

> Whatever Ruskin might write, moreover, the picturesque point of view had been sufficiently engrained in architects of his own age for Barry and Pugin to raise the Houses of Parliament, G. E. Street the Law Courts, Gilbert Scott St Pancras Station, and under Palmerston's pressure, the renaissance Foreign Office. These buildings, however unattractive in detail, are picturesquely suited to their sites, and in the blue haze of the London winter have all the mystery of romance and intricacy and variety that Reynolds desired. The view of the Foreign Office from the bridge in St James' Park in which architecture and landscape gardening are united, might have been sketched by a Claude, imagined by a Vanbrugh, and would undoubtedly have ravished a Price. It is the grandest of the nineteenth century conceptions of the picturesque.
>
> (Hussey 1927: 230)

Here the picturesque is invoked as the defining mode of English urbanism, defining the look of the centre of power, and implying through it a powerful continuity with the past. It does this in an exclusively visual manner, which gives license to edit, to refuse to see, to deny.[10] Clearly, the picturesque in this sense is ideological. It communicates a set of social and political values, yet it does so by suggesting that they are natural, which is to say, outside of ideology.

The view from the Bride of Denmark

The roots of the picturesque lie in an aristocratic mode of perception that exerts power by making its subjects into pictures. But use of the picturesque as a mode of authority does not really explain the modern revivals. In the two revivals I discuss here, the picturesque is used less as a means of asserting control than of ameliorating the anxiety produced by the modern city, both the realistic anxiety of its real spaces, and the metaphorical anxiety about its uncertain future. The first of these revivals of the picturesque is Townscape, the ideology promoted by the *Architectural Review* shortly after the Second World War. Although this revival occurred over half a century ago, it continues to exert an influence on present urbanism: the architects Richard Rogers and Norman Foster have both cited it as an influence, as has the architectural critic Jonathan Glancey, and the environmental journalist Nicholas Schoon.[11] Meanwhile, Gordon Cullen's popular book *Townscape* (1961), which collected his best work for the journal, is still in print.

Townscape presents itself as an explicitly anti-authoritarian mode. Mark Crinson has argued that the picturesque's origins need not mean that it must always be understood as 'evoking an essentially land-owning and landscape-loving national character' (Crinson 2003: 115). In the *Architectural Review*, he continues, 'the Picturesque symbolised English 'allegiance to freedom and liberty' while the monumentalism of the Beaux-Arts tradition embodied the 'absolutism and dictatorship of the French' and the 'reactionary policies of bodies such as the Royal Academy and the *Daily Telegraph*' (Crinson 2003: 116–17). Crinson goes on to argue that as represented at the 1951 Festival of Britain, the picturesque sensibility that informed the arrangement of pavilions, not to mention the relationship of the site to the past, marked a changed attitude to Empire. The exhibition 'changed the focus of experience from a quality embodied by certain kinds of architecture to a mode of apprehension located primarily in the viewer' (Crinson 2003: 117).

I think that this is right, but at the same time I believe that the *Architectural Review*'s approach shows the persistence of the aristocratic view, by which I mean an attitude that holds the city to be an aesthetic object, a source of spectacular pleasure for a privileged observer. This position, amused but fundamentally disinterested, is powerful in terms of the relations it posits between viewer and object. And in terms of my thesis here, it is evidence of an anxious response to the city, a retreat from its complex actuality by making it an aesthetic object. I explore these ideas through an aspect of the journal's own history, represented in Figures 2.2 and 2.3.

These figures show the location and interior of a London public house, the Bride of Denmark in Queen Anne's Gate, SW1. It no longer exists materially, except as a boxed up collection of antiques, but it continues to exist powerfully in the memory of older sections of the British architectural profession. It was rather exotic: as well as the usual dusty bottles, engraved mirrors advertising beer and the paraphernalia of the fully functional bar, it contained, in the account of the present editor of the *Architectural Review*, the fruit of the tree of good and evil, a turtle shell, a painted ceiling by the artist John Piper, numerous stuffed fish and a lion (Davey 1996: 106). It was full of trompe l'oeil effects, the mirrors placed to lengthen or curtail vistas unexpectedly, or introduce unexpected variations of scale. The decoration was similarly unpredictable, lurching between the sumptuous and the calculatedly austere.

In fact it was not a public house at all, but a private folly created by the editors of the *Architectural Review* and installed in the basement of its premises at 9–13 Queen Anne's Gate.[12] Hugh Casson, Nikolaus Pevsner, James Richards, Osbert Lancaster and (probably) Gordon Cullen were among those responsible or it, but the driving force was the dictatorial Hubert de Cronin Hastings, the owner of Architectural Press, and editor-in-chief of the journal from 1927 to 1973.[13] Hastings, alarmed at the demise of the traditional English pub, created the Bride of Denmark just after the Second World War, naming it with site-specificity after Prince George, Queen Anne's husband. Most of it comprised pieces salvaged from post-war London bomb sites, while the lion was Pevsner's, acquired from Lord Moyne of the Guinness family during research for the *Buildings of England* (Davey 1996). It was never in any sense public, but a private interior restricted to the staff of the *Review* and the architecturally eminent. Hastings made his office in the Bride's kitchen, while in the snug bar, Le Corbusier, Louis Kahn and Frank Lloyd Wright carved their names into a mirror with a gramophone stylus provided for that purpose. It was, as one former RIBA president remarked, 'a hard place to get into, even harder to get out of' (Davey 1996).

2.2
Queen Anne's
Gate, London, in
April 2003. The
offices of the
*Architectural
Review* are on the
left-hand side of
the street

2.3
**Interior of the
Bride of Denmark**

To create the Bride required the investment of considerable energy, time and resources. Hastings, for example, not only made himself an expert on the paint used in pubs, but also taught himself 'scumbling and graining' under the direction of an established pub painter (Cruickshank 1991a: 26). It served as offices, and was the public face of the journal; it was not therefore an ephemeral creation, although it may have begun as such, but an integral part of the journal's identity. As such, it put in material form many of the journal's ideas, including, for example, its approach to the picturesque.

The picturesque generally describes landscapes and townscapes, not interiors. But the Bride's location was certainly picturesque, the narrow, irregular, largely eighteenth-century Queen Anne's Gate, a street that also happens, at one point, to frame the superbly picturesque St James' Park. And as a space, the Bride of Denmark was so extensive that it could reasonably be said to be a kind of landscape, and therefore in this sense admissible into the category of the picturesque; it was certainly conceived on an urban scale. It was, in Dan Cruickshank's account, 'a splendid architectural space, a minis- cule piece of ideal traditional townscape, with prospects, enclosure and scale change' (Cruickshank 1991a: 27). At the same time, however, it was a calcu- lated retreat from the urban. Inside, the decorative character produced the feeling of a country pub, an impression that was hard immediately to chal- lenge because the visitor could not see out into the streets, as the pub was installed in the basement.[14]

Like the picturesque landscape, the Bride was calculated in effect, a contrived accumulation of stuff passed off as natural. It was formally irregular. It privileged the visual, indeed its visual effects were calculated to show off the power of the sense of sight, its mirrors being designed to disorient the already confused visitor. It was underwritten by an essentially conservative world-view that emphasised the importance of tradition, here specifically that of the English pub. And related to that, it was imbued with a sense of melancholy or loss. As with the picturesque concern with the *memento mori*, the Bride of Denmark was not a monument to a living culture, but to one profoundly in decline. But most importantly of all, it embodied the aristocratic sensibility of the picturesque: the sense of the world as a pictorial spectacle to be enjoyed in private surroundings by a privileged observer. The Bride in this sense was less the picture than the place from which the picture was enjoyed, the architectural frame for the picturesque view. It is critical in the respect that it was a private rather than a public place, marking out one of the peculiarities of English urban life, its tendency to exclusivity and privacy. As Richard Rogers has frequently remarked, the so-called public life of English cities revolves around essentially private institutions, whereby, paradoxically, to participate in public life one must withdraw from publicity (*Scotsman* 2003).[15] The Bride of Denmark reproduced this tendency exactly, and in fact the same is true of the entire suite of offices of the *Review*, which were done out in a Regency style like a gentleman's club. However, this characteristically English tendency to confuse the private and the public betrays an anxiety about the nature of urban life. In this scheme the city is something from which one retreats, and observes from a distance.

From the safe vantage point of the Bride, the *Architectural Review* devised Townscape, an influential theory of the city derived directly from the picturesque. It was disseminated through a series of regular articles, and a monthly column bearing the title between 1949 and 1971. Gordon Cullen's book *The Concise Townscape* was published by the Architectural Press in 1961. Superficially a formalism, it nevertheless bore a clear ideological ambition, namely the rather unreflected belief that it represented liberty against authority. Townscape, to put it another way, was supposed to be a naturalistic and popular aesthetic, opposed to the unnatural, and authoritarian beaux-arts plan.[16] The key figures were the journal's editor-in-chief, Hastings, Iain Nairn, Kenneth Brown, and most importantly Cullen, a talented draughtsman and the *Architectural Review*'s art editor from 1946 to 1956.

I emphasise the first large-scale use of the term Townscape by the *Architectural Review*, because it is here that an explicit connection with the picturesque is established. The site of this connection is Hastings' editorial 'Townscape' of December 1949, written under his usual pseudonym

Ivor de Wolfe (Wolfe 1949). The declamatory and often bizarre text ran to eight pages. Hastings' premise was his belief that there was no language in existence to describe the built environment as it actually was. In search of a language to do the job, Hastings recovered the picturesque, referring specifically to Uvedale Price – I say recover advisedly, because as he recognised, it had come to have associations with the trivial, 'frivolous embroidery' as he put it. He complained that there was nothing to legitimise the kinds of sentiments he expressed about Cullen's photographs, nothing to describe 'the general field of "OUT THERE"', whereas 'by contrast 'every teacup' seems to have got itself documented and analysed by some "famous expert"' (Wolfe 1949: 355).[17] What followed was an argument for the creation of a new 'English visual philosophy' with the ultimate ideal of creating a ' regional development of the international style'.[18]

Eleven pages of Cullen drawings followed, entitled 'Townscape Casebook' (Cullen 1949). They did not appear to match the grandiose rhetoric of Hastings' text, nor did they attempt to do so. They were simply a collection of sometimes stylish, but mostly low-key and sentimental sketches to illustrate existing good Townscape practice, arranged by perceptual mode. Cullen wrote of the eye as 'fandancer', 'netter', 'agoraphobe', 'movie camera', 'articulator', 'exterior decorator', 'matchmaker', 'sculptor', 'painter', 'traffic cop' and 'poet', and within each category he showed drawn or photographed examples of what he meant.

Let me sketch three examples: the first part, 'eye as fandancer' proposed simply that the grandiose urban vistas associated with the beaux-arts planning tradition should be replaced by a principle of partially screening or implying vistas. Trees and bollards might perform this function, Cullen suggested, as both were able to 'contain whilst revealing: a technique common to many dances and courtship' (Wolfe 1949: 363). As 'movie-camera', the 'eye' perceived the city in serial terms, movement changing the perception of individual elements, altering their relationship to their neighbours. This mobility of composition was a 'drama such as that created by a novelist' (Wolfe 1949: 366). 'Eye as exterior decorator' proposed seeing the city in the same terms as one might see one's home, imagining patterns, possibilities for juxtaposing different objects (Wolfe 1949: 368).

None of Cullen's aesthetic categories was any more than suggestive of mood. But in spite of this conceptual weakness, Hastings wanted Townscape linked to a politics of freedom. Citing Uvedale Price, he tried to recover the picturesque as a 'radical' theory, positing it as a reaction against 'idealism', 'a revolt against that old bore Plato'. It would result, if applied correctly, in a new kind of order resulting from the 'cultivation of significant differences'. It would promote a radical individualism in which objects could simply 'be themselves'. It would give rise to the 'practical surrealism' evidenced by Cullen's photographs and drawings. It would, to a limited extent, blur the boundaries between high and low culture. It would, finally, establish a third order in the developing strains of functionalism, between the romantic or organic tendency associated with Frank Lloyd Wright and the classicising idealism of early Le Corbusier. It would be a new order emphasising the phenomenal world, objectivity and empiricism; those things, those tradition-ally English concerns that could be enlisted in a battle against (foreign) authority (Wolfe 1949: 360).

This interpretation of the picturesque was further elaborated by other members of the *Architectural Review*'s editorial team. Anti-authoritarianism was claimed for the picturesque by Nikolaus Pevsner in *The Englishness of English Art* (1964). He had argued in the Reith lectures of 1955, on which the book was based, for the picturesque to be regarded as a uniquely English contribution to the visual arts; it was, he argued, less an artistic tendency than a mode of vision, one eminently suitable for the practical arts of planning, architecture and landscape gardening. The eighteenth-century landscape garden was one manifestation, but Pevsner also detected the picturesque in modern English urban schemes including the 1951 Festival of Britain (as discussed in Chapter 1), the London County Council housing estate at Roehampton, west London, the town centres of Stevenage and Harlow New Towns, and the plans, as yet unrealised, for the Barbican in the City of London, all of which were illustrated. Pevsner saw the picturesque as having a clear political dimension that effectively illustrated the conditions out of which it emerged. On the one hand was a love of liberty and a distaste for authority. Pevsner quoted the eighteenth-century writer George Mason on the picturesque garden as an expression of 'independency [. . .] in matters of taste and in religion and government' and went on to cite instances of monuments to the American revolution in various gardens of the time. On the other hand, however, the picturesque was a conservative tendency, representative of caution and a desire for continuity with the past; not necessarily bad things, he argued, as when new ideas were introduced they appeared in more developed forms (Pevsner 1964: 196).

J. M. Richards, the *Architectural Review*'s editor, had earlier elabo-rated his thinking about the picturesque for *The Heart of the City*, the report of the proceedings of the 1951 CIAM (Congrès International d'Architecture Moderne) congress at a country house in Hoddesdon, Hertfordshire (Tyrwhitt *et al.* 1952).[19] As with the position of the *Architectural Review*, at CIAM, Richards advocated a formula of Modernism combined with respect for the past. This was not simply an aesthetic matter to do with the respect for old buildings, but a political ideal of continuity with the past, which in his view

underpinned a wider philosophy of anti-authoritarianism. In Richards' contribution to the book, 'Old and New Elements at the Core' he advanced a
humanistic world-view of constant and universal values. 'Respect for old
buildings' was, he wrote, '[. . .] part of the means of maintaining that continuity
of human experience which it is one role of the Core of the town to preserve
[. . .]' (Richards in Tyrwhitt *et al.* 1952: 60). As an example of this, he cited
the Festival of Britain site, in which Whitehall Court (Thomas Archer and
A. Green, 1884), a massive nineteenth-century apartment building on Victoria
Embankment, closed a vista from the Festival site on the opposite, southern
side of the river. The architects of the Festival therefore appropriated what was
generally regarded as a 'bad' Victorian building, feeling that its 'strange, romantic outline' made an effective backdrop for their work. This 'scenic use of existing buildings' had everything to do with maintaining a sense of order that
implicitly transcended political authority (Richards in Tyrwhitt *et al.* 1952: 63).

A critique of Townscape

In Townscape, the viewer's detachment from the urban scene is as complete
as his eighteenth-century ancestor's was from the rural. He need not even
have physical experience of the scene, as was the case in Cullen's drawings
of American towns in *The Exploding Metropolis*. 'Few men have so percep-
tive an eye for the details that make this scale as Gordon Cullen and Iain Nairn
of the *Architectural Review* [. . .]', wrote the urban critic Jane Jacobs in the
introduction, but Cullen's fear of flying meant that never went to the places he
drew.[20] His sketches were picturesque versions of the photographs taken by
Nairn, who, as Jacobs coyly pointed out, 'had done the walking' (Jacobs in
Gosling 1996: 65). Or consider the Townscape position on outdoor advertising,
here in Cullen's 1961 book *The Concise Townscape*. His sentiments, along
with those of his colleagues at the *Review*, were that it was, like all other
popular products, essentially distasteful, but capable of arresting images, in
which case its aesthetic power should be recognised. Describing a possible
development of Piccadilly Circus, he writes of its 'surrealist drama of shapes,
lights and movement' (Cullen 1961: 85). The results themselves were not,
however to be emulated, but accepted with an amused tolerance. Here was
advertising divorced from any sense of function or history, treated as a natural
phenomenon that might give pleasure to a disinterested, educated public,
a public implicitly educated enough to disregard the content of the advertising
messages themselves and enjoy the free spectacle (Cullen 1961: 85).

A more dramatic example of this picturesque detachment would
be the *Architectural Review*'s several discussions of the spectacular quality of

the damage wrought on Britain by the Blitz, first discussed by Richards in the picture anthology *Bombed Buildings of Britain*, and later the artist, and Richards' friend John Piper in the 1947 article 'Pleasing Decay' (Richards 1942; Piper 1947). In the latter, Piper wrote:

> Bomb damage has revealed new beauties in unexpected places – a rich source of information for the planner who would retain picturesque elements from the past that can be opposed in size, colour and shape to the new buildings and groups of buildings, whether by contrast or agreement.
>
> (Piper 1947: 93)

This attitude of detachment whereby the viewer aestheticises any scene, however distressing, is closely related to the surreal. In Hastings' 1949 manifesto 'Townscape', the surreal was one of the values he explicitly promoted, a desire made clear by the photographic image that opens the article (Wolfe 1949). It depicted a small area of a city street, perhaps 10 feet by 10 feet; a heavy cast-iron drain occupied most of the bottom third, the pavement kerb marked the left-hand edge, and the rest was cobbles.[21] Taken from head height with the camera pointing mostly downwards, it showed plenty of detail; the wear on the surfaces and the irregularity of their original placement, and small pieces of unidentifiable debris. In his characteristic style, Hastings described the drain cover as 'fifteen avid little mouths' that will 'suck heedless match-heads [. . .] into the sinister underground organisation of the city' (Wolfe 1949: 354). Here in both the photograph and the text, the city becomes a devouring body, the familiar becoming uncanny, producing a pleasant *frisson* of terror.

Temperamentally, Hastings favoured the surreal, but the mild-mannered Cullen also invoked surrealism in his own work.[22] In his book, *The Concise Townscape* (1961: 51), Cullen depicted a rear view of a man half-disappearing into a doorway from a brightly lit street; only half of his body is visible and there is considerable ambiguity about what he is doing. The fact that it is a male figure in an informal darkened public space, together with the stance – upright, legs spread – suggests public urination or even a sexual act; possibilities that Cullen's commentary, if it did not explicitly encourage, did not completely discount. Here, he wrote 'we glimpse the unknown, the mystery of a city where anything could happen or exist, the noble, the sordid, genius or lunacy' (Cullen 1961: 51) (Figure 2.4). On other pages Cullen deploys familiar surrealist tactics of anthropomorphism and gigantism: on page 81, Cullen produced an image of a monk in front of a gigantic sculpted hand, the index finger of which points directly to the sky. Cullen wrote in the caption that

2.4
**Image from *The Concise Townscape*
(1961): Gordon Cullen**

the gigantism of this image produced a 'shock [. . .] as of some sudden violence of nature or of unreality' (Cullen 1961: 81) (Figure 2.5).

Now as an aesthetic mode, the surreal has the same detachment as the picturesque. Susan Sontag, writing in 'Melancholy Objects' described the tendency of the surreal to flatten the world so that everything, however grotesque, became legible as *object trouvé* (Sontag 1978: 46). Like the picturesque, this aestheticisation of the world is not value free, but develops explicitly from a bourgeois social position in which the viewer is essentially detached from what he sees, uncommitted and uninvolved. His gaze is that of fascination with the other. Surrealism, Sontag wrote 'is a bourgeois disaffection'. While it appears through its subject matter to support the rights of the 'underdog [. . .], the disestablished or unofficial reality', in actual fact it treats its subjects as an 'exotic prize to be tracked down and captured by the diligent hunter with the camera'. And the subjects themselves, 'sex and poverty', are the 'homely mysteries obscured by the bourgeois social order' (Sontag 1978: 54).

Townscape is a gentle surrealism, certainly. There is nothing in Cullen's vision of the explicit sexuality of May Ray's photographs, for example. But there is much in common with his work and the images that illustrate André Breton's novel of urban drifting, *Nadja* (1928). In that work, the city of

2.5
**Image from *The Concise Townscape*
(1961): Gordon Cullen**

Paris appears as a series of depopulated stage sets, chosen for their ambiguity: advertising hoardings appear decontextualised, meaningless and strange; fragments of clothing and debris appear separated from their bearers; curious objects and fragments of drawings allude to a magical world beyond the everyday. All help produce a sense of the *merveilleux*, the psychological condition Breton wanted to make available to the privileged few who had managed, albeit temporarily, to dispense with the bourgeois conventions of viewing the world (Breton 1991).[23] Now this is an agreeable aesthetic game, but as Sontag suggests, the surreal mode may only be open to those who are essentially detached from what they are seeing. Cullen's gaze, like Breton's, is that of the flâneur, that 'voyeuristic stroller' of Baudelaire who, (as Sontag put it), 'discovers the city as a landscape of voluptuous extremes' (Sontag 1978: 55). The surrealist mode can only, Sontag continued, 'deliver a reactionary judgement; can only make out of history an accumulation of oddities, a joke, a death trip' (Sontag 1978: 75). The surreal therefore, paradoxically, affirms rather than critiques the established social order. The same can be said of the picturesque.

At the *Architectural Review*, Townscape affirmed a specifically English social order. The mode of vision it proposed is one of privileged play, an ideal to which Cullen and his colleagues subscribed. Cullen's urban metaphors in the book *The Concise Townscape* spoke of a comfortable bourgeois existence, the city conceived as a series of dinner parties and pleasant strolls. Work did not feature at all, except as an occasional spectacle for the tourist: see the images of Italian market traders on page 21 or the Devonshire fishermen on pages 113–14, in both cases an amusing sight rather than an image of labour. In this scheme the city became a metaphorical dinner party. 'Let us suppose', wrote Cullen, thinking of the relationships between buildings,

> a party in a private house where are gathered together half a dozen people who are strangers to each other. The early part of the evening is passed in polite conversation on general subjects such as the weather and the current news. Cigarettes are passed and lights offered punctiliously. In fact it is all an exhibition of manners, of how one ought to behave. It is also very boring. This is conformity. However later on the ice begins to break and out of the straightjacket of orthodox manners and conformity real human beings begin to emerge. It is found that Miss X's sharp but good-natured wit is just the right foil to Major Y's somewhat simple exuberance. And so on. It begins to be fun. Conformity gives way to an agreement to differ within a recognised tolerance of behaviour.
>
> (Cullen 1961: 11)

This passage lays bare the social basis of his theory, through a series of assumptions: that an English dinner party is a supremely natural image; that a party in a private house (as opposed to say, a restaurant) is understood as an appropriate or normal place to socialise; that the rules of the party are understood by the guests *a priori*; that the guests will be of high social status ('Major Y'); that there is a generally understood social dynamic where, after a time, a certain deviation from good manners is encouraged as a means of reinforcing the rules. Townscape's preoccupation with social order, with the dynamic of agreeable social behaviour, speaks of wider anxieties about the nature of city life. Its recovery of natural urban forms, and agreeably natural urban behaviour must be set against the lack of these things at home in the contemporary English city.[24]

Poundbury

This powerful vision remains, I argue, embodied in the picturesque in later architectural revivals, and nowhere more so than at the new town of Poundbury.
Underwritten by the architectural theories of HRH Prince Charles and Léon
Krier, Poundbury is undoubtedly picturesque. It is, like HRH Prince Charles'
manifesto-like book, *A Vision of Britain* (HRH the Prince of Wales 1989), preoccupied with the city view above all else: the visual dominates all other
senses (Figure 2.6). It contrives an appearance of the natural, manifest in the
concern to be seen above all as an organic extension of the town of
Dorchester. Appropriating the vernacular of the architecture, and its pre-
modern plan, it outwardly denies that it has been formed through anything
other than natural processes of accumulation over time. It is calculatedly anti-
formal – 'variety, movement, irregularity, roughness and intricacy' are all valued
in the surfaces of the buildings and the streets. Poundbury exhibits the
picturesque in its essentially aristocratic viewpoint: its concern for the visual
presupposes an essentially leisured, privileged observer who consumes its
sights – up to and including its inhabitants – as a visual entertainment.

      The picturesque is central to HRH Prince Charles' theory of archi-
tecture. His intervention in architecture began on 29 May 1984 at Hampton
Court at a dinner to mark both the 150th anniversary of the Royal Institute of

2.6
**Poundbury,
Dorset, in
January 2003**

British Architects, and the award of its most prestigious prize, the annual Gold Medal, to the Indian architect Charles Correa. HRH Prince Charles had been expected to make a light and complimentary speech, but instead he used the occasion to attack his hosts, specifically their competition for the extension to the National Gallery and its result. The winning design, by the firm Ahrends Burton Koralek (ABK) was singled out for attack: notoriously he thought it resembled 'a monstrous carbuncle on the face a much-loved and elegant friend' (HRH the Prince of Wales 1984). The design itself was 'a kind of municipal fire station, complete with the sort of tower that contains the siren'. The controversy that resulted meant the abandoning of the Gallery's commitment to the ABK scheme, and, finally, the selection of the more restrained and historically contextual design by Robert Venturi and Denise Scott-Brown.

HRH Prince Charles continued to take an interest in architecture, making a further controversial speech on 1 December 1987 at the annual dinner of the Corporation of London's Planning and Communication Committee. There he attacked, more generally, architecture and planning in post-war London, claiming amongst other things that the damage inflicted by the Luftwaffe in 1940 had been benign by comparison with the self-inflicted wounds made since. When the German raids destroyed buildings, they 'didn't replace them with anything more offensive than rubble [. . .] planning turned out to be the continuation of war by other means' (HRH the Prince of Wales 1987).

HRH Prince Charles' views on architecture were summarised in a ninety minute television programme he made with the BBC in 1989, 'A Vision of Britain', which coincided with a book of the same title, and an exhibition at the Victoria and Albert Museum. An anti-modern tirade, the book argued for a return to the materials and methods of the pre-industrial age. The loss of pre-modern views of the City of London was a cause of particular regret. The luxuriously illustrated book included a double-page reproduction of a Canaletto from the Royal collection at Windsor, *Thames with the City in the Background from the Terrace of Somerset House*, painted 1750–1; superimposed above this, on a translucent parchment, is an image of the exact same view in a contemporary monotone print, bound at the centre only so one may compare the two (Figures 2.7 and 2.8). A grainy monotone, it depicts the City's lumpy office towers having obliterated the delicate forest of church spires represented by Canaletto. It is a dramatic comparison, but deeply unfair: Canaletto's London, all blue skies and glittering water, appropriates the Venetian mode of urban representation, in which the purpose is to seduce. The photographer of the 1980s City uses the high contrast and grain of the high-speed news photograph to signify brutal modernity. The City has certainly changed, but the modes of representation serve entirely different purposes, the one affirms, the other denigrates.

2.7
London: The Thames from Somerset House Terrace Towards the City (1750–1)
Canaletto

2.8
Photograph of the Thames from Somerset House

HRH Prince Charles' attack on the architectural profession was well-timed and popular – the television programme was watched by seven million viewers. He argued that architects had become largely self-regarding and self-serving, bolstered by an uncritical professional press (HRH the Prince of Wales 1989: 9). He thought that it had failed to communicate its values effectively to a wider public and that it had become the tool of a distant élite. His view was countered by an increasingly aggressive RIBA through its Modernist president, Max Hutchinson, who published a reply to HRH Prince Charles in 1989 as *The Prince of Wales: Right or Wrong? An Architect Replies*, in which he argued for the necessity of architecture to represent the age in which it was produced (Hutchinson 1989).

HRH Prince Charles developed his position further in 1988 by turning to property development. On Duchy of Cornwall land on the fringes of Dorchester, he proposed to build a new town, Poundbury, in which his architectural principles would be materialised. Krier produced the masterplan, which was revised over the following three years in conjunction with Andres Duany, an American urbanist with experience of building new settlements; Duany drew up the comprehensive design code.[25] The land comprised about 400 acres immediately adjacent to the town centre and it was to be developed as four distinct, more or less self-sufficient urban units with about 800 households in total. In contrast to Modernist practice, the living functions of work, residence, circulation and recreation were mixed, on a pre-industrial model, so that it ought to be possible to live entirely within each urban unit.[26] In any case, no function of the unit ought to be more than ten minutes' walk from any other. It was the antithesis of the modern zoned city.

Formally, it was in every respect picturesque.[27] Krier's plan reiterated the pre-industrial form of Dorchester, so streets would be narrow and curvilinear, with special attention to landmarks and vistas. There would be no long axial views and no large open spaces. A sense of enclosure was to be encouraged in the public realm, so views would generally be curtailed by a landmark such as a tower, or a curving street would indicate its own continuity (Figure 2.9). All buildings were to be sited close to the street instead of being set back, with services and car parking to be concentrated at the rear. There would be considerable attention devoted to the façades of buildings. No single style would predominate, but there would be an effort to evolve a consistent typology, as had been achieved at Seaside in Florida.[28] Buildings would be generally small in scale, three to four storeys, with the exceptions of the church, the market tower and the rotunda, all of which were imagined as public landmarks. There would be no large areas of public space in the town itself. Land use would be three to four times as intense as in a modern housing estate. Consistent with this, no special provision would be made for the private car. Parking would be permitted on the streets, and different kinds of circulation would intentionally not be separated. Finally, Krier encouraged a sense that landscape framed the whole town. Perspective drawings from 1991 show Poundbury as a single image from the green common on the outskirts; it is dense and compact, formally defined by the (as yet un-built) market hall tower.

In my discussion of Townscape and the *Architectural Review*'s take on the picturesque, I argued that although ultimately it confirms the aristocratic world-view, it nevertheless presents the picturesque as a model of anti-authoritarian urbanism. I suggested that enlisting the picturesque in this ideal was a response to particular post-war anxieties about the city, specifically the city imagined as a site of overbearing authority, of fear and political repression. Poundbury also enlists the picturesque in what seems to me an anxious way, but the fear it responds to is a late twentieth-century one, that of *lack* of authority, of disorder of both social and architectural kinds.

2.9
**Poundbury,
Dorset, in January
2003**

Images of Poundbury show an intense relationship between the picturesque mode and civility. The town has, in common with the American new urbanist settlements in Florida, a strict code to preserve its appearance of happy accident. Drawn up in conjunction with Andres Duany, it imposes a model of behaviour that verges on the authoritarian. Here is a small extract:

> The following items shall *not* be located such that they will be visible from the streets: clothes driers, meter-boxes, air extractors, wall-ventilation openings, dustbins or roof-top solar collectors or soil pipes. Where airbricks are essential to satisfy building regulations, these shall be of terracotta, painted cast iron, or unpainted drilled stone. Vent stacks clearly visible from the streets shall be enclosed within chimneys or lead-clad. The following items are specifically forbidden: bubble skylights, prefabricated accessory buildings, permanent plastic sub-blinds/awnings, plastic commercial fascias and lettering and illuminated signs [. . .] external individual television aerials and collectors are not permitted.
>
> (Krier 1992: 264–5)

Now this set of rules demonstrates the extent to which the physical form of the place is bound up with modes of behaviour. The code abolishes all outward signs of modernity, so modern forms of waste collection, heating and lighting must be concealed behind a pre-modern façade. These restrictions in themselves need not involve much modification of behaviour, but the restriction on satellite dishes, a form of television aerial that cannot be easily concealed, actively limits the broadcasting that can be received in the town along class lines (in 1992 when the code was published, the channels available through satellite dishes were mostly sport, soft pornography and light entertainment; low cultural forms which would not accord with Poundbury's sense of moral purpose). Approved activities receive appropriate built form such as Krier's curious market tower (Figure 2.10). This not only acts as a civic landmark, its four obelisks marking Poundbury's highest point, but a representation of civic life. Its tall, ogee-arched, vaulted ground floor presupposes a traditional market; the large vaulted room on the second storey, lit by fifty-eight triangular openings, is a room to deal with the market's financial business. This landmark structure is not really therefore a folly, but the frame for a desired social economy. The actual existence of the market and associated activities is crucial to Poundbury's success. The market hall, part of the structure that was built, does in actual fact perform more than a symbolic function, holding local events, and performing a disciplining function on the town's social life.

For an image of what was hoped for at Poundbury, I turn to a perspective view of the centre made in oil by Carl Laubin, a British-based

2.10
Market Tower, Poundbury, 1991, architect: Léon Krier

2.11
Poundbury,
Dorset, in January
2003

American architect who while working for Dixon:Jones had developed a side-line in architectural paintings, encouraged by Jeremy Dixon[29] (Figure 2.12). His fantastic images for Dixon and Edward Jones of their Royal Opera House development had been widely published, and he later did work for such diverse clients as the neoclassicist John Simpson, and Norman Foster, as well as a series of architectural *capricci*. These are unusual works in their materials and purpose: although the later works, after Laubin had left the architectural firm, were done as *capricci*, the earlier paintings, of which *Poundbury* was one, were made as part of the design process, an alternative to both the standard architectural drawing, which Laubin felt was difficult for the general public to read, and the architectural model, which tended to present an aerial (and hence unrealistic) view. The medium of oil painting allowed the representation of a place from the point of view of its users or inhabitants; it also allowed the representation of wear or decay, aspects of a building's life that would clearly affect habitation but could not be depicted by conventional means (Laubin 2003).

2.12
Poundbury, oil on
canvas (c.1992):
Carl Laubin

Laubin's painting of Poundbury is best known in reproduction. The dimensions of the original were roughly 30 by 40 inches, and like many of

Laubin's paintings of the time, it was made as part of the design process, before the architecture was realised, rather than as a discrete art object (Laubin 2003). Laubin worked from Krier's drawings, and to get a sense of the quality of the building materials, he visited local Dorset villages. The content of what was painted was based on these experiences, and also on the circumstances of the artist's life – he lives in a village of similar size and texture to that the designers of Poundbury hoped to emulate. The depiction of street-life, criticised in some quarters, was based, so Laubin claimed, on his own day-to-day experiences (Laubin 2003).[30]

As a painting it is nevertheless extremely finely done. It depicts a view of the centre along a street, with the Market Tower just to the right of centre. Below the tower is a simple market hall, open on all sides. The buildings that line the street are all Georgian in their façades, simple in decoration and rising no more than three storeys from the street. The roofs are red tiled, the walls faced in a warm red brick, with stone facings at ground level. The street is narrow, suggesting a passage suitable for pedestrians and cyclists, but wide enough for only one car. This is not a monumental place. The street curves gently to the right towards the tower, and is closed at the end by a three-storey building of indeterminate type. It is a reasonably well-populated scene, nineteen figures visible of varying ages; it speaks of a quiet order in which the only sign of modernity is a small red Post Office van at the end of the street – letter-writing being a Good Thing, and the Post Office a fine civic institution, this is an acceptable modern intrusion.

This image has much in common with the other images Laubin produced at the same time – especially his fantasy of Paternoster Square for John Simpson – but it is nevertheless important in fixing a visual idea of Poundbury that connects the aesthetic of the picturesque in architecture with social order. Poundbury is definitely urban, but it is a different kind of urbanity from that feared to exist in the big city. Here everything is human-scale and slow moving; the bicycle is the principal mode of transport for citizens. Work, leisure and residence are intertwined and maintained in a happy balance. The only visible work, that of the market traders, who wear white smocks, is unalienated and leisurely. The lone child, a boy, depicted in the bottom right hand corner, looks longingly at the cakes in the bakery window. Yet his desire, as yet unsatisfied, speaks of an ordered world in which the pleasure of cake eating, and by implication other pleasures, can be deferred. The boy's restraint signifies a self-disciplined, ordered world. Here, overall then, the picturesque mode is concomitant with a natural social order. Heterogeneity – such as it exists here – is present as if to confirm a natural order.[31]

Laubin – who has never visited his subject – presents an image of perfect civility, an ideal that Poundbury tries to enforce through a textual code, and through the framing role of its buildings.[32] In reality this has not been without problems, as Turnbull (1997) reported in *The Times*: the code demanded, for example that a dovecote built above a village shop be used as such, against the wishes of the shopkeeper herself.[33] Turnbull also suggested that the waste-collection service ran into problems after it emerged that the narrow streets prevented access by the standard size garbage vehicles. The architects' somewhat unhelpful response was to suggest that the council should get smaller vehicles specifically for Poundbury (Turnbull 1997: 25).[34]

But these problems also suggest authoritarianism, a charge levelled against the American new urbanist settlements, especially Celebration, which was built by the Disney corporation outside its Disney World theme park in Florida.[35] Authoritarianism is also a charge that has been put to Krier in a series of symposia on the new urbanism organised and published by *Architectural Design* in 1993 (*Architectural Design* 1993a: 27).[36]

Krier's reply was not to reject outright the charge, but to argue that the codes were necessary, and that the resistance to them was a peculiarly English problem ('My problem in England is that everybody seems to be against the codes' (Krier in *Architectural Design* 1993b: 19)). He explained:

> The idea of authority has to come back to the planner because if you give up these certainties the authority does not vanish into thin air but is taken up by others, by the accountants, by the engineers who tells you how many cars you need, and by the sociologists or philosophers. Authority is established by certainties, which in planning terms means codes.

> (*Architectural Design* 1993b: 26)

In other words, the building of a new town like Poundbury cannot happen without authority, and that if it is not the authority of the planner that is imposed, then it will be that of some other, possibly less desirable, group. Life, in Krier's view is inevitably governed by codes and he cited examples of new settlements of the historical past where codes were necessary. Elsewhere he denied that this imposition of authority on the part of the planner amounts to the same thing as political authoritarianism, as, he wrote, the same neoclassical forms in public building have been used in Washington DC as well as in Hitler's Berlin:

> There exists neither authoritarian nor democratic architecture. There exists only authoritarian and democratic ways of producing and using architecture . . . Architecture is not political, it can only be used politically.

> (Krier in Ellin 1996: 17)

This sidesteps the questions posed earlier by the analysis of images of Poundbury, and the analysis of the code. The images speak of a desire to impose a well-defined social order. There is nothing to suggest that this is anything other than an order with benign purpose, but it is order nonetheless, and it is unclear what mechanisms if any exist to manage dissent, or what relationship this place has with the idea of democracy. Personally, I do not think there is anything more sinister about this place than any other well-designed suburb, but the fact that architecture is clearly intended as a frame for civil life, with a highly complex code to enforce that idea, suggests that order must be more illusory than actual. The population of Poundbury is, to a large extent, self-selecting, with the exception of a small component of social housing, so it is a population that is likely to accept this code. But that does not mean that the code is any less authoritarian in its aims; the true test of its nature will happen as the town adapts to change. Poundbury, in summary, is a settlement in which the picturesque mode is used for authoritarian purposes. As a response to the anxiety about the urban, it uses the more reactionary aspects of the picturesque to contrive a fantasy of an ordered past, a deep, pre-industrial England in which modernity has simply been abolished.

Conclusions

I have shown in this chapter that there are a number of ways in which the picturesque has been invoked in the modern English city, some of which are more authoritarian than others. However, all variants enlist it as a response to anxiety about the urban. In the earliest example I cite, Townscape, the retreat into a naturalistic urbanism speaks of a flight from the memory of the city as a site of uncontrollable political authority, an idea that received modern expression at the Festival of Britain. At Poundbury, the picturesque is invoked to recreate a social order of the pre-industrial past in order to correct the perceived chaos of the present. Both invocations of the picturesque are characteristically English; both involve, crucially, a retreat from the urban and all its complexity. The aestheticisation of the city that the picturesque facilitates is not an engagement with the urban, but the reverse.

I want to conclude by suggesting that this picturesque view of the city remains highly pervasive, and that the dispute between ostensibly modern and anti-modern positions seen about HRH Prince Charles' interventions in the architectural debate in the 1980s actually occludes much wider agreement. Consider, finally, the image of Trafalgar Square (see Figure 6.6, p. 145) produced by Richard Rogers for his 1986 scheme to improve London.

Here is a professedly Modernist architect whose scheme for the National Gallery extension had been condemned by HRH Prince Charles, and who intervened himself in the architectural debate against HRH Prince Charles in favour of a renewed commitment to Modernism; yet despite these credentials, the Trafalgar scheme is immensely polite. Its only large-scale change, the removal of traffic from in front of the National Gallery could easily be construed in anti-modern terms, and the artist, Laurie Abbott, has even gone further, repressing the only Modernist building in the view, New Zealand House, a twenty-storey 1960s tower built by Matthew Johnson-Marshall and Partners. There is, in short, very little in this to contradict the picturesque aesthetic advanced by HRH Prince Charles.

Chapter 3

The free city

Introduction

The main focus of this chapter, the new town of Milton Keynes, sits somewhat uneasily in this book. An hour by train to the north west of London,
straddling two existing Buckinghamshire towns, Wolverton and Bletchley,
it does not physically resemble any of the other places I describe. Centreless
(at least in popular perception) and, with the one exception of the central
shopping mall, architecturally unspectacular, it might well seem to mark a
retreat from the urban rather than an accession to it. To the architectural
historian Kenneth Frampton it was no more than a 'collection of more or less
well-designed housing estates', which is to say, not a city at all (Frampton
1992: 286). Certainly, it resists those things that have lately become commonsense urban thinking: the idea of centre, the architectural spectacle, the neighbourhood, the pedestrian, the street café.[1] The architecture that exists is
for the most part inward-looking and self-effacing, and it was only in the
mid-1990s, with the construction of a cultural quarter on its central axis
that the city developed any sense of spectacle.[2] It could be said with justification that it belongs to an earlier age of garden cities and post-war new
towns, in which issues such as air quality and sanitation created a desire
to decant urban populations into the quasi-countryside where such things
could be better managed. After half a century of the NHS and of clean air, the
old cities are not of themselves especially harmful places to live, and some
of their oldest and grimiest parts have seen their populations modestly
revive. New towns, after the gloomy experience of Skelmersdale, of
Runcorn, of Cumbernauld – and internationally of Brasília and Chandigargh –
are out of favour (Brett 1980; Bendixson and Platt 1992; Glendinning and
Muthesisus 1994).

Yet Milton Keynes belongs here for several reasons. First, it is as much a product of the present as it is of the 1960s. It is said to be the fastest-growing urban area in Britain, and given that it lies in a prosperous arc on the outer fringes of London, it is likely to continue to grow (Schoon 2001: 140).[3] It will, if government targets for growth are adhered to, reach a population of 500,000, making it twice its original size, and larger than the established cities of Bristol, Liverpool, Manchester, Newcastle and Nottingham (Hetherington 2003, *Observer* 2003).[4] Second, it stands in distinct relation to the garden city and new town projects: apart from its newness, it is formally and demographically quite unlike any of them, and is the only one, with the possible exception of Cumbernauld, to be conceived on an urban scale.[5]

Third, and most importantly, Milton Keynes can be regarded as a response to the anxious condition of the English city that I described in Chapter 1. It responds, I think, to the realistic anxiety about the city in England, the city as an anxious space in itself, somewhere that is not inhabited with ease. And it responds to the metaphorical anxiety described, in which the city occupies an uneasy cultural position in England, the city as an unquestionable material fact that is also somehow foreign or unnatural. As a response to these anxieties, Milton Keynes is qualitatively different to the others discussed here. Superficially, it may look like an anti-urban response to the problem, a capitulation to an anti-urban culture. This is emphatically not the case, for it was conceived as a self-contained city, not a suburb.[6] But its urban character is distinctive. Unlike the picturesque cities imagined in the revivals of 1949 (Townscape), 1971 (Civilia) or 1991 (Poundbury), Milton Keynes did not appropriate a traditional, and supposedly reassuring, urbanism from the English past. Nor did it look for inspiration to the well-maintained traditions of European urbanism to be found in southern Europe. Nor was it a response of monument-building, of *grands projets*, to embellish existing cities.[7] Instead, a modified form of the urbanism of the western US was imported. Despite the predominance of suburban housing, the other outstanding aspects of the city – the grid, the low density, the reliance on the private car as a means of transport, and the fetish of circulation in search of consumer goods and services – were innovations for an English city, certainly in combination like this. Milton Keynes amounts to the most comprehensive and thorough attempt to reimagine the English city of the late twentieth century, and as such it warrants consideration here.

Although Milton Keynes can be reasonably thought a contemporary artefact, I am interested here in the moment when its architects begin to imagine the life of the city in detail. I concentrate therefore on the drawings of the central city made in 1974 by Helmut Jacoby, a highly regarded German draughtsman.[8] His visionary perspectives were made for the Milton Keynes Development Corporation, the public body that co-ordinated the design of the city. They were widely published, in official pamphlets and brochures, and a range of journals and newspapers; they were made to appeal to a wide constituency, both professional and non-professional, the disinterested as well as the curious. Derived from the architects' plans, they very accurately represented what was built. But more importantly for the present discussion, they represented an index of aspirations and desires pertaining to city life. They imaged a (then) novel life of abundance, leisure and consumer choice, which had been alluded to in the text of the city's plan. Jacoby seems to have been particularly encouraged to imagine the life of the city as much as its architecture.[9] It is these latter aspects of the perspective drawings that concern me most here rather than their architectural qualities. As with other images I consider in the book, they are seen to function as an optical unconscious, laying bare what cannot be said by other means.

The city

Milton Keynes was the last, and by far the biggest of the British new towns built after the Second World War.[10] After Milton Keynes, the idea of new towns per se fell into disfavour; the urban policy of both Labour and Conservative administrations was directed toward the amelioration of the problems of the inner city, to which the new town movement was thought to have contributed (Bendixson and Platt 1992). Milton Keynes was commissioned in January 1967 by the Labour government of Harold Wilson; the development corporation was set up in March of the same year under the Labour peer Lord Campbell of Eskarn. The site, a 40-square-mile deformed rhombus, lay between two existing Buckinghamshire towns of little architectural interest, the largely working-class Wolverton, which had an important railway workshop, and Bletchley, the centre of British military intelligence during the Second World War, and, increasingly, a dormitory town for London. The site contained a number of smaller settlements including the picturesque villages of Stony Stratford, Woughton Green and Milton Keynes, the latter giving its name to the new city. The total population of the existing settlements was 40,000, which was predicted to grow to 250,000 by the end of the century. The site was bisected by two important trade routes, the M1 motorway and the West Coast railway line linking London and Glasgow. The Grand Union canal also crossed the site, and was periodically discussed as means of freight transport. The geography was unremarkable, with little variation in height, no rivers or large bodies of water, a mild climate and no major historic monuments. It was according to Derek Walker, who was to become the city's chief architect, a 'bloody boring' site (*Architectural Association Quarterly* 1974–5).

Four teams of consultants were invited to compete to design the city. The competition was won by the firm of Llewelyn-Davies Weeks Forestier-Walker Bor, who submitted their report in 1970, having made public some preliminary findings in 1969.[11] The response from the architectural profession was unfavourable at this stage, setting the tone for the city's persistently poor image in the professional press. The 1970 report said little about individual buildings; like Lúcio Costa's 1957 plan for Brasília, it concentrated on an overall form, and a design philosophy (Costa 1957, discussion in Holston 1989: 59–98). The report opened with a set of six principles on which the city should be built:

i.   Opportunity and freedom of choice
ii. Easy movement and access, and good communications
iii. Balance and variety
iv. An attractive city
v.   Public awareness and participation
vi. Efficient and imaginative use of resources.

(Llewelyn-Davies *et al.* 1970: 13)

'Freedom of choice' is perhaps the most important of these principles, for it identifies a move from a negative philosophy of planning towards one that was essentially permissive.[12] The earlier new towns, along with other large public services, were conceived on a 'predict and provide' basis, in which the state, via its appointed development agencies, decided the material needs of the population. Llewelyn-Davies and his team presented the alternative view that such needs could not be known in advance, but ought to be met in a framework flexible enough to accommodate them; not an easy task, as he admitted (Llewelyn-Davies *et al.* in Bendixson 1969: 103). However, the consultants were agreed that 'no committee of experts should try to dictate the future pattern of life in the city'. This was 'not a new idea' but it was new 'to take it seriously' (Llewelyn-Davies *et al.* in Bendixson 1969: 103). Ideally therefore, the 'final form of the city should be an expression of people's wishes, hopes, tastes, and it is a first principle of our planning to make this possible' (Llewelyn-Davies *et al.* in Bendixson 1969: 103). These were, in the words of one commentator on the interim report of 1969, 'unusual and humble' objectives (Bendixson 1969: 108).

Many metaphors have been employed to describe what Milton Keynes formally resembled: 'an open ended umbrella' (Llewelyn-Davies in Banham 1976: 359); 'a huge tartan picnic blanket thrown down on the soft Buckinghamshire countryside' (Bendixson 1969: 107); 'a piece of coarse netting dropped askew on the map' (Banham 1976: 359); 'an instant Los Angeles to be laid over the agrarian landscape of Buckinghamshire' (Frampton 1992: 286). The result, unlike any existing English city of any size was nevertheless 'consistent and comprehensible', and remains clearly identifiable from the air (Banham 1976: 360).[13]

The plan for Milton Keynes emerged from an internal debate during 1967 about mobility, during which a powerful faction within Buckinghamshire County Council advocated a dense, architecturally dramatic linear city between the two existing poles, linked by the fashionable transport of the period, a monorail.[14] The city's high density would make free public transport viable. This scheme was (as far as it could be deduced from the plans) spectacular, but reiterated Modernist tropes familiar from Le Corbusier's Ville Radieuse of the 1920s, from Brasília, and from the post-war redevelopment of the Barbican in the City of London. In the plan, this city was all megastructure; a single architectural form contained all imaginable services, and its single axis and means of transport disciplined all movement.

By contrast, the Llewelyn-Davies plan showed a preference for a city in the form of a loose network, or grid (Figure 3.1). This was to be rectilinear in the centre, providing, according to the architectural historian Robert Maxwell, an image of 'geometrical rigour' that was 'astonishing in its purity of form' (Maxwell 1974–5: 1). But the centre was only a small part of the whole. The rest of the plan described a city of exceptionally low density, comprised of suburban housing rising to no more than three storeys.[15] Its principal arteries wound picturesquely around the contours of the landscape.[16] Its grid described kilometre squares, which, uniquely for a new town, were not zoned but might contain any combination of buildings for housing, work or recreation. These functions were therefore dispersed throughout the settlement, rather than concentrated in any one place. None of these in any way resembled a neighbourhood, a deliberate policy aimed at spreading wealth through the city (Llewelyn-Davies et al. 1970: 16). The city's inhabitants, it was thought, should roam throughout the city for the best services. This, it was thought, was what affluent people did, and the city should reinforce their behaviour rather than try to restrict it.[17] In other words the city not only provided an image of mobility, but also enforced it. Like Brasília, designed in 1957, mobility would be (in theory) achieved by universal and growing access to private cars, penetrating 'every point in the city' and offering 'its

The Plan for
Milton Keynes

MAP C
THE STRATEGIC PLAN

3.1
**The Plan for
Milton Keynes
(1970), architect:
Llewelyn-Davies
Weeks Forestier-
Walker and Bor**

users a freedom of choice and opportunity which more and more people will want – and be able – to take advantage of' (Llewelyn-Davies *et al.* 1970: 15).

Although Milton Keynes was conceived of as a finite settlement in the first instance, its structure, particularly in its emphasis on mobility and freedom of choice, was underwritten by a belief that cities above all were fundamentally indeterminate; they were formed by change, and so ought to embrace it. Milton Keynes was geometrical, but was clearly capable of infinite extension along the same pattern without destroying the concept; although circumstantially limited, it was conceived of in endless terms. In 1951, the architects had discussed this possibility in an essay for the *Architectural Association Journal*, published under the name of Llewelyn-Davies, but actually written by John Weeks (Llewelyn-Davies 1951). The essay proposed that architecture should, as a matter of course, accept indeterminacy, as obsolescence was a building's only certainty. Architecture should, he argued, make use of modular components and serial structures to create 'loose fitting and extendable building envelopes' that could be readily adapted (Hughes and Sadler 2000: 97). Later citing John Cage's serial music and Andy Warhol's serial art as influences, Weeks and Llewelyn-Davies built the Northwick Park hospital in north west London (1961–74) on indeterminate principles. As a building type particularly subject to change, the hospital was conceived as a series of modular units with a standard width, but not length, which could be extended as space allowed (Hughes and Sadler 2000: 96–101).

Now for the general population, indeterminacy as an idea was underwritten by certain new beliefs about labour patterns. In particular, it made assumptions about growing leisure, or the demand for leisure. The Milton Keynes Development Corporation certainly believed that automation would result in a rationalisation of working hours, which in turn implied 'that more time than ever will be spent at leisure. We think this trend can only accelerate. Shorter working weeks and longer holidays will be the norm' (MKDC 1974: 3). This was underpinned by an assumption that the majority of the population would be below the age of thirty (Llewelyn-Davies *et al.* 1970: 3). Hence the profusion of leisure centres, then a new architectural type, dispersed throughout the city. Hence also the small, but telling, proposal that allotments in the development area be renamed as 'leisure gardens'. The concept of 'allotment' brought to mind a time of scarcity that could be ameliorated through hard labour; it also carried connotations of paternalism, class and old age. All this would be transcended through the coming age of leisure.

Above all, Milton Keynes was to be modern. Derek Walker, the city's chief architect, wrote later that 'Our existing cities are the shell of a society at least 30 years extinct [. . .] the modern way of life has no physical expression except for in Milton Keynes' (Walker 1982: 9). The city was not only therefore simply a new form, but an attempt to imagine a qualitatively new and different way of life.

Representing the city

Now in saying this, I am arguing that Milton Keynes presents a different case to both the Modernist city in post-war England and the more recent assertion of traditional city forms. The problem for the historian is how to recover a sense of its difference, when the architectural reception of the city now, as much as its popular reception (if it does not treat it as a joke), stresses its lack of differentiation from its surroundings (see Frampton 1992: 286). Maxwell (1974–5) gave some sense of the shock and surprise that the original plan was capable of generating, as did some journalists later at the opening of the central shopping centre in 1980 (for example, McKean 1980).[18] But one of the most persuasive ways of recovering a sense of the city's otherness is by considering the official images of it produced at the beginning of its construction. These images were made for popular consumption before anything much had been built. They were designed to attract potential residents, particularly from London; they were preoccupied less with the architecture of the new city than the urban lifestyle that it would make available. My interest in them has to do with the manner of their representation, which, it seems to me, indicates some deep and unresolved doubts about what the city represents. There is a sense of anxiety and unease in these pictures, which if anything their artist cultivates.

Let me present three of these images. They were drawn by Helmut Jacoby in 1974, a draughtsman employed by Derek Walker on his appointment as chief architect by the development corporation in 1972. Jacoby, based in the US during the 1950s and 1960s, had provided images for architects including Philip Johnson, Eero Saarinen, I. M. Pei, Marcel Breuer and Kevin Roche, in effect providing a visual index of American Modernism.[19] He was probably the most highly regarded architectural renderer working anywhere at the time and his involvement with Milton Keynes was crucial in establishing the city's image.

The first image reads straightforwardly. It depicts the central city seen from above, twenty rectilinear blocks of low-rise, campus-like buildings separated by tree-lined avenues (Figure 3.2). The largest of these structures, the Miesean shopping centre, actually completed in 1980, is clearly visible as a white rectangular block in the lower half of the image.[20] Lower down, there is the (un-built) city park complete with faux-prehistoric burial mound and ornamental pond.[21] Further to the top of the image, the giant covered stadium stands out, a vast but self-effacing space-frame structure concealing a 65,000-seat bowl.[22] But what is striking about the city as Jacoby saw it is, apart from the formality of the grid, is its politeness, its discretion, its relative lack of differentiation from the surrounding countryside. If anything – and this illustrates one of Llewelyn-Davies' public aims for the city – the centre is actually greener than the country, showing a higher density of planting than the farmland (Self 1972: 114). It merges imperceptibly with its surroundings. There are no monuments. No one part of the centre stands out. It cultivates the appearance of a network, in which hierarchies are rhetorically eschewed in favour of circulation. Here, rhetorically speaking, any part of the centre is as open as any other.

The grid of roads both images the penetrability of the city, and facilitates it. So too does the foreground image of a helicopter in flight, from which the view is imaginatively made. The machine, a Hughes 300C, is a light, low-powered two-seater built for urban use; the passenger seat in this case is occupied by one of Jacoby's stylised figures, a young man in a fashionable business suit of the time. Prefiguring a real attempt by the development corporation to establish a helicopter service from Milton Keynes to Heathrow airport, the message is clear – this is just another way of getting around, albeit a self-consciously modern one.[23]

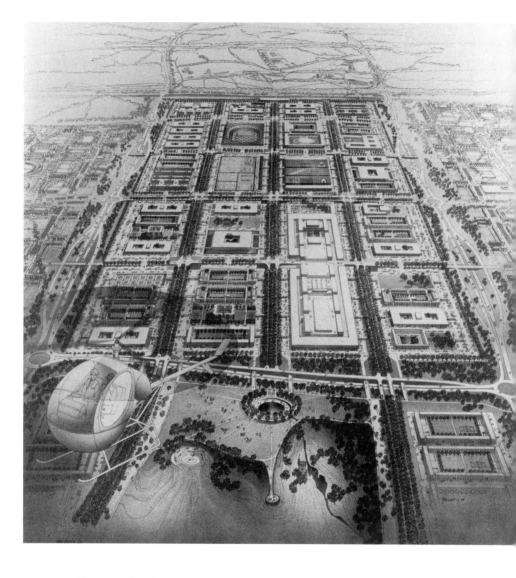

The second and third images, progressively more ambiguous in the order in which I present them, depict interiors of leisure centres, a prolific building type in Milton Keynes. One shows the interior of the City Club, a vast leisure complex proposed by a developer, Ultramarine in 1973, in response to a brief from the development corporation (Figure 3.3). Ultramarine's plan was unprecedented in scale. They imagined a 65,000 seat covered stadium, itself untried in Europe, surrounded by restaurants, bars and exhibition spaces. In order for the stadium to be profitable, there would need to be 40,000 visitors per week, but, the developers argued, it might be the single element that would create 'pride' in the city (Bendixson and Platt 1992: 136–40). A revised

3.2
Rendering of central Milton Keynes for the Milton Keynes Development Corporation
Helmut Jacoby

proposal made after concerns were raised by the development corporation about crowd-control in such a megastructure resulted in the fragmentation of facilities on a horizontal, park-like layout within the central area grid, and the addition of two swimming pools, an ice rink, an indoor ski slope, a hair-dressers and a bookstore. The board of the development corporation, initially sceptical, were convinced of the validity of the proposal after discussions with representatives of Madison Square Garden in New York, Tivoli in Copenhagen and Wembley Stadium, the latter being the nearest British equivalent. Derek Walker, an enthusiast for the project, thought it might provide a 'soul' for the city in the same way the cathedral did for Coventry. The plan was in effect killed by the economic recession of the mid-1970s, although elements of it, the indoor skiing, for example, survived and have been realised. But these things survived in discrete, separable buildings that spectacularise their primary function, not as elements of a single complex that would compress and synthesise all imaginable culture.[24] At the club, the official pamphlet stated in 1974, 'somebody can have a hard game of football, relax in a sauna bath, meet friends for a drink in the bar, look at an exhibition and eat in a restaurant' – all in the same place (MKDC 1974: 15).

Jacoby's image, made in 1974, shows a fragment of the first version of the City Club, the arcade, a very large but light, single-storey, space-frame structure with exposed vertical I-beams and roof trusses in the manner of Mies van der Rohe. There is a suggestion of a transparent convex roof,

3.3
Rendering of City Club, Milton Keynes for the Milton Keynes Development Corporation
Helmut Jacoby

which would confirm a generally understood vocabulary of arcade form. The image describes the view from the first floor balcony, looking down towards the activity below.

It is, perhaps intentionally, hard to summarise the scene: hetero-geneity, albeit within the imaginative limits of the designers, is the key idea. There is a lot going on, and although most of it falls into predictable pat-terns of consumption and display, no single activity dominates. It is a public space of a kind, although one whose tone is set by popular culture rather than history or civic duty: giant images of the lunar astronaut Neil Armstrong and the rock guitarist Jimi Hendrix loom from the walls, while a television screen above the bar shows a film. There are people promenading in fashionable clothes, eating and drinking, and dancing to a jazz band. In this image, the City Club is self-consciously modern, framing activities that are rhetorically, if not actually, unlimited.

Simultaneity is important here: the performance of the jazz group (which might normally suppose reverent and single-minded appreciation) is now one of an abundance of activities with which one is free to engage at whatever level.[25] Everything is, to appropriate Walter Benjamin's statement about architecture, apprehended in a state of distraction (Benjamin 1973: 241; Gilloch 2002: 190). Consumption is radically undifferentiated. There is simul-taneity as well, it could be said, in the interpenetration of inside and outside, such that it is unclear where the building or frame begins and ends. Birches line the mall; other vegetation spreads from the roof, seemingly unattached to anything on the interior; the band plays in an intermediate zone that is neither outside nor in. Meanwhile, a Boeing 707, unmistakable signifier of glamorous intercontinental travel, zooms over the club, passing through, but as much part of the scene as anything else.

It is all slightly exotic (the imagery is by and large American, taking note of the aircraft, the astronaut, the music, the musician) and slightly surreal (there is a large stars-and-stripes hat behind a mass of vegetation, bearing the strange message 'Look out Sam!' – why?), but never overwhelmingly so. This is more or less a shopping mall, and the different activities presented are all assimilable to the idea of consumption. There is no sense, for example, that this public space could ever be the site of political activity. And as Bendixson has pointed out, the architecture has a sense of order and restraint that can be said to have been calculated to dissuade dissent. The stadium is covered by a 'rectangular space frame of the utmost severity' while the activ-ities of the club proper were 'set out as strictly as the square on a chess board' (Bendixson and Platt 1992: 140). As the historian Patrick Joyce has argued with respect to the nineteenth-century city, the idea of freedom that is presented here is at the same time a code that disciplines social behaviour (Joyce 2003: 189–90).

There is nonetheless a sense of unease about this scene, as if the figures represented are not entirely comfortable in their roles. This unease is, I think, further developed in the third image I draw your attention to. It describes a further scene of leisure activity, Wolverton Agora, a public venue which actually exists, now mostly in the form of a covered market (MKWeb 2004) (Figure 3.4). Like the City Club arcade proposal, this is a large space frame structure with exposed metal roof trusses, providing a central public arena, though it is smaller and architecturally less spectacular than the City Club. The roof, for example, is opaque, and although Jacoby permits us to see out to the street entrance, he does not give the same impression of the inter-penetration of inside and outside. The finishes, as far as we can tell in this monochrome image, are mostly brick and tile, which, if in the dark browns common in British public buildings in the 1970s, would have made for a warm but gloomy environment.[26] But this image is more detailed – if ultimately highly ambiguous – about the nature of the public life that the new city would frame. We have moved first from the level of generalisation in the helicopter view, to a generalised sense of consumer culture, and now to a sense of culture on an individual level. Here the viewer the viewer looks across the central arena of the Agora from a corner of the street level balcony, and in this image, true to the ideals of the plan, the architecture effaces itself in favour of the action.[27]

The architecture may be unspectacular but the action is not. It is a circus of sorts, with a small standing crowd witnessing a trainer standing on

3.4
Rendering of Wolverton Agora, Milton Keynes for the Milton Keynes Development Corporation
Helmut Jacoby

the back of two baby elephants, one foot on each, while on the other side of the arena, a giraffe and a pantomime horse stare each other down as two acrobats perform handstands. In the centre, a couple dressed as king and queen occupy a throne on a floral float, led by a cowboy firing two pistols in the air. Above them an airship – or a barrage balloon – floats, accompanied by inflatables in the forms of Humpty-Dumpty, Donald Duck, Pluto the Dog and what may or may not be a giant baguette. But are they inflatables at all? Merging seamlessly into the melée at the far left of the image on the balcony is Mickey Mouse, or rather, it seems, someone in a Mickey suit. The whole scene is watched by a pair of lovers, with whom we are asked to identify. As they lean distractedly over the balcony, the man cups his right hand over the woman's breast, and seems to gaze down into her cleavage while she looks down at the circus action. Her loose blouse is mildly suggestive of sexual availability. A bottle of beer stands half drunk, the smaller of their two glasses poised tantalisingly half over the edge of the balcony cornice.[28] In the ambiguity of the imagery and its apparent (yet opaque) symbolism, it is a remarkably rich image.

Given its instrumental nature, it would be easy to dismiss this image as ephemeral. But like Jacoby's other images of Milton Keynes, it is done on a large scale, and shows an intense reading of the architect's draw-ings; it deserves to be taken seriously. The number and detail of the figures also mark this out as an unusually highly worked perspective. It has had an afterlife too, appearing in virtually all the official publications where the idea of the City Club is cited, as well as a volume of Jacoby's own renderings.

If we do take these images as a serious attempt to represent the life of the city before it was built, then the uneasiness in the representation is curious. By this I do not mean that they are badly drawn (they are not), nor that they are drawn with a lack of attention relative to the other parts of the image (they are very detailed). Rather, I mean that the representation of the life of the city betrays anxiety about what the new city stands for. It is as if the artist has realised, but cannot say explicitly, that the theory that underpins Milton Keynes will result in a radically different kind of city to the familiar, one in which class boundaries and boundaries of taste might be collapsed, and distinctions between notions of high and low cultures broken. With this poten-tial for radical change comes, naturally, unease, which the artist deals with by depicting it in ironic terms.

How can this be shown? In all of Jacoby's work, not only that of Milton Keynes, there is a tendency to stylise the figures; his treatment of hair, for example, turns it into a solid shape, brittle and opaque, like meringue. But the stylisation of the figures is exacerbated in the Milton Keynes images.

Not just that, but their number, variety and detailed character means the figures constitute something like a crowd, or even a society. This fact demands that they must on one level to be taken seriously, rather than just an indicator of scale (the usual role of the human figure in architectural drawings), yet on another level, they seem absurd. Irony seems to me to be the right word to apply to the figures in the City Club. They are reduced to the level of clothes-horses, parading a ridiculous array of contemporary fashions in an arena where public life has become a spectacle of meaningless consumption.

The same could be said about the Wolverton image. Jacoby correctly identifies this as a working class part of the city. Of the existing settlements in the development area, it was the only one with any appreciable industry, a railway works. The ambiguities of the scene – the apparent seduction of the main female figure, the calculated blurring of boundaries between 'real' and 'sculptural', the reduction of working class entertainment to the most crass forms of kitsch, illustrates to the artist's (and by extension, the architects') essential discomfort with what is depicted. It is not their culture, and it shows.

I would make no claim for these images as art, for they are clearly instrumental in the purpose of promoting the city, but their ironic tone makes them worthy of comparison with the great images of late-nineteenth-century Paris by Georges Seurat. In *La Grande Jatte* (1884–6) for example, the affluent middle class are shown at play on a Sunday afternoon; their preoccupations with their clothes and correct deportment gives the scene a sense absurdity below the painting's superficial grandness that subverts the sense that this scene of leisure can be read straightforwardly. The companion piece to *La Grande Jatte*, *La Baignade* might be reasonably taken as a frame through which to view Jacoby's Wolverton image. In this case, Seurat shows the working class at play in an image of relative repose and calm, subverted by the realisation that the bathers have chosen the point of the Seine where the great collector sewer of Paris deposits the waste of the entire city.[29] Likewise, Jacoby's image is dominated by a few large figures and is characterised by monumentality and repose, yet these qualities are subverted by the fact that the subject matter of the image is a very low-grade culture. In summary, in the cases of both Seurat and Jacoby, the artist is essentially alienated from his subject matter; in each instance, it appears absurd; the means of dealing with it is the adoption of an ironic tone.

Milton Keynes' sources

This young, free, mobile, indeterminate, city of consumption was in many respects an attempt to materialise the planning theory of Melvin Webber. In December 1967, the Milton Keynes consultants invited Webber from Berkeley where he held a professorial chair in planning theory, to speak at a seminar.[30] As Robert Maxwell wrote later, he was fascinated by the

> relation between mobility and place; if the mobility is achieved by private car, place becomes stopping place, and all places come to have the same quality as temporary stages in a long car journey, with the disembodied aspect of destinations perceived through the car windscreen.
>
> (Maxwell 1975)

In Webber's view, elaborated in the essays 'Nonplaces and the Nonplace Urban Realm' (1963) and 'Permissive Planning' (1968) there was no longer any meaningful connection between the realm of the social, and spatial form. This was for the simple reason that in a mobile, affluent society, one's social relationships were not limited by one's spatial location. A professional – he gave the example of a university scientist – may have working relationships that span several countries, but which are as meaningful as those close by. In fact, his local relationships might be quite weak by comparison (Webber 1964: 113). He continued,

> a highly specialised man may turn from a transatlantic telephone call to arbitrate an intra-office personnel problem, to read his mail from customers in various places, then join the motorists in the peak hour traffic rush, before reassuming his roles as parent, news-paper reader and member of a friendship circle.
>
> (Webber 1964: 118)[31]

Webber's imaginary organisation man inhabited not a city, precisely, but an 'urban realm', defined as 'neither settlement nor territory, but heterogeneous groups of people communicating through space'. The 'spatial extent' of each of these realms would remain, Webber thought, 'ambiguous' (Webber 1964: 114).[32] At the highest levels, the urban realm would be the most spatially diverse and extensive, as the example above shows (Webber 1964: 118). Importantly for the question of urban design, Webber conceived of the urban realm as an essentially horizontal arrangement, both conceptually and spatially (Webber 1964: 118). A society would function best if the relationships of its members were allowed to flourish, wherever they are; the richness of a society had little to do with its spatial form, much to do with the ease with which such relationships could be conducted, extended and developed.

Good communications rather than building were therefore paramount. Planning needed to be rethought as a consequence. Instead of a preoccupation with land use in predetermined geographical places, and a body of essentially restrictive law to enforce that division of land, planning should become a continuous process based around continuously revised goals. Peter Hall described his theory of planning in terms of 'goal setting, forecasting of change in the outside world, assessment of chains of consequences of alternative courses of action, appraisal of costs and benefits as a basis for action strategies, and continuous monitoring' (Hall 1996: 330). The city become urban realm was thus a de-centred network, indeterminate in both geographical temporal extent and time; a process in space and time, not a place.

Webber was the single greatest influence on Llewelyn-Davies, and in terms of the final form of the Milton Keynes plan, his ideas were most clearly materialised in the refusal of a neighbourhood structure: the neighbourhood was precisely that coincidence of social relations and place that Webber argued could no longer meaningfully exist.[33] The city's affluent, mobile residents would – in fact, were obliged to – choose from a smorgasbord of public services spread across the entire city. Webber, of course, is only one element in an intellectual constellation that informs Milton Keynes. There were, as Jencks described, many corresponding ideas in contemporary planning discourse where the city is rethought as an undifferentiated array or network, horizontally rather than vertically organised, explicit in its refusal of traditional urban hierarchies. Among the most widely read of these theories was Harvey Cox's *The Secular City* (1965) which argued that the loss of neighbourhood-type local identities was in fact something to be celebrated for it marked a further step away from the 'superstition and the cosmologies of closed societies'. The qualities Cox most valued were therefore, controversially, 'uprootedness and pragmatism', these things best describing what he called the secular city (Jencks 1985: 329). Jencks relates Cox's thought to the philosophy of Karl Popper, who in *The Open Society and its Enemies* (1966), had similarly argued for an anti-tribal society, in which superstition and prejudice were replaced by an essentially anonymous rationalism. There should be no utopian or holistic schemes, for they would require irrational belief. Instead, as in Webber's planning theory, belief would be replaced by an ideology of constant self-criticism and monitoring. Jencks usefully summarised these and other perspectives thus: 'the positive use of anonymity and mobility replaced the agonising over their existence' (Jencks 1985: 329).

It could be said that these theories were rooted in the intellectuals' experiences of one remarkable modern city, Los Angeles. By the mid-1960s, LA presented a form markedly unlike anything in Europe, or even the eastern US.[34] Its population was less than half of what it was to be at the end of the twentieth century, but its spatial pattern was well-established: polycentric, horizontally dispersed, mobile, (relatively) free of planning restrictions, and so geographically extensive it had three distinct meteorological climates. Downtown, the traditional heart of any American city, was only worth a 'note' here, as Reyner Banham put it in 1972 (Banham 1972: 201). In LA, the city and periphery were conceptually blurred.[35]

Although historically one of the American cities most settled by those of British descent, the English relationship with Los Angeles had long been uneasy. Banham quoted from the English journalists Adam Raphael and James Cameron testifying to the city's perceived incivility; the city was, variously, a 'Babylon' beneath a corrosive smog, and a 'stinking sewer' (Banham 1972: 21). Banham's enthusiasm was shared by Peter Cook of Archigram, Peter Hall and Cedric Price, but few others. To assert in English architectural discourse that the city had value as an urban model was controversial in itself. For Llewelyn-Davies to describe the Milton Keynes plan as a 'modified Los Angeles system' was therefore to invite trouble (Banham 1976: 359). But Llewelyn-Davies referred to both his own positive experience of the city, and that of Melvin Webber, who regarded LA as a deeply civilised place. It may not have had the architectural density of New York, but it was, Webber thought, no less urbane, making rich social and cultural networks possible via its excellent communications (Jencks 1985: 330). His planning theory, whereby the concept of the city as place was superseded by the city as place-*less* urban realm, was informed by this experience.

In England, the experience of LA undoubtedly informed the polemical essay 'Non-Plan: an Experiment in Freedom' published in the 20 March 1969 issue of *New Society*. Its authors, Banham, Peter Hall (a planner), Cedric Price (an architect) and Paul Barker (the editor of *New Society*) argued that the restrictive British planning system had become fixated on trivial matters of architectural taste instead of strategy that improved the lives of those it purported to serve. They argued that their experience of southern California showed that a system in which taste was not an issue, and people were relatively free to build what and where they liked, had in fact produced a better quality of environment than that of urban England. They proposed a series of experiments in England, limited in time and geographical area, in which normal planning controls would be abolished: after a period to be determined, the experiment would be reviewed, and continued or not as appropriate. The experimental areas were named to cause intentional offence, each one identifying a cultural figure and geographical area with which a particularly bucolic idea of Englishness was associated: Constable Country, Lawrence Country and Montagu Country, envisioned by Banham, Hall and Price respectively.[36] Each imagined that a low-density sprawl would result, inhabited by a highly mobile population whose consumption of goods and services was wide ranging and eclectic. Activity was spontaneous, social attitudes progressive and leisure time abundant. Industry would dissolve seamlessly into spectacle. 'Montagu Country', the renamed Southampton–Portsmouth conurbation was a riot of pleasure: the Fawley oil refinery would be the site of a *son-et-lumière* show witnessed by an audience of stoned waterbus passengers (Banham *et al.* 1969: 441).

Los Angeles was, for the open-minded, intellectually progressive planner, the best example of what Jencks referred to as the 'open city'; a polycentric, open-ended, changeable metropolis that favoured 'grids or webs over the concentric form of traditional cities' (Jencks 1983: 346). In these ways, the experience of Los Angeles informs the city of Milton Keynes. But these experiences concern the city at the level of plan or map, the city less as material form than a process, or experiential realm. This is clearly important, but it says little about the sources for the architecture; here LA and Milton Keynes have little in common. Llewelyn-Davies imagined a city in which individual buildings would not much matter in themselves. There would be no monuments; indeed little that was in itself demonstrative. The aerial view of the city drawn by Jacoby in 1974 shows a place whose architecture is calculatedly unspectacular, merging seamlessly with the surrounding countryside.

Let us return to the City Club as a model of the city's architecture. As we saw earlier, this was to be a hi-tech, temporary, lightweight and flexible structure that, although very large, had no claim to monumentality. No exterior image of it was ever published, and all the images of its interior show a building that at least sought to represent the dissolution of boundaries between inside and outside, between architecture and landscape. It was to be rigorously self-effacing. The idea of the City Club itself took some explanation, evidenced by the initial scepticism of the board of the development corporation to the idea (Bendixson and Platt 1992: 136–40). What, they wondered, was the difference between this and a species of indoor funfair? Did not the radical compression of high and low, of corporeal and cerebral cultures signify a destructive levelling of culture? And did not the interpenetration of inside and outside signify an openness to impurity? Could such an impure, heterogeneous structure be allowed to stand in for the city metonymically as Derek Walker would have liked?[37]

In terms of built structures, The City Club most closely resembles the Centre Georges Pompidou in Paris, the giant cultural centre built by

Richard Rogers and Renzo Piano between 1971 and 1977. Like the City Club, this is a structure premised on its flexibility. Its structure – a series of giant steel columns suspending four vast, open floors, is designed to allow for almost any kind of activity from performance to exhibition to study to retail to the consumption of food and drink. And it does house all of these functions in a way that rhetorically compresses high and low culture, as Jean Baudrillard's critique of it hyperbolically makes clear (Baudrillard in Leach 1997: 210–7).[38] In this scheme, culture is altered from being the expression of a privileged élite, essentially removed from the larger population, to something that is open to all and may take almost any form. It may be consumed in a distracted way too to take up again Benjamin's metaphor – in fact, it positively encourages distraction (Benjamin 1973: 241). No longer does the consumption of culture necessarily demand prior knowledge, concentration and silence. The paradigm of consumerism takes over. The scheme's radicalism is real, for it really does alter the way culture is apprehended. But its radicalism is arguably the radicalism of capital. In these ways, it resembles the form of the City Club, but unlike it, it is a monumental building in spite of itself. Spectacular and sculptural, its colour and scale disrupt the sober nineteenth-century grid.

It could be said that the Pompidou drew on two earlier designs for cultural centres, neither built, but widely discussed (see Hughes and Sadler 2000: 5): Cedric Price's 'Fun Palace' of 1960, and Michael Webb's 'Sin Centre' of 1962. Webb, who shortly afterwards helped found Archigram, designed a twenty-storey megastructure for Leicester Square devoted to leisure (Figure 3.5). A 'biologically functionalist parody', it was an organic-looking glass skin, inspired by Buckminster Fuller's geodesic domes, inside which servicing was fetishised, the air conditioning ducts, piping and wiring displayed openly like bodily organs. 'Sin' was an exaggeration of course. This was a department store with a dance floor and bowling alley attached. And it was a building, albeit a somewhat odd-looking and unfeasible one (Frampton 1992: 281–2; Jencks 1985: 282).

In some ways more subversive was the innocently named 'Fun Palace' designed by Cedric Price and Joan Littlewood for a site in London E15 in 1960 (Figure 3.6).[39] In the words of its authors, a short lifespan 'community toy and learning machine' rather than a building, it shared several key characteristics with the Milton Keynes City Club. Like the club as it appeared in Jacoby's drawing, the Fun Palace utilised a vast space-frame in which the servicing was clearly visible (Jencks 1985: 285). Into the gigantic interior, Price imagined an extraordinarily heterogeneous range of activities, by no means all of which could be assimilated to the paradigm of consumption:

ARRIVE AND LEAVE by train, bus, monorail, hovercraft, car, tube or foot at any time YOU want to – or just have a look at it as you pass. The information screens will show you what's happening. No need to look for an entrance – just walk in anywhere. No doors, foyers, queues or commissionaires: it's up to you how you use it. Look around – take a lift, a ramp, an escalator to wherever or whatever looks interesting. CHOOSE what you want to do – or watch someone else doing it. Learn how to handle tools, paint, babies, machinery, or just listen to your favourite tune. Dance, talk or be lifted up to where you can see how other people make things work. Sit out over space with a drink and tune in to what's happening elsewhere in the city. Try starting a riot or beginning a painting – or just lie back and stare at the sky.

(Price in Hughes and Sadler 2000: 23)

Here is the rhetoric of consumer choice hyperbolised. Everything is available for consumption, from childcare to urban violence to pleasurable apathy, all safely, if loosely, contained by the palace. Price's implication was that space was given over to the public for the purposes of experimentation in urban living; the results of which might or might not lead to social change, although the context of Price's other work (an inflatable replacement for the houses of Parliament, a university on rails for the Potteries) suggests that he rather hoped that it would (Hughes and Sadler 2000: 26–7). At Milton Keynes, the rhetoric of the City Club is milder, exercised on filling up all the leisure time

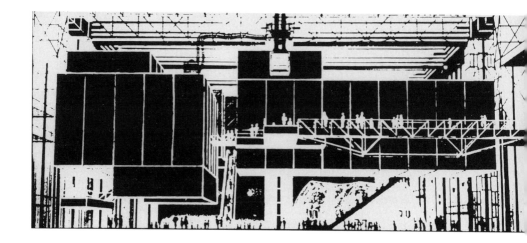

hopefully released by the cybernetic revolution.[40] Yet the hyperbole of choice is the same in both cases, and quite radically, both cases allow for, even celebrate that most direct of challenges to a northern Protestant culture, idleness. 'Just lie back and stare at the sky', Price wrote (Hughes and Sadler 2000: 23). A Milton Keynes development corporation leaflet of early 1974 permitted much the same: 'If your dream is to do absolutely nothing it would be difficult to find a city as spacious, relaxed and happy for you to achieve it in' (MKDC 1974: 27).

3.6
Fun Palace, 1960, architect: Cedric Price and Joan Littlewood

Against Milton Keynes

As a discursive object, Milton Keynes can be said to be embedded in a set of ideas that give it theoretical legitimacy: the planning theory of Webber and other advocates of what has been termed the open city, the *post hoc* rationalisation of Los Angeles by English architects and architectural critics, the radical buildings of Webb and Price. More generally, Milton Keynes could be said to illustrate a modern world-view that was essentially secular, that elevated the values of freedom and mobility, that accepted the market as a fact and encouraged participation in it, that in Freudian terms encouraged the free play of the libido. Pleasure was enormously important in the theorisation of Milton Keynes, and includes things a northern European Protestant society would regard as vestigially sinful, such as lust and idleness. These pleasurable aspects of the new city were amply illustrated by Jacoby, who seemed to understand its libidinal potential. But they are present in the original documentation by Llewelyn-Davies and his colleagues, with its emphasis on freedom.

If there was a philosophical text that might be said to underwrite these preferences, it could be said to be *Eros and Civilisation* by Herbert Marcuse, a socially libertarian argument that revisited Freud's *Civilisation and its Discontents* (Marcuse 1956). Marcuse's book attacked Freud's premise that civilised society was only made possible by the collective repression of the libido (Eros), arguing that such repression was in fact unhealthy, and would ultimately, through a Freudian return of the repressed, lead to societal collapse. Better, argued Marcuse, to give free rein to the libido; freedom from repression would radically change the basis of western civilisation, but would produce a healthier society. Marcuse's work, first published in 1956, was widely taken up by the so-called counter culture in the 1960s, a fact he reluctantly came to accept.[41] Curious as it may seem given the bland form of the actual city, Milton Keynes belongs in the libertarian critical constellation around Marcuse and ideas of freedom.

This view of the city as an essentially libertarian place was not without its critics. Banham described the *Architectural Review*'s 'implacable hostility' to both Los Angeles and 'its putative offspring up the A5 beyond Bletchley' (Banham 1976: 359)' meaning of course Milton Keynes. In his 1972 book on Los Angeles, he opened with powerful critiques of the place from two British journalists writing in 1968 in *The Guardian* and the London *Evening Standard* respectively. Adam Raphael thought it was 'the noisiest, the smelliest, the most uncomfortable, and most uncivilised major city in the United States. In short, a stinking sewer' (Banham 1972: 15). James Cameron, meanwhile described the city as no more than an endless sprawl of

> hamburger stands, banks, topless drug stores, hippie hide-outs, Hiltons, drive-in mortuaries, temples of obscure and extraordinary religions, sinless joy and joyless sin, restaurants built to resemble bowler hats, insurance offices built to resemble Babylon [. . .].
>
> (Banham 1972: 16)

Now these opinions (which needless to say represent only a tiny fraction of the total negative criticism of Los Angeles) were driven by a powerful moral sense. What caused offence was partly the physical discomfort of any large city, the noise, the pollution and so forth. But much more offensive was the peculiar character of LA itself; its tendency to flatten received cultural hier-archies, its elevation of pleasure and individual gratification, its essential godlessness. So it is with Milton Keynes – a review of the shopping centre on its opening in 1979, for example describes it as flashy, inauthentic, bogus and American; resurrecting a moral critical vocabulary that might as well have come from Ruskin (McKean 1980).

Now there are plenty of critics who make the same general arguments in relation to Milton Keynes. But germane to the argument already
made here is the extent to which the authors of Milton Keynes acknowledged
their own difficulties with the libertarian concept of the city. The perspective
drawings of the city made by Jacoby, are, as I have argued, clouded by a
sense of unease. Although in theory they promote the city, they adopt a mode
of representation that is essentially ironic. The reason for this, I suggest, is
twofold: first, the unavailability of a mode to describe a lifestyle that does not
exist in the present moment; second, a fearfulness on the part of the architects about what the proposals actually mean. The representational tone they
adopted – irony – suggests that they did not see themselves inhabiting the
city they created; they wished to establish some distance from it, and irony
was a ready means of so doing. The architects may have an intellectual attraction to the libertarian ideas that underpin Milton Keynes, but the unease in
their representation betrays a real anxiety about how such libertarianism
might be materialised.[42]

Milton Keynes might therefore be said to raise moral questions.
These questions were, no doubt, uppermost in the minds of those who made
a critique of the city, and I will turn now to the most extensive, although
possibly also the most oblique, of these. In 1971, the year after the detailed
plan for Milton Keynes, the *Architectural Review* published a comprehensive
attack on it, from the point of view of the picturesque. This was of 'Civilia: the
End of Sub-Urban Man', a scheme for a new town on an East Midlands
slagheap, published in 1974. It occupied a special issue of the journal, mostly
written by Hubert de Cronin Hastings, with illustrations by the journal's picture
editor, Kenneth Browne. It was Hastings' valedictory statement, his last intervention before he retired from the journal after 46 years, and it followed the
pattern of the other interventions described here already, on 'Townscape' and
the Italian city (Wolfe 1949; *Architectural Review* 1962).

Hastings adopted his usual pseudonym of Ivor de Wolfe, and the
text was as windy and bizarre as always, another exercise in doom-laden
circumlocution. But its key principles were clear enough. As indicated by the
essay's subtitle, it was an attack on sprawl, a tendency the *Architectural
Review* thought had been exacerbated by the most recent generation of
new towns. Hastings directly attacked the enthusiasm in certain architectural
quarters for the form of Los Angeles, relating it to Milton Keynes. The
Buckinghamshire new town was a key representative of the 'demon' of
sprawl. An 'autistic little demon if ever there was one who might yet be got
into a corner and quietly garotted before he manages [. . .] to skewer London
and Birmingham on one cloven spear like an open-ended Kebab' (Wolfe 1971:
334). The written manner is peculiar to Hastings, but the sentiment prescient,

and the pose of doomsayer familiar from, for example, the much later writings of Richard Rogers. Without the 'major act of environmental reconstruction' of Civilia, we would simply 'say goodbye to England in the coming Millennium' (Wolfe 1971: 334). England is tellingly identified here with the countryside.[43] The policy Hastings advocated was 're-centralisation', 'building public works called cities', on the understanding that what had been built so far in the new towns programme had not been cities at all, but recycling what would now be called 'brownfield' land, and building at a density never before seen in Britain.

The city of Civilia was large – a million inhabitants, four times the projected size of Milton Keynes. It was also to be extremely densely popu-lated, occupying just sixteen square miles, making it precisely one hundred times as dense as then vaguely fashionable LA (Wolfe 1971: 354). In form, it deliberately aped the medieval hill towns of central Italy, using its conical slag heap as an armature.[44] Because all modern servicing and communications were kept off-site at the base of the town, space was freed for a highly picturesque network of winding streets and stairs, gangways and pedestrian plazas. The architecture was skilfully collaged from photographs of contem-porary buildings by the *Architectural Review*'s picture editor Kenneth Browne. It was both spectacular and intimate. Its vertiginous buildings were made to inspire awe, but this is set against a vast array of picturesque viewpoints and spaces for contemplation. Like Milton Keynes it was new, and set somewhere in the Midlands. But it was dense where Milton Keynes sprawled; it was vertiginous where Milton Keynes was flat; it permitted circulation only by foot and boat, where Milton Keynes favoured the car; its architecture was spectacular, where Milton Keynes' was self-effacing. Kenneth Browne's extraordinary images illustrate these points of difference (Figures 3.7 and 3.8).

Like the residents of Milton Keynes, the residents of this place seemed mostly to be on holiday, but their leisure was subtly different. Residents of Milton Keynes were freed from work by automation, living in an as yet unrealised future. Civilia's were free already; they never really had to work because they belonged to the rentier class that produced the *Architectural Review*. Their leisure was arguably that of the sophisticated bourgeois – the polite stroll, the coffee and conversation in the terrace café, the boating trip. There were no spaces for large public assembly here (like the City Club), because their privileged residents did not need them. Neither were there spaces for large-scale consumption, because this activity fell outside the interests of the city for whom it was built. Milton Keynes was described by some as a bourgeois city, but compared with Civilia, it is a place of the rabble or the mob. Constantly on the move, constantly distracted by the proliferating consumer culture, Milton Keynes' citizens never develop the deep sense of place inculcated by the picturesque city.

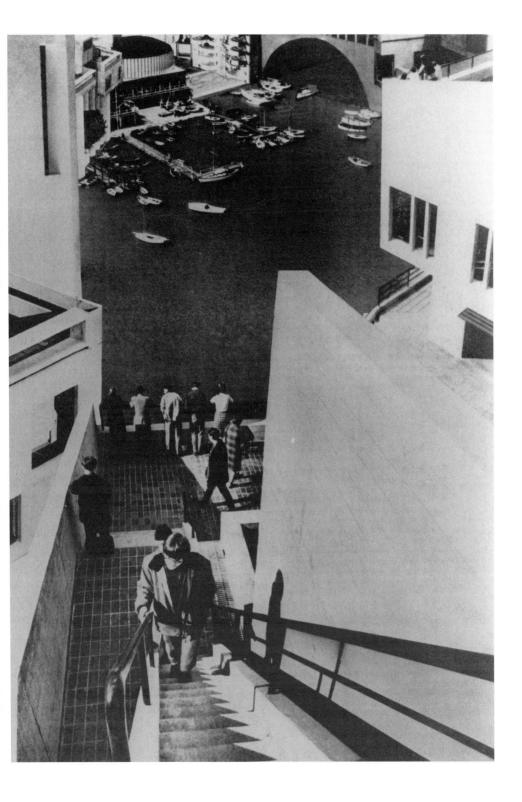

Like de Cronin Hastings' other writings, 'Civilia' read now seems only partly serious; the absurdity of its terminology seems knowing, while the hyperbolic vertiginousness of Browne's buildings, and the surreal character of the city's street-life in his images recalls the contemporaneous animated collages of Terry Gilliam for Monty Python. For certain, what we know of Hastings suggests a man who was concerned above all with theatrical effect, manifest not only in his plans for buildings, but in his theatrical character (see discussion of him in Chapter 2). Yet for all this, in Civilia's picturesque character, and in its powerful reassertion of the bourgeois public realm, of the city as a playground for the privileged, it is oddly prescient.

How might Civilia be construed as an attack on the moral ambiguities of Milton Keynes? Let me sketch out some ideas. To begin with, it was a city plan that, in the true spirit of the picturesque, confined itself to the visual. Restricting the idea of city to the creation of an image, it could absolve itself of those difficult problems of use and inhabitation that so preoccupied the authors of Milton Keynes. What mattered was contained within the purified domain of aesthetics; base desires could be safely kept out. To continue, Civilia was a plan that actively repressed such things as consumption and circulation. There were apparently no big retail stores here, because they would not be appropriate for the picturesque image; similarly, barely any roads (banished to a subterranean zone, where they cannot be seen); no provision for large-scale entertainment including spectator sports. In summary, Civilia dealt with the moral uncertainties of the libertarian city by banishing them. How did it banish them, exactly? By recreating the bourgeois public realm of an idealised past. In the powerful viewpoint of the Civilia images, the city – as it invariably was in the *Architectural Review* – was an object of spectacular consumption to be enjoyed by a privileged observer. Milton Keynes' architects were well aware of the *Review*'s attack on them, and declared Civilia to be 'a curious stockpile of stacked up medieval modern' which was 'curiously arbitrary and limp in terms of city planning – all frou frou photomontage and the golden word game' (Walker in *AAQ* 1975). More seriously they recognised its class origins, the picturesque aesthetic marking the reactionary reassertion of bourgeois taste in city planning: 'they raise the question of who is architecture for? Who is the consumer of architecture if one regards it as a product?' (Woodhead in *AAQ* 1975). Taking up the picturesque in such a profound way was, the Milton Keynes architects thought, indicative of a profound suspicion of, and hostility to, the modern world. One of them, Chris Woodhead, wrote in 1974:

> The worries the *AJ* people had were far deeper than worries about architecture, they were triggered by a much deeper worry,

I suspect, which is to do with the nature of modern life, the nature of modern institutions, a fundamental dislike of the twentieth century, of western technological culture.

(Chris Woodhead in *AAQ* 1974–5)[45]

Finally, this spectacular reassertion of bourgeois values is justified in moral terms. Occupying a fraction of the land area of the profligate Los Angeles, it is a means of saving the earth. By re-centralising the urban populations, the antique oppositions between town and country can be recreated. It is a perfect manifestation, in Modernist dress, of the aristocratic world-view of the picturesque.

Conclusions

I want to make two general points in conclusion. First is to say that this account of Milton Keynes has been focused on the city as a philosophical proposition, rather than as a material fact. The libertarian ideas that I say underpin it, and the uneasiness in its representation have little to do with the actually existing city, which in many respects works well. In retrospect, it also can be said to have little to do with the idea of the open city, or the non-place urban realm, or non-plan, ideas that suppose it to be a process rather than a monument, whose limits are indeterminate and porous. The fear that this might actually be the case is part of Civilia's motivation – Hastings lambastes Milton Keynes as an alien growth that will, if unchecked, fill up all of the gaps between London and Birmingham.[46] In fact, the city has done nothing of the sort. It remains legible, quite unexpectedly, as a discrete object in the landscape, an oasis of order and sense quite distinct from the usual ad hoc way of planning a town. It may have, perversely, elements of the picturesque, as Banham once pointed out, but it remains conceptually distinct, and in reality really nothing to do with Los Angeles at all.[47]

Second, for all the appearance of modernity that Milton Keynes still evinces, the hard picturesque revival of Civilia much better describes contemporary English practice. The high moral tone, the concern for aesthetics above all, the emphasis on the centre over the periphery – all these themes have been powerfully asserted in contemporary discourse. Along with them, as I hope to have shown, is a privileged world-view.

Chapter 4

The Mediterranean city

Introduction

As described in Chapter 2, one architectural response to English anxieties about the urban has been a retreat into picturesque aesthetics. Realistic fears about the safety of city space, and unease about the position of the city in English culture have led to the rethinking the city in distinctly non-urban terms. Townscape proposed a re-reading of the city in terms of nature, Poundbury the reinvention of the pre-industrial city, as if the revolutions of the nineteenth and twentieth centuries had not happened. Both instances of the picturesque sought to deny the facts that had produced urbanity in the first place.

A further response, the subject of the present chapter, has been the appropriation of urban models from continental Europe, especially the Mediterranean world. This appropriation has always existed more on a rhetorical level than on a material one. What concerns me here is not so much the importation or adaptation of foreign architectural forms as the anxious rhetoric that surrounds it. Like the revival of the picturesque, this is also a form of retreat, for it also denies the actual urban qualities of the existing English city. It also comes with its own attendant anxieties, namely the fear that the foreign is inevitably superior, and that in some putative urban competition, English cities are falling behind.[1] This particular fear has been key for architects such as Richard Rogers; it is a familiar narrative in the news media. It has become increasingly significant for the architectural profession as a whole: the RIBA held its annual conference in 2003 in Rotterdam as a means of exemplifying and debating the perceived gap between urban practice in

England and in continental Europe. The fear of the other is, needless to say, mixed with desire for it. The anxiety that Barcelona or Milan might represent some superior urban civilisation is combined with a desire for the life of these places – to build in them, to own property in them, to consume them as sophisticated tourists, to withdraw to them when the English problem becomes too much.

In this chapter, I explore this English desire for the Mediterranean historically through three cases: the phenomenon of the Grand Tour; the *Architectural Review*'s advocacy of what it termed Italian Townscape; and most importantly, the RIBA's award of the Gold Medal, the highest prize in architecture, to the city of Barcelona. It is a paradoxical and complex desire. Historically, it has been an aristocratic phenomenon, centred on the appreciation of the ancient world at the expense of the contemporary. Desire for the other was always tinged with revulsion at the habits and beliefs of the natives. Appreciation of the architectural spectacle produced by the Church, for example, was combined with a suspicion of Roman Catholicism. But this has begun to change in a post-imperial context, and the anxiety that the Mediterranean world may now exemplify better ways of living and building, is very real.

The traditional English understanding of the Mediterranean world was highly selective. It was historically aristocratic, and it remained essentially privileged, based on familiarity through cultural tourism and vacations: in other words, forms of leisure experience rather than work. It rated the visual, especially architecture, over other forms of culture. It elevated the past, and disdained the present (Haskell in Wilton and Bignamini 1997: 10). The ancient world was consumed as an ideal, forever lost. As Elsner and Rubiès have argued in their cultural history of travel, such voyages in search of what has been lost have long been essential to the construction of Western culture's sense of itself. The other may take many forms – the exotic east for the eighteenth-century tourist, the middle ages for the Victorian – but the desire for it, and its cultural role is, more or less, constant. 'Romanticism', they write, 'fulfils a need in the history of European culture as perhaps the last bulwark of modernity against secularism [. . .] (Elsner and Rubiès 1999: 4).[2]

The desire for the Mediterranean in contemporary architecture has many of these traditional qualities, although it is now linked to anxiety about English urban identity: 'If we lag behind the pace of European change, London's future will be circumscribed' (Rogers and Fisher 1992: 219). England is, Rogers thinks, about twenty years behind the rest of Europe in these terms.[3] In one sense England lags because it lacks the superficial Mediterranean pleasures of the square, the street café, the food and the weather. But it also supposedly now lacks the civic culture of the Mediterranean city, a culture which England supposedly used to have in abundance. England's polite society was much admired, as were its institutions of the public realm – its railways, its libraries and lavatories – all of which contrived a sense of civic stability (Glancey 2001). The contemporary desire for the Mediterranean is therefore tinged with a sense of loss of what England once was; Barcelona is appreciated with mourning, because it represents a past that cannot be recovered (Davies 1990). While the Grand Tourist looked on the ancient world with something like nostalgia, its loss did not threaten the present, but for the contemporary architect, the appreciation of the Mediterranean raises real anxieties about the present. In this important respect, the contemporary English appreciation of the Mediterranean departs from earlier models.

The Grand Tour

Although Italy was long a place of religious and educational pilgrimage, the modern desire for the Mediterranean could be said to begin with the eighteenth-century phenomenon of the Grand Tour, in which Italy, as has been recently described, was treated as a vast museum in a picturesque setting (Chaney 1998: xi).[4] The Grand Tour is extremely well documented from the British point of view, less so from the Italian.[5] In summary, the Grand Tour was a quasi-educational tour of Europe taken by wealthy young men until the Napoleonic wars made continental travel difficult. Travel to the continent for religious and political purposes had been routine to an educated élite for some time, but it was drastically expanded and institutionalised in the eighteenth century as an ideal form of education to which every upper-class young man would aspire. It had a practical rationale: English universities were in poor shape at the time.[6] There were more professionally focused tours for architects which made use of some of the same facilities and sights, although these were quite serious in intent, and were directed at the acquisition of specific professional skills and knowledge (Salmon 2000: 26–112).

The English Grand Tour typically lasted three years, and took a route by carriage from England, through France, and then to northern Italy via a sea passage from Marseilles. From Genoa or Livorno, the entry point to Italy, the party would travel to Rome, then south to Naples, north again to Venice, and then home via the Apennines and Germany. Each Tour was based on a prolonged stay in Rome. The Grand Tourist was accompanied by a guide known as the 'bear-leader' whose role was not only to provide instruction about the historical sights to be visited, but also moral guidance in what were considered to be challenging circumstances (Hibbert 1987: 20). Some Tourists

were accompanied by tutors of considerable intellectual standing – the econ-
omist Adam Smith, for example, was bear-leader for the third Duke of
Buccleuch (Hibbert 1987: 20).[7] But more often, the bear-leaders were 'fussy,
incompetent clergymen, pedagogues or place-seekers [. . .] quite incapable of
controlling their high-spirited young charges' (Hibbert 1987: 21).

Whatever the deficiencies of the guide, and whatever the distrac-
tions of brothels and booze, it was a broadly systematic means of acquiring an
education, represented by a Tour experience, a textual infrastructure of books
and maps, and a service infrastructure of English-run inns and stores. The
Grand Tour articulated a profoundly aesthetic view of the world, focused
almost entirely on the viewing of architectural ruins. It had procedure; monuments were to be surveyed in a particular order, and in a manner appropriate
to one who would one day inherit family possessions.[8]

Through the eighteenth century, the Tour became increasingly
narrow, focused ever more specifically on the ruins of the Roman Empire. It
was nevertheless underpinned by a modern, cosmopolitan politics. It was the
European élite who went on the Tour, and they, irrespective of their home
nation, shared the same educational background: they read the same texts,
came to the country with the same well-cultivated sense of superiority, and
once in Italy visited much the same sights. The Grand Tour was 'not only a
requisite part of a wealthy young man's education, whether he was an aristo-
crat or not', but 'an experience which identified him as a member of a
cosmopolitan community of Enlightened Europe' (Calaresu in Elsner and
Rubiés 1999: 141). Dr Johnson pronounced that 'a man who has not been in
Italy is always conscious of an inferiority' (Chilvers 1990: 196).

The British cultural relationship with Italy was the most developed
of any European nation. In Rome at the end of the eighteenth century, the
British outnumbered any other foreign group, with a population of 2,000
(Richardson and Smith 2001: 125). In one account, this amounted to 'a peaceful British invasion of Italy' (Wilton and Bignamini 1997: 21). There was no
question of the importance of it as an educational institution for the formation
of a cultivated élite, an 'invisible academy' that helped facilitate the career of
Joshua Reynolds for example, who, it has been argued, would not have been
president of the Royal Academy without his Italian experience (Wilton and
Bignamini 1997: 31). As an educational institution, the Grand Tour fostered and
disseminated a specific aesthetic. It cultivated the values of the picturesque: a
taste for the landscape work of Claude Lorraine, Nicholas Poussin, Gaspar
Dughet and Salvator Rosa was especially well developed in England as a
result. In the work of these painters, Italy was in different ways represented
as a land of ideal forms in which the landscape formed a backdrop for mytho-
logical or biblical scenes (Wilton and Bignamini 1997: 40). Claude and Poussin

represented Italy as a place of timeless and mysterious beauty in which the contemporary world played no role. In the first half of the eighteenth century, alongside this already developed landscape tradition, a new tradition of urban representation emerged to meet the specific demands of the English market. The key artists included Canaletto, Bellotto, Vernet and Panini (Wilton and Bignamini 1997: 40). Canaletto's particular success amongst the *milordi* resulted in the artist residing in London from 1756–65, where he applied his mode of architectural fantasy to English subjects, especially the river Thames (see Chapter 2).

These paintings provide evidence of the durable aesthetic produced by the Grand Tour. The city is reduced to an essential view, the river Arno in Florence, the Doge's Palace or the Grand Canal in Venice. The city appears not as a social phenomenon, but as an architectural theatre set on which colourful, but historically unspecific action may take place. The large scale of these works, and their high tone and brilliant colour make a seductive scene that the beholder feels he can enter and symbolically possess. Here, in summary, is an aesthetic which reduces the city to an image with a cultivated sense of timelessness, the city as an aesthetic fantasy, which unlike the actual city with its unfamiliar customs and unscrupulous natives, can be easily consumed.[9] The Grand Tourists were in no doubt about their superiority, vis-à-vis contemporary Italy, and the power of their gaze is represented by the nature of the imagery that they cultivated.

The *Architectural Review* and Italy

Frank Salmon has described the way in which architectural tourists of the eighteenth century brought back plans and drawings of classical buildings, which were then used directly to inform English designs (Salmon 2000). However, what concerns me more here is not so much architecture per se, as the understanding of city life. This was not so much a concern of the eighteenth-century tourist, but it assumes a much greater importance in subsequent revivals of interest in the Mediterranean world.

The Grand Tour's aesthetic mode persists in the gentlemanly world of English architecture long beyond the eighteenth century. At the *Architectural Review*, it took material form in the journal's suite of offices in Queen Anne's Gate. Apart from the calculatedly bizarre Bride of Denmark in the basement, the place was done out in a regency style, while the journal's attitude to the past made connections between the Georgian and modern periods, disparaging the immediate past.[10]

Consider, for example, the special issue of the *Architectural Review* of 1962, which discusses Italian Townscape (*Architectural Review* 1962). In many ways, this is a continuation of the 1949 thesis of Townscape. Like that piece, 'Italian Townscape' begins with a peculiar essay by the journal's editor-in-chief, Hubert de Cronin Hastings, writing as Ivor de Wolfe.[11] It advocates the dense urbanism of Italy as a model, for openly aesthetic reasons, rather than ones concerned with the four functions identified in orthodox Modernism.[12] Townscape's concerns were, Hastings summarised, 'foils, focal points, projections, vistas closed and vistas open, truncation, change of level, perspective, silhouette, intricacy, anticipation, continuity, space, enclosure, exposure, the precinct profile, rules of thumb [. . .]' (*Architectural Review* 1962: 441).

Townscape was not therefore a matter of architecture, or building, or even town planning, all nominally rational disciplines, but of art. The images, better than anything else, represent an ideological mode that here relates the architectural interest in Italy with an essentially powerful, quasi-colonial world-view in which the native population seems to exist for the purpose of giving visual pleasure to the English visitor. The Englishman does not gaze upon the Italian as an equal subject; instead, the Italian and his surroundings are made into a scene, a spectacle for visual consumption. The visual mode in operation in these pictures corresponds almost exactly to the mode of the eighteenth-century painter of townscapes. In both scenarios, that of the eighteenth-century Grand Tour, and of the modern appropriation of Italy in the *Architectural Review*, Italy becomes the supreme picturesque subject. Consider, for example, this heavily cropped image of Florence from the article, which depicts a view of the centre from a bridge crossing the river Arno (Figure 4.1). A horse-drawn cart, heavily laden with hay, passing towards the

4.1
Image of Florence from *Architectural Review*, June 1962

centre on the left of the image gives local colour, and suggests the persistence of a pre-industrial way of life. In fact, apart from the suggestion of the
tarmac road, there is nothing in the image that could have not been imagined
by Bellotto.

Barcelona

I turn now to my central case in this chapter, the example of Barcelona, the
capital of the Spanish autonomous province of Catalonia.[13] If the English
reception of the reconstructed, post-Franco city describes, as I suggest here,
a continuation of the ideology of the Grand Tour, it also marks a departure from
it. Spain was never a significant part of the Tour, and its appropriation as a site
of 'cultured' tourism is a recent phenomenon. The part of Spain that interests
me here, Catalonia, is culturally and linguistically distinct from the rest of the
country too; whatever the arguments about independence there have been
since the dissolution of the Franco dictatorship, it has presented itself to the
rest of the world as a distinct entity. So we need to be careful not simply to
give the impression that Catalonia exists in some uncomplicated Mediterranean framework. But at the same time, the reception of Catalonia by those
outside, particularly those in northern Europe, has profound similarities with
an earlier understanding of Italy. If therefore I seem to elide the differences
between Italy, Spain and Catalonia, and imply a transnational Mediterranean
world, it is because in the English architectural discourse around those places,
such differences are elided.

The English interest in Barcelona has been remarkable in its enthusiasm, although little discussed of itself.[14] Its clearest expression was in the
award of the 1999 RIBA Gold Medal to the city, the world's most prestigious
architectural award (See *Architectural Review* 1999). This was the first time it
had been given not to an individual, or group of individuals, but a city.

The case of Barcelona would seem in large part to affirm the
thesis of the Grand Tour. It demonstrates a longing for the Mediterranean
world on the part of a foreign cultural élite. A higher form of culture is
presumed to exist there, and knowledge of it is presumed to be an important,
even crucial, part of an architectural education. At the same time, along with
the important pleasures of attractive food and weather, it is, as was the
Grand Tour, continuous with an idea of leisure, in this case because urban
Spain has become attractive as a destination for middle class English tourism,
and property ownership.[15]

However, Barcelona is a departure from the paradigm of the Grand Tour in several other respects. It does not constitute a place that is especially difficult or expensive to get to. For the English, it is in some ways the most accessible of foreign city destinations, served by an array of discount airlines.[16] By some measures it was the European city most visited by tourists in recent years, surpassing the much larger and more established capital cities of London and Paris.[17] There is no question now that it, and not the seaside of the Costa Brava, is the 'motor' of tourism in the region, so visitors to the city do not by any means solely comprise a cultured élite – quite the reverse (Robira 2002: 175).

But the most significant departure from the Grand Tour paradigm is the nature of the English visitor's gaze on Barcelona. If I may be permitted a series of generalisations about the city based on its reception in the popular media, then I would say the following: the visitor looks upon the city with pleasure – but this pleasure is mixed with something like shame about the state of his or her own urban world. If the Grand Tourist went to Rome to admire the ruins of an ancient civilisation, he generally disparaged the present. The food and accommodation were invariably described as poor, and the indigenous population thought untrustworthy and unscrupulous, to be exploited at best. The situation with regard to Barcelona is almost completely the reverse. It is the modern civilisation that is admired, not that of a repressive and often bloody past. The modern city is thought clean, efficient and conscientious with regard to its duty to preserve its monuments, and bold in its approach to the future. Its government likewise impresses in its organisation and achievements, and its enlightened patronage of architects, all contrasting with the situation that is available at home. Its food and weather, needless to say, are thought excellent. The desire for Barcelona is therefore motivated by the desire to emulate, or replicate something that exists elsewhere; the city shames the English city; it exists as an ideal to be emulated.

In the following, I explore the desire for Barcelona through two aspects of the city, first the nature of the place in an exotic discourse around Spain and Spanishness, in which Catalonia plays a special role. Second, I consider Barcelona through recent architectural discourse in which the city appears as a moral place. The astringent quality of some of its recent architecture is discussed in this context. I conclude with a discussion of the limitations of the Barcelona model, in particular the way its vivid social life is dependent on authority, both in terms of social structures and state institutions such as the police. The desire for Barcelona is nostalgic and, as such, highly problematical. It is an outstanding example of what Nan Ellin has described as the romantic impulse in postmodern urbanism. In advanced capitalist societies, globalisation, she writes, has produced a search for 'urbanity, a usable past, a sense of community, a neighbourhood, a vernacular, diversity, meaning, inno- cence, roots, origins, certainties, leadership, and heroes' all of which add up to what she describes as a 'romantic resurgence' (Ellin 1996: 1). All of these things are strongly present in Barcelona because its evolution and economic position are different from those of northern Europe. Things are possible there, which are no longer possible in the north; forms of urban life still exist in ways that have long since died out elsewhere. At the same time, its late absorption into the European Union means that it has modernised with all the latest technology and equipment. Its combination of tradition and super- modernity is, for the most economically developed nations, irresistible. Yet it is the product of special circumstances, economic, political and social. Its most attractive characteristics cannot, I think, be reproduced elsewhere through architecture alone.

In general Anglo-American discourse, which is to say tourist guide- books, travelogues and reports in newspapers, Barcelona tends to represent outlandish social possibilities, behaviours and customs which are recognisable because they are (just) western and Christian, but unimaginable at home. Its position is in some respects comparable to the near east that Edward Said described in *Orientalism* – exotic and other, culturally produced by the west (perhaps with the complicity of the locals) for consumption by a western public but geographically and culturally familiar enough to allure rather than alienate (Said 1978). Spain was never a western colony in the same way as these countries of the near east, but its cultural position for an Anglo- American public is similarly uncanny. Amongst other things, this is manifest in an interest in the remains of the Islamic civilisation above everything else. In this scheme, the Alhambra palace at Granada is elevated to be the monument of greatest cultural significance.[18] Foreigners tend to exoticise Spain's landscape too. The architectural historian Christian Norberg-Schulz, unaware it seems of his objectification of the country, wrote in 1985 that the 'vegetation strikes us as being most unusual [. . .]' being strongly reminiscent of that of 'Arab countries'. 'We may safely say as a result,' he continues, 'that the Iberian peninsula was predisposed for the Islamic invasion' (Bofill 1985: 18).

Catalonia occupies an ambiguous position within this exoticising tendency. The region's geographical proximity to France, its trading and cultural links with that country and northern Europe in general, its relative wealth, its inclination – expressed by graffiti artists on motorway destination boards – to regard the rest of Spain as 'Africa' – make it relatively less open, one would think, to objectification as exotic.[19] Yet this is scarcely the case, considering the vast literature that connects Barcelona and ideas of the irrational, the scatological and the surreal. For the art critic Robert Hughes, it is Catalan food that emblematises these essential characteristics: the passion for eating almost any kind of sea creature, and the consumption at Christmas of chocolate turds (Hughes 1992: 27). For Hughes, and virtually all other foreign observers, the Catalan irrationality is symbolised too by the allegedly schizoid character of the people, expressed in the terms *seny* and *rauxa*. The former, defined as 'commonsense' or 'nous', signifies their usual sober condition, the latter the state of Dionysian excess permitted on feast days (Hughes 1992: 24–6; Rowe 1997: 45). For the northern European, Catalonia is discursively an odd, surreal, irrational place. It implicitly unlike the sober north, accepting as a matter of course of excessive behaviours inconceivable at home. These things define Catalonia's exoticism.[20]

According to foreign critics, Barcelona's architecture represents this exotic character in material form. Charles Jencks wrote in a 1977 article on new Barcelonese architecture for the *Architectural Review* that Catalonia's people, due to their geographical situation between the exotic Iberian peninsula and the rest of Europe, are open to influence and were 'open and convivial and exceptions to the national average. The high architecture is correspondingly more exuberant, creative and vulgar than exists in Spain' (Jencks 1977: 160). Specifically, he thought that the city's geographical position at the apex of deep Spain, North Africa and the rest of Europe produced, as at Venice, a hybrid architecture. For Norberg-Schulz, this idea led to the capital's ability to simultaneously perceive itself and other cultures as 'other', a double defamiliarisation: 'Catalan culture expresses an Iberian world (hence an exotic one) but it also give this world a particularly 'fantastic interpretation due to its intermediate location' (Bofill 1985: 18). It is therefore an architecture predicated on a relationship with the other. The Eixample, for instance, the nineteenth-century extension to the city above the gothic quarter, is the bourgeois place that Gaudí's architecture apparently subverts – but is also clearly a form of restraint or frame for it. His work, however fantastic, never threatens the rational grid of the streets. The so-called *Mançana de la Discòrdia* (block of discord) that contains three of the most fantastic monuments of Catalan *Modernisme* never disturbs the respectability of the rest of the grid.[21] Here then is an architecture for which the exotic is critical to its identity, but nevertheless holds it in a state of restraint.

But the tendency to exoticise is a foreign imposition, and may lead to some unlikely interpretations. Gaudí's Sagrada Familia cathedral was appropriated by hippies in the 1960s, as an example of psychedelic architecture (Figure 4.2). Robert Hughes writes: 'a good morning in Barcelona in 1966 was a joint on the serpentine encrusted bench of the Güell Park, and then a descent to the city to groove on the façade of the Sagrada Familia [. . .]:

urban mountaineering for the stoned tourist' (Hughes 1992: 466). Here the foreigner's appropriation of Catalan architecture leads to a bizarre misunderstanding of its intentions, for Gaudí's work was meant as an expression of both his conservative Roman Catholicism and his Catalan nationalism. The psychedelic use of the Sagrada Familia would, no doubt, have left him appalled.

A further example of the exoticisation of Catalan architecture cited by Hughes, is the contemporary work of Ricardo Bofill, a Swiss-trained Catalan architect whose local work includes the international airport at El Prat.[22] Hughes centres on the Walden 7 housing project at Sant Just Desvern just outside central Barcelona to the west, reached by Diagonal (Figure 4.3). Located in a ruined cement works, which also houses Bofill's offices, Walden 7 presents an extraordinary image: a 60-metre tall lattice of a building, pierced by large holes. Essentially open in structure, there are views right the way through it, making it calculatedly immaterial-seeming; it is wider around its middle than its base, so from several angles it appears to defy gravity. Its form is designed to frame a modern, individualistic, erotically liberated mode of living. Each of the tiny (30 m²) apartments ('cells') can be linked to another. Bofill imagined that as residents' relationships evolved or devolved, they could

4.2
Sagrada Familia, Barcelona (begun 1882), architect: Antoni Gaudí

4.3
**Walden 7, Sant Just Desvern
(1970–5), architect: Ricardo Bofill**

grow within the block, acquiring or discarding apartment units around them as necessary (Bofill 1985: 46).

Bofill writes of the importance of surrealism in his work, 'the paradox of stairways that lead nowhere, absurdity of elements suspended in the void, spaces both powerful and useless, whose strange proportions become magical through a sense of tension and disproportion' (Bofill 1985: 58). All of these characteristics of Walden 7 show up in Hughes' critique of the building, but where for its architect they are evidence of its strength, for the critic they represent the reverse. For Hughes, the building is literally a ruin because its tiles are falling off, caught by nets that are now themselves, Hughes claims, falling to pieces.[23] This structural failure, which seems to be borne out by even the official photographs of the work, allied to the reluctance of its inhabitants to live in the way its architects intended, complete a thoroughly dystopian scenario, although one that has clear parallels with the long and ruinous history of the Sagrada Familia.[24] In both, Catalan identity is critically linked with a cult of the irrational, in which the largest and most ambitious projects are said to exist in the condition of ruins. Buildings are valued not for their use value, as it were, but their capacity for symbolism, especially where that symbolism disturbs the established order.

The moral city

Some of the foreign attraction to Barcelona is therefore its capacity for exoticisation, exemplified by the city's links with surrealism. The architecture of Gaudí and his contemporaries forms part of a surrealist tourist route, including public artworks, and museums dedicated to the work of Picasso, Miró, and some 90 km up the coast in Figueras, Dalí.[25] In each of these, but especially in the latter, architecture helps contrive an idea of the surrealist *merveilleux* that is promoted as essential to Catalan identity.

But the idea of Barcelona as a quintessentially surreal city co-exists paradoxically with a more recent understanding of it as a moral one. It is this understanding, I argue, that led to the award of the RIBA Gold Medal in 1999, more specifically to those individuals in the city who had made its reconstruction possible: the three socialist mayors, Narcis Serra, Pasqual Maragall and Juan Clos who had supplied the political will, Oriol Bohigas, the city's chief architect, and José Antonio Acebillo, the director of a number of urban initiatives between 1980 and 1993 (*Architectural Review* 1999: 17–19).

In this scenario, which I wish to emphasise, the city exerts a moral power over the English architectural profession, and far from subverting normal urban life, it reinforces a traditional bourgeois morality. In so doing, it acts as one important model for future English urbanism, up to and including a model of urban politics, in much the same way as the ancient world provided a model of political life for the Grand Tourist.[26] Barcelona's élite, especially Bohigas (who was a regular visitor to London), fully participated in their city's role. They admonished English cities for their contemporary failures; they helped inculcate a sense of nostalgia at what England had lost; and they reinforced an impression that the Catalan capital was now uniquely advanced in urban matters (Davies 1990). On making the RIBA award to Barcelona, the Institute's president, David Rock, said:

> the award conveys so many messages – messages about a building's context being an integral part of architecture, messages about the crucial role that architects play in city planning, about the significance of a client body so knowledgeable and appreciative of architecture and about the power of the mayoral role. Past and present, work and play are happily intermeshed in a new totality that is more than its often splendid parts, and is better connected even to sea and mountains.
>
> (*Building* 1999)

The award spoke of the self-interested, but reasonable desire on the part of architects for a similarly well-informed and wealthy client as the city of Barcelona. But as Rock's citation suggests, it was also made out the belief that there was a correctness about what was being achieved in Barcelona, a sense of duty, and of moral rectitude, qualities which had long been absent from the English practice of architecture. It is this that needs further investigation here.

What do I mean by this term morality? How is it exemplified by Barcelona in the rhetoric around it? How is the moral city realised materially in Barcelona's architecture? What are the limits of the moral Barcelona as an idea, specifically in its relation to English urban architecture? I use the term morality to signify a philosophical realm concerned with the regulation of human behaviour. Architecture has always been concerned with this in one way or another, and there is much debate about it even between figures with ostensibly similar political positions. For the architectural historian David Watkin, architecture should be an exclusively aesthetic matter: its interference in the moral realm is for him an aberration of the modern period, an example of the hubris of Modernist architects and their belief that architecture may solve social problems (Watkin 1977). For the equally conservative philosopher Roger Scruton however, as I will show in Chapter 6, architecture has a critical role in enforcing good public behaviour, defining and policing the public realm, a position which he shares with some unlikely figures also discussed here: HRH Prince Charles and Richard Rogers (Scruton 1994).

All of these in different ways are concerned with architecture as a means of enforcing the moral city: in other words a state of good manners, involving polite public behaviour, and rituals which regulate it, underpinned by secular (but Christian-derived) beliefs about society and tradition. Morality in this case also has to do with the quality of new architecture and urbanism itself, in particular the continuation of the Modernist belief in truth to materials and formal restraint. Hence the severe quality of many of the new buildings in Barcelona was in contrast to elsewhere in Europe and the US, where the postmodern concern for the façade dominated.

Barcelona as moral city is theoretically underwritten by a number of well-known concepts. Broadly, it exemplifies a pan-European interest in the revival of pre-industrial forms of urbanism as a means of challenging the Modernist city (Ellin 1996). Some of these represent a conservative social agenda, as I described in Chapter 2. Bohigas stated that his work in the 1960s, through which he established what became known as the Barcelona School, was influenced by the English New Brutalism and particularly, Italian neo-rationalism (Davies 1990: 24).[27] The latter, seemingly premised on a desire for moral certainty, was articulated through the clear and familiar architectural forms. As Robert Delevoy has described, the neo-rationalists

> were trying to find the fundamental types of habitat: the street, the arcade, the square, the yard, the quarter, the colonnade, the avenue, the boulevard, the centre, the nucleus, the crown, the radius, the knot . . . so that the city can be walked through. So that it becomes a text again. Clear. Legible.
>
> (Delevoy quoted in Ellin 1996: 10)

The moral implications of this approach are clear, and they apply to a variety of post-war approaches in European urbanism. But for a text that underwrites the specific conception of morality that Bohigas and his colleagues wished to convey at Barcelona, I turn to the New York-based British architectural historian Kenneth Frampton. Against a developing discourse legitimising postmodernism in architecture, Frampton has continued to assert a belief in the Modernist traditions of truth to materials, truth to structure, and ideals of morality that derive from these. He regards the postmodern assertion of the façade as essentially dishonest, and as a capitulation to the values of the market. A greater integrity, a greater moral value is represented by an architecture that privileges structure over surface. His idea of 'tectonic culture' is a very late manifestation of a Modernist utilitarianism (Frampton 1995).

However, it is Frampton's earlier essay 'Critical Regionalism', published in various versions from 1983 onwards, that I position as a justification for Barcelona as a moral city. In its revised form, as the penultimate chapter of the widely read *Modern Architecture: a Critical History*, Frampton approvingly cites modern Catalan architecture, with a special emphasis on Bohigas' work of the 1950s (Frampton 1996: 314–27). Frampton's point is, broadly, that an architecture of resistance is still possible. In spite of the pervasiveness of capital, architecture does not have to simply affirm, but can stand in critical relation to the society that it inhabits, in the same sense that the work of key Modernists offered an alternative view of the world. But in order to form this critical position, architecture must accept certain limits.

Frampton summarises 'Critical Regionalism' with these points: first, that architecture must be a marginal practice in order to be critical; second, that it must be 'consciously bounded', in other words that it understands or acknowledges the limits of site or history; third, that it should respect commonly used local materials or forms, without resorting to the vernacular; fourth, that such an architecture is only likely to occur in certain limited places, 'cultural interstices' Frampton calls them, places which 'in one way or another are able to escape the optimising thrust of universal civilisation' (Frampton 1992: 327). A little later, in the last lines of the book, Frampton restates this conclusion, paraphrasing the words of one of the Barcelona architects, Solá-Morales, involved in the reconstruction of the city. 'The art of architecture becomes a [. . .] kind of reality reserve, a place where man can still find material and spiritual repose; a kind of enclave capable of resisting as *other* the destructive onslaught of technological modernisation' (Frampton 1992: 343).

Some of the limits to Frampton's own argument were addressed by Fredric Jameson, who wondered in a reply to 'Critical Regionalism' if its claims to radicalism were not overstated. Was not, he wondered, Critical Regionalism's sensitivity to place analogous to the capacity of global capital, in what he terms its 'late' phase, to adapt to local circumstances? Critical Regionalism could be the architectural equivalent of 'the EPCOT syndrome raised to a global scale', he wrote, thinking of the Florida theme park which presents vignettes of life in foreign countries for touristic consumption (Jameson in Leach 1997: 255): in other words, Critical Regionalism as a post-Fordism of architecture; a tendency that far from offering resistance to the power of global capital, actually confirms it. As Jameson points out, one of the problems of Frampton's argument is that the concept of Critical Regionalism vis-à-vis wider social and economic processes is left untheorised, so the reader is left unsure in what precise ways and how the process of resistance is operated, except in the most general aesthetic terms (Jameson in Leach 1997: 249).

Perhaps in the end this lack of specificity is important, because it permits Barcelona to play – with great success – an ambiguous role. On the one hand it can stage itself as the moral metropolis, exemplar of continuing Modernist resistance against the prevailing culture; on the other, on the other, it can stage itself as a capital-friendly location, for the resistance it stages is only of an aesthetic, and therefore non-threatening kind. And indeed the city has been enormously successful in attracting investment since the end of the Franco regime.[28]

This ambiguity runs through the official presentation of the city by its leaders. Consider, for example, Oriol Bohigas' speech to the RIBA in 1999 when he accepted the Gold Medal on behalf of Barcelona, subsequently published in an edited form by the *Architectural Review* as 'Ten points for an urban methodology', with a brief introduction indicating the journal's approval (Bohigas 1999). It was, the journal said, 'a manifesto for good city making', the word 'good' here carrying a certain moral load (Bohigas 1999: 88). Summarised, Bohigas' ten points are:

1   the city is an expression of politics, and in the case of Barcelona, it is the political continuity afforded by a tradition of socialist mayors that has made possible the transformation of the city
2   the city is a collective phenomenon
3   conflict and difference are essential characteristics of the city, and it was a mistake of earlier Modernists to try to neutralise them through zoning
4   in physical terms, the city is conterminous with its public spaces
5   a city should have a clear identity that is the sum of the individual identities of its neighbourhoods
6   a city should be legible, that is spatially easy to understand by its citizens
7   the city should be built around the individual, site-specific architectural projects
8   the central city should be reasserted over the periphery
9   architecture should be functional as well as aesthetically radical
10 the city should be an architectural project.

Bohigas' manifesto is underwritten by a horror of buildings produced most directly by the actions of the market.[29] Bohigas wrote of 'a superabundance' of it 'constructed in our horrible suburbs, along our holiday coasts, on the edges of our motorways, in our shopping centres'. It was, he continued 'a very bad architecture, the worst in history which destroys cities and landscapes' (Bohigas 1999: 91). It was a long-held belief: in an interview for the *Architect's Journal* nine years previously Bohigas stated that for him the signal case against the free flow of capital was the architecture of London's Docklands, 'the most horrible architecture in the whole world at the moment' (Davies 1990: 24–5). (The critique of Docklands was undoubtedly a great attraction for British architects at that moment; it was a place from which many in the profession felt excluded or alienated.[30])

Bohigas' position, revised and reworked many times over the decades, identifies Barcelona therefore with a pan-European urbanism that is distinct to the American. Bohigas' belief in the traditional European city stands in opposition both to the city of the free market he saw exemplified in the US, and to developments in London's Docklands. The European tradition was 'very different from what a famous British politician said, that there was "no such thing as society", only individuals and the state' (Bohigas 1999: 9).[31] Very different too from an emergent view, through the work of Manuel Castells, William J. Mitchell and others, that the city was simply dissolving through the use of information networks, rendering the material nature of the urban irrelevant, assuming that if people can work from home, they will (Castells 1996;

Mitchell 1995). This, Bohigas argued, was 'anthropological and ecological nonsense [. . .] a vision put forward by those who are opposed to giving priority to the collective and in favour of the privatisation of the public domain' (Bohigas 1999: 9).[32]

And yet, Bohigas' manifesto restricts its radicalism to the realm of aesthetics. Capital is problematical mostly, it seems, because it makes for an ugly urbanism. And paradoxically, what Bohigas seems to favour is, crudely put, a model of urbanism that freezes the city at an earlier point of capitalistic development. The city he favours bears an uncanny resemblance to the nineteenth-century city. Many of Bohigas' improvements draw explicitly on the model of the Eixample, while the renewed commitment to parks and open spaces as a means of punctuating the dense urban realm is a familiar Victorian model, familiar throughout the developed world. Bohigas' theory, to summarise, seems to desire the (better) aesthetic consequences of nineteenth-century urbanism, without the context – it is a de-politicised, de-historicised revival for touristic appropriation, as fantastic, in its way, as Léon Krier's work at Poundbury, or the saccharine Americana of Celebration.[33]

How was the moral Barcelona materially exemplified? Specifically, there were three ways in which it occurred: first, in the targeted investment in visible signs of civic power such as the street, public transportation and public spaces, whereby the idea of public order is made visible. Many of the 160 projects realised by the Office of Urban Projects (OPU) under Bohigas between 1981–7 were of this kind (Figures 4.4 and 4.5). Second, it occurred in the respect for the built fabric of the past, through which, in spite of a turbulent and bloody history, a sense of continuity and tradition was maintained. Concentrating on individual projects, many of them projects of restoration and enhancement of the existing urban realm, Barcelona's reconstruction under Bohigas involved barely any demolition. In particular, the old street grid was maintained and enhanced: the grid of the Eixample, lined with imposing, regular apartment buildings is the paradigmatic representation of a regulated bourgeois life.[34] Faced with a variety of choices (including the continuation of the Modernist city planning policies of the 1960s, or a laissez-faire approach, both of them essentially anti-urban in character), the city's architects opted for the enhancement of the nineteenth-century bourgeois realm of the city, and used it as a model for the city's extension. The Martorell Bohigas MacKay masterplan for the Olympic Games, for example, used a modified version of the nineteenth-century plan to extend the city to the sea. In so doing, a largely industrial area was replaced with an extension of the bourgeois realm – an important symbolic transformation that identifies the future of the city with the realm of consumption, rather than production (Buchanan 1986: 59).

4.4
**Plaça Reial,
Barcelona (c.1842,
refurbished
early 1980s),
architect: Francesc
Molina i Casamajo**

As already discussed, the rational grid restrains architectural eccentricity, while its long axial views and wide pavements make surveillance easy. Its proliferation of street cafés, kiosks and corner stores both contribute to and police the life of the street.

The third way in which the moral city was exemplified occurred through the realisation of high Modernist architecture at a time when else-where in the west, especially in the US, Britain and Europe, architects showed a postmodern preoccupation with the façade. In Barcelona, by contrast, with occasional exceptions such as El Prat air terminal, architectural postmod-ernism was ignored in favour of the continuation of a vigorous, local modern tradition along the lines of the 'Critical Regionalism' argued for by Frampton (Davies 1990: 24).[35] This was materialised in a variety of key structures from the mid-1980s onwards. Arguably the most symbolic of these was the 1986 reconstruction of the German Pavilion by Ludwig Mies van der Rohe from the 1929 International Exhibition, a building which now houses the Mies Foundation (Figure 4.6). A structure of international significance, it is made mostly of marble and glass, cruciform in plan, and set between two reflecting pools of water; it has no curves whatsoever, and no angles other than right angles; it contains virtually nothing other than a Barcelona-design chair by Mies himself in leather and aluminium, and a sculpture by Georg Kolbe. The architects responsible for the reconstruction were Christian Cirici Alomar, Fernando Ramos Galiano, and Ignasí de Solà-Morales Rubió (González and Lacuesta 2002: 18). The latter undoubtedly regarded the project in moral terms, a means of establishing the city's position at the heart of a revived Modernist project; it was he who Frampton quoted at the end of his essay

4.5

**Plaça del Mercè, Barcelona
(*c.*1982), architect: Lluís Mestras,
Ramon Sanabria, Pere
Casajoana, Rosa María Clotet**

4.6

**German Pavilion
at the
International
Exhibition,
Barcelona (1929,
reconstructed
1986), architect:
Ludwig Mies van
der Rohe**

'Critical Regionalism' as describing the purpose of architecture as resistance. This small, spare, precious, anachronism of a building was clearly intended to be seen in those terms.

Architectural Modernism and the morality associated with it persists in more contemporary designs however, such as the important Plaça dels Països Catalans (1982) (Figures 4.7 and 4.8). An unashamedly élitist piece of work, it is formally extremely restrained, and popular only with skateboarders who find its open spaces and freedom from visitors ideal. Shortly after its opening, Peter Buchanan, the most dedicated advocate of Barcelona in the English architectural press, admitted that it was probably baffling to the general public, but no matter, for it was nothing less than one of the masterpieces of twentieth-century Modernism: an architectural equivalent of the music of Webern (Buchanan 1984: 45).

The Plaça dels Països Catalans is simply a public square just outside Sants railway station adjoining the busy Carrer Tarragona; it is a scruffy, heterogeneous zone of the city, neither old town nor Eixample, defined by large, cheaply built private apartment buildings of the 1950s. The square was built in 1981–3 by Albert Viaplana and Helio Piñon with the late Enric Miralles, and it consists of an attempt to make a coherent modern form out of a disparate and hostile site, which initially comprised car parking, roads, and residual space on a platform over the railway tracks leading into the

4.7
Plaça dels Països Catalans, Barcelona (1982), architect: Albert Viaplana, Helio Piñon and Enric Miralles

4.8
Plaça dels Països Catalans, Barcelona (1982), architect: Albert Viaplana, Helio Piñon and Enric Miralles

station. The platform could take no substantial weight, so a major building was out of the question. The architects wrote, 'at the outset we were desolate. Anyone who knows the place would understand' (Bohigas *et al.* 1991: 175). They decided that the only appropriate solution was a large public space, and that is what was built. Its main elements are a large area paved in granite, two juxtaposed steel mesh canopies, the tallest of which is 15 metres in height, a sinuous row of steel benches, and a fountain in the form of two rows of stainless-steel pipes which – in theory – gush water directly onto the plaza. There are assorted other elements – lighting, bollards and so on – but the overall effect is exceedingly spare, and for the time when western architecture elsewhere was preoccupied with the revival of existing forms, extremely modern. It has not worn well. It was first refurbished in 1991–2, and at the time of writing, a further refurbishment was due (González and Lacuesta 2002: 116). As my contemporary photographs show, it is not well patronised, particularly in comparison with the Parc de l'Espanya Industrial a few metres away. It is dirty, strewn with litter and well covered in graffiti, while its openness provides little relief from either the sun or the surrounding traffic.

Whatever the functional qualities of this piece of architecture, it is nevertheless an important material exemplar of the moral city. Some might say it was an unsuccessful contribution to the public realm, but it is undoubtedly a large one – and simply being a *space*, free of any commercial activity, it acts as punctuation for the everyday flows of capital and goods around. As a public square, by its nature it carries connotations of bourgeois morality, so its benches, its open spaces, and its fountain suppose correct, generally understood and shared forms of public behaviour that maintain and police urban sociality. And as I have just argued above, its form carries the moral charge of architectural Modernism. It is a hard piece of work, and, and meant as such; its forms are meant to unsettle and challenge in the spirit of the avant-garde, but their difficulty is understood as exemplary of moral correctness, an awkwardness that punctures the dishonest surfaces of everyday life. In all these ways, Barcelona was seen by the English architectural profession to keep the Modernist faith, and for a large part of that profession it was immensely alluring.

Barcelona's anxieties

Now, the foreign, especially English, desire for the Mediterranean world is, as I have argued here, a response to anxieties about the urban at home. The peculiarly English anxieties about the experience of the city, and of its place in the national culture have a clear response in the experience of southern Europe where, in spite of real problems of public security, there has been no flight of the bourgeoisie to the suburbs, no turning away from the urban, no flight from modernity and Modernism. Barcelona's cultural position is as secure as it has ever been. The English desire for this southern European urban life is therefore predicated on anxiety about life at home: what it demands from Barcelona is a solution to domestic problems, or at least an image of that solution.

The English desire for Barcelona is an English phenomenon: it superimposes English desires onto a foreign city, and in so doing it masks Barcelona's own anxieties about the urban, communicated in its local newspapers and news media, and in local academic debate, and in that of foreign academic Hispanicists. I sketch out these anxieties by way of a conclusion. First is the relative lack of space available to residents. Barcelona's population density – approximately eight times that of Greater London – is one of the highest in the developed world. It makes possible a great range of public services, but it also creates urban conditions that are extremely crowded from a northern European, and especially English, perspective. This is a historical issue, resulting from the city's geography, and its remarkable population growth during the 1960s and 1970s. Approximately 650,000 new residents were added to an already very dense city in the 1960s, creating extraordinary pressures on housing. Rooms, beds or the use of a bed might be sublet;

rooms might be subdivided or apartments sublet without cooking rights; more than one family might share an apartment, or build illegal shacks on the urban periphery, or stay with friends or relatives. Multiple employment, or *pluriempleo* was, and remains, common. These pressures to some extent still exist: both the birth-rate and internal migration have slowed, but the nature of the labour and housing markets in Spain make it unusual for children to leave home until married. This makes for a very different attitude to urban space; the street becomes much more intensively used, becoming in effect an extra room. The pressures on domestic space, which still far exceed those of northern Europe, mean that there is often literally no place for socialising in private homes. All socialising, including the forming and maintenance of sexual relationships, must be done outside the family home, and often more or less in public (Kenny and Kertzer 1983: 143–8). Barcelona's high density creates a plethora of attractions for the visitor – but as a model of urban living, it is highly pressured and contains its own anxieties.

The second of Barcelona's anxieties concerns the fact that in large part Barcelona's economy has been restructured around tourism, for foreign visitors. This is tourism of both the cultural kind – visitors to museums and cultural events – but also visits to trade fairs and commercial events, many held on the site of the 1929 exhibition at the Plaça d'Espanya. This is not unique to Barcelona, but as has been argued in a variety of local publications, the replacement of the older, industrial economy by the new one has a number of significant urbanistic consequences. Tourism is very good at creating architectural spectacle. The major contributions to Barcelona's twentieth-century urbanisation have been the result of touristic spectacles: the hilly park of Montjuic was created as an integral part of the 1929 International Exhibition; the second Mediterranean Games of 1955, and the 1982 World Cup added to this infrastructure; most spectacularly of all the 1992 Summer Olympic games saw the creation of an entirely new urban quarter by the sea, as well as the renovation of the port. Tourism has defined a new paradigm of the city (Robira 2002:163). But tourism forces the urban spaces of Barcelona, and the citizens within them to perform roles: specifically the city becomes a theatrical spectacle, its urban spaces stage sets, and its citizens actors (Robira 2002: 91). This theatrical paradigm leads to a physical emphasis on the centre over the periphery, a centre which must (whatever the city authorities' rhetoric about social inclusion) become ever more available for consumption; meanwhile, the poverty that all great cities concentrate must be ever more dispersed to the periphery, where it cannot be seen. The Socialist council in favour of social and spatial equality for citizens has overseen the implementation of a economic paradigm that in many ways inhibits these aims (Robira 2003: 83).

The third anxiety about Barcelona is the question of authority. It is also in some respects an authoritarian view of urban life. Although the city and the public are in Bohigas' view declared to be conterminous, the city is not regarded as an expression of the public, but rather, an expression of the idea of the public held by a political élite. So although the experience of Barcelona is one in which the idea of the public is elevated, and is architecturally framed by the provision of new public spaces, the role of the public in designing or choosing those spaces is extremely limited. Speaking in London the year after the RIBA speech, Bohigas declared both that 'the city is the place of freedom but not exactly of liberty' and that there is a 'general problem with public participation'. Most methods of public consultation do not work, he said [. . .] 'and when people do give their opinion it is usually a mistake' (Melhuish 2000). The Barcelona experience is therefore strongly connected with visible political authority, experience of which, thanks to Spain's authoritarian history, is much more a part of urban tradition than it is in Britain.

The English appropriation of Barcelona is in effect a kind of exoticisation, for it makes a partial reading of the city to assuage domestic anxieties. But its understanding of the other occludes its own anxieties about the urban. The surface of Barcelona is highly alluring, but it is built on high densities, on an idea of city as spectacle, and above all, on structures of authority and control, each of which exemplify distinct, localised historical processes. The English understanding of Barcelona, like the Grand Tourist's understanding of Italy, is in large part therefore built on fantasy.

Chapter 5

The city in ruins

Introduction

> Decline has turned into collapse and Liverpool threatens to become
> the first de-industrialised city in the nation.
>
> (Parkinson 1985: 9)

> It was once said by Marx that there were only two choices in his
> day – socialism or barbarism – today the choice is socialism or
> nuclear annihilation.
>
> (Derek Hatton, deputy leader of Liverpool City
Council 1983–6, in Hatton 1988: 31)

If there is one English city that can be described as quintessentially anxious,
it is post-war Liverpool. Here is a city whose entire existence seemed to be in
doubt by the middle of the 1980s. Its population had dropped from 850,000 to
480,000 since the Second World War, effectively halving; its unemployment
rate since the 1930s had been generally double the British average (Parkinson
1985: 11–13); the industries on which its traditional wealth had been based
(docks, shipping, ship-building) were in steep decline; its civic government
was politically divided, and, by the early 1980s, insistent on a damaging course
of confrontation with central government; in July 1981 it was the scene of the
worst urban riots in mainland Britain for a generation, disturbances which
resulted in one death, and the unprecedented use of tear gas by the police to
try to quell the revolt.

These events and processes were arguably all the more disturbing
because of the grandeur of their context. At its peak at the end of the nineteenth century, Liverpool had more millionaires than any other city apart from

London, and its wealth was materially represented in the miles of handsome terraces to the east of the commercial centre, in the spectacular mansions of Princes Park and Grassendale, and the tree-lined boulevards of Toxteth. It was the latter that represented the most dramatic scene of all: the extraordinarily grand Princes Road, a piece of South Kensington above the Mersey, was the centre of the 1981 riots, and was still a ruin twenty years later. It was not only the residential architecture that made Liverpool's economic decline especially stark, but its commercial buildings too. The Albert Dock, the central image of this chapter, was the grandest of all Victorian industrial buildings. Listed Grade 1 by the government in 1952, it was highly regarded by Nikolaus Pevsner who wrote in the South Lancashire edition of the *Buildings of England*, that for 'sheer punch' there was 'nothing to touch it' (Pevsner 1969: 167). (Pevsner was equally laudatory about the city's civic buildings. He thought St Georges Hall, which crowns the plateau by Lime Street station, to be the greatest neoclassical building in all Europe.) In 2003, the city proposed that the Albert Dock be considered as a World Heritage Site by UNESCO, a status that would value it equally with Stonehenge, the Great Pyramids of Giza and the Taj Mahal (Carter 2003).

Liverpool's decline in this context has produced a special fascination for outsiders. The travel writings of expatriate Americans Paul Theroux and Bill Bryson have popularised its ruinous qualities (Theroux 1985; Bryson 1996). A local councillor, Keith Hackett, complained that one of the city's problems was the entertainment value of its decline, as if its purpose had become the production of morbid thrills for tourists.[1] And yet, the city has willingly collaborated in this process. The standard architectural reference book on the city, *Seaport* by Quentin Hughes, an architect in the university's famous department of architecture, presented an image of an entropic city, all soot, decay, moss, rotten wood and steam trains, the whole lot crumbling into the Mersey (Hughes 1964). First published in 1964, it was reissued in 1969 and again in 1993, and remains the standard photographic reference work on the city's architecture. The same is true in the opening quotations of this chapter. Michael Parkinson, a locally based historian, rehearses the rhetoric of collapse in his study of the problems of the 1980s. Above all, Derek Hatton, the de facto leader of the city council between 1983 and 1986, presents an apocalyptic scenario, in which Liverpool becomes the true fount of resistance to global capital. Hatton's is an essentially theological position which (as we shall see later) legitimised a reckless and damaging conflict with central government (Hatton 1988).

The condition of Liverpool in the 1980s may therefore be said to be profoundly anxious: its continued existence was both rhetorically and actually in doubt, and vast areas of it, from to Toxteth to Wavertree to Vauxhall, were ruinous, creating anxious space. It is against this background that the cultural complex of the Albert Dock was created. At the time, one critic thought it 'the most important museum to open in Britain in living memory' (Januszczack 1988: 37). The political will to create it was immense, it did not lack for funds and it involved national organisations (the government and the Tate Gallery) much more than it did local ones. The Tate was above all an ideological project, which was a model for other urban developments in the 1980s. The problem I address here concerns its form: in the absence of any other positive urban models for the development at the time, the aesthetic it appropriates is curiously like that of the English country house – which is to say, not an urban model at all.

Liverpool

The apocalyptic rhetoric of Derek Hatton was based on observable processes. At the time Hatton staged his takeover of the council, the city's population had declined 73 per cent over thirty years with further decline was occurring at a rate of 10,000 per year (Middleton 1991: 75). Some of this was, as with other cities in the UK (and the rest of the developed world) migration by the wealthy to areas just beyond the city's boundaries, in Liverpool's case principally to the Wirral peninsula on the south side of the Mersey. But Liverpool's metropolitan population had also declined, a pattern rarely repeated elsewhere. The city's business remained principally that of the docks. But although the container port of Seaforth at the northern extreme of the Mersey estuary handled as much cargo as the city's docks had ever done, being largely automated, it was no longer a major employer, neither did it any longer provide secure employment, as a protracted industrial dispute in the 1990s showed.[2] The city's other main businesses, manufacturing and food processing, were equally troubled. The closure of Tate and Lyle's sugar refining plant in 1980 left large areas of wasteland in inner city areas such as Vauxhall. Unemployment on Merseyside in 1985 was 27 per cent, twice the national average (Parkinson 1985: 13); GDP per capita was around 75 per cent of the UK average throughout the 1980s and 1990s. Figures such as these led to the area's qualification in 1994 for Objective 1 funding from the European Union as one of the EU's poorest regions, a qualification it shared with Greece, Spain, Ireland and southern Italy.[3]

This economic weakness was compounded by decades of political uncertainty. A once mostly Conservative city had become politically divided, hung (with no overall control by any one party) throughout much of the 1970s. A budgetary crisis was precipitated by this, and by the incoming Conservative (central) government's approach to local councils, which it regarded as badly run and in need of reform. The first of a series of fiscal reforms to local government saw the imposition of budgetary controls by limiting the amount that councils could gather from local property taxes, or rates; councils would be forced to economise to balance their books. Liverpool's political weakness during the 1970s, and its declining tax base, put it in an especially difficult position. The ruling Labour party included a powerful group belonging to Militant Tendency, a far left faction within the main national party, who, under Hatton, produced a strategy of confrontation with central government. They were preoccupied with the provision of jobs and houses, and campaigned on the provision of basic material goods. Curiously, they were as suspicious as the right-wing tabloid press of so-called 'loony' councils, whose politics centred on concepts of equal rights.[4] Militant, mainly working class and socially conservative, was uncomprehending of, if not hostile to, the politics of racial and sexual justice, which it saw as a distraction from the business of class war. Between 1983 and 1986, their tactics included the setting of an illegal budget, and the symbolic sacking of all public employees in Liverpool, before the leadership was expelled by the national Labour party, who felt that Militant were impeding their chances of national electoral success.[5]

The Militant leadership of Liverpool regarded their city as unique, and they abandoned normal municipal solidarity with other cities.[6] Central government also treated Liverpool as a special case. After the Toxteth riots of July 1981, which lasted two weeks, caused one death, hundreds of injuries and £11 million of damage, a badly frightened government set up a special government department for Merseyside, headed by a cabinet minister, Michael Heseltine. Heseltine brought a party of journalists to the area in late 1981 to publicise the scale of the task he had. Of Wavertree, in the east of the inner city, he said: 'it was an appalling eyesore. You drove through Liverpool; you looked at this terrible place, and you drove on' (Middleton 1991: 90).

The government also set up the Merseyside Task Force, which shortly became the Merseyside Development Corporation (MDC), to coordinate private investment in the city. Initially chaired by Basil Bean, it was the first of Britain's Urban Development Corporations (UDCs) (Middleton 1991: 81). The UDCs were not regulatory or planning organisations, rather government-appointed corporations whose primary task was to bring disused land and buildings into effective use. Their creation, by a Conservative government with an ideological commitment to the values of the free market, was resisted by local councils who saw them, correctly, as usurping large parts of their role. Their principal task was market-orientated: removing the negative value of their land. UDCs did not generally build, but equipped land for building.

Their principal task was not to spend public money, but to use public funds as leverage for private funds, with the ratio 1:4, public to private, as the rule of thumb (Middleton 1991: 299).

The extent of the deterioration of the public realm in the original area covered by the Task Force was described by Michael Middleton: the original population had declined to 400, and the extent of the public facilities in the area were 'one public toilet and two telephone boxes' (Middleton 1991: 81).[7] Merseyside Development Corporation, the UDC for Liverpool, had two flagship projects, the Garden Festival of 1984, which reclaimed a large area of waterfront to the south of the central city, and the redevelopment of the Albert Dock, which the MDC had acquired in 1982, and developed in conjunction with Arrowcroft, a property developer. The Garden Festival was a temporary project, criticised by some locally for being ineffective in alleviating long-term social and economic problems ('we want jobs not trees', a frequent complaint) (Middleton 1991: 82).[8] The Dock redevelopment was long-term and ambitious, a restoration of the material fabric of the dock complex to make a cultural space for the city.

The Albert Dock

The Dock comprises five cast-iron-framed, brick-faced pavilions, each of seven storeys, including basement and mezzanine floors. The pavilions enclose a rectangular 'piazza' of water. The brick walls are immense, 4 feet thick at ground level, 2 feet thick at the top. The fireproof floors are brick vaulted. Each is essentially U-shaped in plan, allowing, on the river frontage, the penetration of carting bays. On the dockside, the façade incorporates some classical elements. There is a colonnade all the way around, described by massive cast-iron Doric columns. A vast Doric portico on the façade of the Dock office marks the city entrance to the complex. The centre of each pavilion is marked by a gentle arch.

The Dock was poorly regarded when a working building – in 1858 the critic J. A. Picton had dismissed it as 'a hideous pile of naked brickwork' – but as the mouldering ruin that it gradually became until its closure to shipping in 1972, it was much praised, not only by Pevsner (Picton in Hughes 1964: 18). J. M. Richards and the photographer Eric de Maré were among the first to introduce its charms to a wider public in their 1957 special issue of the *Architectural Review* on industrial architecture, an issue which later became their book *The Functional Tradition*. They argued that buildings of these kinds were precursors of modern architecture (Richards 1958). By the time they were writing, the Dock was more or less disused. Built in the age of sail, it was too small for most twentieth-century cargo vessels, and James Stirling later recalled that just after the Second World War it had become by default a marine bone-yard, a place where ship parts were heterogeneously stored: an excellent playground for small boys (Stirling *et al.* 1994: 133).

The MDC acquired the Albert Dock in 1982 and set about turning it into a cultural complex, in consort with Arrowcroft. The principal cultural facility of the Dock was to be a branch of the Tate Gallery. The Gallery's involvement with the Dock in fact predated its acquisition by the MDC. Under the directorship of Alan Bowness, the Tate (in common with other national collections) initiated a policy of de-centralising its collections in 1968, although little progress had been made, while outposts of the Science Museum had been set up in York and Bradford. In 1980, Bowness visited several northern cities including Leeds, Manchester, Sheffield and Liverpool with a view to creating a Tate of the North. Liverpool was chosen as the site, principally because money was available from the MDC[9] (Tate Gallery 1986: 21). But there were historical connections with the city too (Henry Tate, the gallery's principal benefactor, was a Liverpool sugar merchant) and the building offered ample, albeit compromised, space.

The Tate's trustees visited the city and the Albert Dock in November 1981, and while the city's social and economic condition unnerved them, they allowed the project to go ahead in 1984. They were offered a third of warehouse 'C', a pavilion on the north-western corner of the dock, nearly adjacent to the emerging Maritime Museum. They were relatively successful in securing funds, much more so than they had been for extensions to the Millbank base: MDC provided half of the £9.5 million construction costs, £2 million was raised from the private sector, £0.5 million directly from central government, and the remainder, £1.8 million was raised by the Trustees.

The official rationale for the de-centralisation of the collection stressed the benefits for the community of the 'north of England', who, in order to be fully civilised, required the benefit of modern art on a regular basis. It was considered not enough that northerners were within a three-hour train ride of London or Edinburgh, the only other cities in the country where such collections might be found. The Tate also emphasised the quality of the building – they knew, on seeing the monumental structure, with its classical design, that they 'had found the right place'.[10] But most of all, the Tate candidly admitted, 'money could be found'[11] (Tate 1986: 21–4). The 1981 riots, and the fundraising structures that had been put in place as a result, enabled things to happen at Liverpool that were impossible anywhere else.[12]

Once the decision had been made, the Trustees invited James Stirling to take an interest in the project, given that he had just completed designs for them for the Clore Gallery at Millbank, the new gallery housing the

5.1
**Early sketch for
Tate Liverpool
(*c*.1984), architect:
James Stirling**

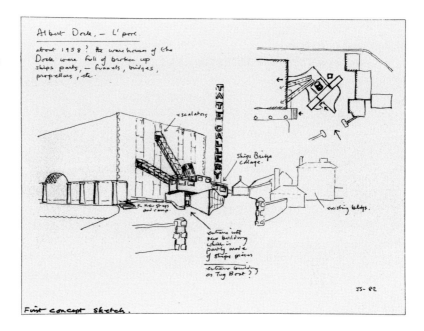

Turner bequest. Stirling had been raised in Liverpool – he claimed to have been conceived in a bunk of a steamer moored at the Pier Head – and knew the docks well, the Albert Dock in particular being an early playground (Buchanan 1988: 20). He recalled visiting in the late 1950s, finding it 'full of broken up ship parts – funnels, bridges, propellers, etc.' (Stirling *et al.* 1994: 133). An early sketch seems to make reference to this remembered condition (Figure 5.1). He imagined a new entrance to the Tate's pavilion on the north wall, made of a ship's bridge and two gangways. The final design in fact made only limited intervention to the warehouse exterior, the bright blue portholed façade and lettering by the graphic designers Pentagram behind Hartley's colonnade being the only sign of the gallery's presence.

Inside there were further characteristic signs of the architect. A bright blue and orange balustrade signalled the coffee shops on the mezzanine, memorably described by one critic as the 'ample buttocks of some colossus' (Weston 1988: 34). But this aside, for Stirling it was an unusually discreet job (Figure 5.2). In the first instance, the Tate occupied three floors of the original pavilion, providing 4,000 m^2 of gallery spaces, education rooms and the shop and café, all built around a central service core. A decision was made early on to leave the original brick stair shaft at the south end of the building, and from there flowed the idea that only the most necessary interventions would be made. The mezzanine floor between ground and first floors was therefore removed, apart from a small section at the entrance (the 'buttocks').

Heating and lighting ducts were contained within a specially designed unit that runs the length of each gallery ceiling.

Other than that, interventions were kept to a minimum: the brick structure remained in large part exposed, to great effect in the ceilings; columns were painted grey, but otherwise left exposed, as was the elaborate and delicate structure of the top floor ceiling, a network of steel spars. In the beginning, this part of the gallery was not open to the public, although it has since been incorporated into the gallery as part of the exhibition space. Where it was necessary to replace existing elements, such as windows, which were badly decayed, the existing forms were replicated using modern materials (Cruickshank 1987: 58). The gallery was opened by HRH Prince Charles on 24 May 1988, a grey and blustery day. He arrived by boat, consciously emulating his Victorian predecessor Prince Albert on the opening of the original dock.

5.2
Tate Gallery, Liverpool (1988, refurbished by Michael Wilford 1998), architect: James Stirling

Loft-living

The siting of art galleries in former industrial buildings has become so commonplace that we have lost sight of both how recent this phenomenon is, and how odd. It was an observable phenomenon in 1960s New York, but only became a common mode of organising public gallery space in the 1980s, when the raw quality of the surfaces was still something of a shock. Its peculiarity as a mode derives from this sense of shock, by which I mean the disjunction between the elevated, sublimated culture of art, and the raw or downbeat surroundings.[13] The use of industrial space in public galleries nevertheless often resulted from a humanistic desire to heal the urban wounds left by industry. Liverpool is a particularly clear case.

There are two American precedents for the re-use of industrial space for cultural purposes. One is as part of what in the US became known as Rousification, after the work of the developer James Rouse. In Baltimore and Boston, both cities with architectural and historical parallels with Liverpool, Rouse used public funds to lever private capital to redevelop decayed areas, particularly those with redundant nineteenth-century industrial buildings. Rouse's Inner Harbour at Baltimore was a model for Liverpool. As Peter Hall has described, the economic model was tourism: 'Bored suburbanites', he wrote,

> would come in droves to a restored city that offered them a quality of life they could never find in a shopping mall. Yuppies . . . would gentrify the central areas close to downtown and inject their dollars into restored boutiques, bars and restaurants. Finally, the restored city would actually become a major attraction to tourists, providing a new economic base to the city
>
> (Hall 1996: 348).

Now, Rousification explains the economic framework of the Albert Dock, in particular the shift from a place of production to one of consumption. But it does not completely explain the visual appearance of the Dock, specifically, the preservation of the architecture. The model for that, I suggest, is the loft. The loft is an essential text in Liverpool's case, because, although a foreign import, it provides a model for humanising a ruined situation; or to put it another way, reprising the argument of this book, it provides a way of assuaging the anxiety resulting from de-industrialisation.

The origins of the loft lie in the New York art world of the 1950s. Artists in the latter part of the decade began to adopt such spaces in downtown for studio use.[14] Later they began to live in them as well, contravening zoning regulations.[15] The buildings were, in plan, generic Anglo-American late nineteenth-century warehouses, similar to those found from San Francisco to Manchester to Calcutta. Framed in cast-iron, of seven to eight stories, they had large, relatively unencumbered spaces and highly decorative façades which aped Renaissance *palazzi* (the cast-iron façade was a New York peculiarity).

For artists the advantages were numerous. Large spaces could be had for little money, and the lack of the normal amenities of bourgeois life did not matter: proximity to industrial fabricators and timber yards was more important than a good grocery store. The loft phenomenon developed in the 1950s with artists such as Robert Rauschenberg, and the group around the performance artist Allan Kaprow, and later through the artists of the Minimalist generation.[16] Rauschenberg's loft was memorably described by Calvin Tomkins:

> [T]he loft was about a hundred feet long by thirty wide. A row of supporting columns ran down the middle but otherwise it was a clear, unobstructed space. Tall, grimy windows let in the distinctively white light of downtown New York – also the roar of trucks on Broadway. Near the windows was big, ramshackle wire cage containing a pair of kinkajous [. . .] beyond the cage stood a group of large objects – a car door, a window frame, a roof ventilator mounted on wheels – components of an unfinished five part sculpture [. . .], paintings, combines and sculptures from the recently concluded Jewish Museum retrospective were stacked against the wall farther along. There was a big table in the middle of the room, its surface cluttered with magazines, pictures clipped from magazines, felt pens and pencils, and tubes of paint, and other materials. Toward the back of the room, a counter projecting from the end wall formed an alcove for a refrigerator, an electric stove and the bed – a mattress laid on the floor. All the rest of the loft was work space.
>
> (Tomkins 1980: 83, 111)

This was a hard place, evidently, and a rather strange one for anyone used to bourgeois city life. But it was also romantic. Kaprow's accounts of happenings in New York lofts in the early 1960s locate these buildings as places of urban theatre in which anything might, and probably would, happen (Kaprow 1993: 15).

At first, the loft was a private affair and it would have been unusual for a gallery visitor to be familiar with them, unless they knew artists personally. But from the early 1960s, the loft space came to be more familiar; consumed as image, if not as fact. The pop artist Andy Warhol and his entourage occupied a series of industrial buildings, each called the Factory, from November 1963 onwards. The first was a former hat factory close to the United Nations headquarters on the East River. Warhol's talent for publicity ensured that it, and future Factories became, in effect, a theatre set for fashionable New York society. With every interior surface painted silver, and given over to socialising as much as artistic work, Warhol made clear the loft's potential for domestication by New York's upper classes. By the end of the 1960s, commercial art galleries had begun to rent space in SoHo.[17] A decade later it was effectively colonised as the prime location for commercial galleries in New York, accompanied by development of commercial lofts for high-class apartments.

By 1970, writes the sociologist Sharon Zukin, 'as the bare polished wood floors, exposed brick walls and cast iron façades of these "artists' quarters" gained increasing public notice, the economic and aesthetic virtues of loft-living were transformed into bourgeois chic' (Zukin 1982: 2). The loft, for some years a sign of bohemia, had been assimilated by that to which it once stood in opposition. This process was accompanied by rising land values, rising rents and the rapid zoning (by economic, and then legal means) of industry out of the areas they had once occupied. The loft phenomenon was little more than an interior style by the end of the 1990s, characteristic of New York, but one of a number of possible aesthetic and lifestyle options. Loft-living was formalised, expensive, based around high-class residential and retail uses and hostile to the industry that once occupied its spaces.

It was a New York phenomenon primarily, but spread to other American cities and, then, much weakened, as a developer's style for new apartments to London, and other British cities by the mid-1980s (see Wright 1993). Even in this diluted form, it nevertheless represented a clear set of values, which were no longer bohemian for sure, but distinct from earlier bourgeois modes of living in the city. It was first, writes Zukin, an attempt to find a more 'humane habitat' than that provided by Modernist architecture with its imagery of rationalism, efficiency and mass production. Ironically, it was the modern factory that was to provide the alternative. Regardless of its history as a place of mass production, or the role of mass production in the making of its outward forms (the cast-iron façades, for instance), in relation to the Modernist apartment block, the loft building was perceived of as a place with individual character (Zukin 1982: 68). Then there was nostalgia: 'Like Gothic ruins in the nineteenth century, artefacts of the industrial age now inspire nostalgia for the past' (Zukin 1982: 73). Or to put it another way, 'disuse . . . lends enchantment' (Zukin 1982: 76). As Robert Harbison put it in *Eccentric Spaces* 'we visit the docks in London but not in Rotterdam because commerce is romantic only when it has vanished' (Harbison 1977: 131).

Overall, Zukin writes, lofts describe a wider shift in developed economies from an industrial mode of economic production to a post-industrial, or more broadly postmodern one, dominated by the service sector' (Zukin 1982: 112). Specifically they emblematise an aspect of this which she terms the 'artistic mode of production' or AMP. This means of economic production is centred on art in the belief that it is not simply a consumer product, but a means of capital accumulation and socialisation. Its effects on cities are (Zukin 1982: 178):

1   to transfer urban space from the old world of industry to the new world of finance
2   to transform local labour markets
3   to lower economic expectations amongst those engaged with the AMP (artists and arts administrators will tolerate relatively low levels of pay, and relatively high levels of job insecurity)
4   to 'reduce the immediacy of industrial society and its problems to a distant historical perspective'
5   finally, to make it 'impossible to consider a return to any version of the old urban-industrial infrastructure'.

Returning to the Albert Dock, we can see these processes in action. At the same time as the development was being planned, the company behind the Tate's wealth, Tate and Lyle, continued the withdrawal of its sugar refining business from Merseyside. The major sugar refinery was closed in Vauxhall, just to the north of the city centre in 1980, at the same time as the Tate trustees were considering sites for a possible northern outpost of the gallery (Middleton 1991: 87). The last remaining refining plant was closed in Bootle, a little further to the north, in April 1984, when the gallery's construction had just begun. It involved the loss of 90 jobs, and the refining business was moved to Tate and Lyle's existing plants elsewhere (*Financial Times* 1985). The Gallery, and the Dock in general, created a series of low-paying, insecure jobs, for those with a liking for the arts. And through these measures, the past became little more than a surface (Walsh 1992: 3). For Peter Hall, the result of this kind of development is a kind of theatre:

> Like theatre it resembles real life, but it is not urban life as it ever actually was: the model is the Main Street America exhibit which greets entering visitors at the California Disneyland, sanitized for your protection, wholesome, undangerous, and seven-eighths real size.
>
> (Hall 1996: 351)

The Albert Dock as ruin

One text through which the Albert Dock can be interpreted is therefore the idea of loft-living. Not only does the Dock appropriate some of the style of the loft space for its galleries, but it does so as part of a process that has a world of production replaced by one of consumption, or as Zukin has it, the paradigm of manual labour is replaced by the 'artistic mode of production'. The world that appears through these loft spaces is familiarly called post-industrial.

The Albert Dock is partially described by the term post-industrial. But there are aspects to the Albert Dock that do not so easily fit the description, and we ought to look for models of interpretation that more adequately represent its peculiar context, particularly its Englishness. The loft arose out of quite different circumstances to the Albert Dock. New York, its place of origin, was bankrupt in the 1970s, but never a failing city in the same manner as Liverpool.[18] It was always the United States' largest metropolis, its commercial centre, its largest port and the centre of its news media and publishing industries and art world; overall, therefore, it was always the centre, never the periphery. The loft, as developed there in the in the interstices of capital and space, was another essentially commercial product of the city, a means of producing valuable real estate. It was then exported elsewhere in weaker forms. Liverpool was a consumer, rather than producer of the loft idea. Not only that, but it could be said that the loft was *imposed* in a quasi-colonial manner by the political centre. Through the loft look, Liverpool had a new identity defined by authority.

We therefore need a different kind of text through which to interpret the Albert Dock. It is referred to by Sharon Zukin: when a city de-industrialises, she writes, 'the urban-industrial infrastructure submits to the rules of the picturesque' (Zukin 1982: 180). Making use of the argument I made in Chapter 2, we can say that the picturesque does three things which are clearly in evidence at Liverpool: it responds to a problem by aestheticising it; it invokes a gaze that is highly privileged; and it signifies a withdrawal from the urban as much as an accession to it. Using this definition of the picturesque, we can see that the Albert Dock, as much as it seems to be an importation of the American idea of the loft, is actually something rather different. As an idea of the city, it makes use of home-grown ideas more than imported ones.

How can this argument be substantiated? Consider the Albert Dock as that quintessential emblem of the picturesque, the ruin. As already seen, the Albert Dock on its opening was criticised for being a Disneyfied version of the past, an industrial site 'prettified and touristified' for consumption by unthinking visitors. Undoubtedly the building has been tidied up. But if one considers the Albert Dock as more than a building, but an urban space with a discursive existence as much as a material one, then it retains many of the characteristics of a ruin. The Dock's situation, for example: the sea, invariably choppy and grey, not only presents a classic image of romantic yearning, but it is also at this geographical point a kind of ruin. Once thick with ships, with Mersey ferries dodging in and out, it is now more often than not, empty. The ferries intermittently punctuate the void to provide an experience for tourists. Across the Mersey are the ruins of Birkenhead's industrial base, the one remaining shipyard, Cammell Laird, now in receivership. Back on land, one's gaze is drawn from the dock to the Pier Head, and the Liver Building, the Cunard Building and the Dock Office, all monumental early twentieth-century buildings abandoned by their original owners, and only partially re-let.[19] Or to the west one looks on the 'Ropewalks', a mile of abandoned and ruined warehouses and vacant lots, struggling up the hill to the Anglican cathedral.[20] There were plenty of signs of change at the time of writing, not least the award in 2003 of the status of European Capital of Culture for 2008. But up until the end of the twentieth century, almost everywhere in Liverpool still acceded to the condition of a ruin. One could not visit the Dock and not be conscious of the dereliction that surrounded it; there was nowhere in any direction that did not offer some of the character of a ruin. The Dock itself may have recovered its integrity as a building, but the same could be said of little in its immediate surroundings.

Consider then the Dock's discursive existence as a ruin. Although it may exist materially in a restored state, as a discursive object it is undoubtedly ruinous. It was the knowledge of it as a ruin, built up over decades in a variety of publications, that attracted the architectural critics to the Dock, and also rather repelled them from what had been achieved by the refurbishment. Many regretted that the Dock proper was no longer materially ruinous. Dan Cruickshank, writing before the completion of the Tate, noted that 'it has secured a sound future' but that it had also 'lost something of its power it possessed during its life as a working monument to functional design', a power 'later replaced by the romance of decay' (Cruickshank 1987: 60). This was Peter Buchanan's point a year later on the opening of the gallery itself. He wrote that its gallery spaces were fine, but that the Dock in general had lost something: 'at least when derelict and threatened with destruction, the Albert Dock was not just powerfully poetic in its solidly stoic and noble forlornness but still stirred the imagination to cram it with ships and goods from around the world, with bustling activity and sweaty toil' (Buchanan 1988: 18). As Waldemar Januszczack noted in a review for the *Architect's Journal*, the nobility of the ruin had been replaced by tourist tat: 'Everywhere you look there are nautical heirlooms in perfect stages of (useless) preservation, capstans, tall ships, lock gates, lifting gear, cranes, pulleys scattered carefully about the cobbles of the Albert Dock like onyx ashtrays in an Italian living room' (Januszczack 1988: 37).[21]

And it was the ruin that attracted the project's main architect, James Stirling, who, in his original sketches for the gallery, recalled the maritime bone-yard of his childhood. Stirling's account of his relationship with Liverpool: his own alleged origins in the bunk of a steamer at the Dock, and his memory as a child playing in the ruins of the Dock amongst ship parts when it was used as a convoy refit depot. This remarkable childhood experience led Stirling to propose, in an early sketch for the project, an entrance via a set of ruined ship parts – a bridge, gangways and so on. The idea was quickly rejected on conservation grounds, a pity according to Jenkins (1992), as it would have been a way of acknowledging the Dock's history and the powerful image of its post-war derelict condition.

In fact there is no critique of the reformed Dock that does not make some reference to its previous existence as a ruin, as if this condition is simply inescapable, as if it is the *job* of this structure to be ruinous, and to represent in material form the idea of industrial decline. Now, this has deep roots: in 1942, for example, J. M. Richards, editor of the *Architectural Review*, was advocating a world-view in which the ruin had as much place as the newly built. This had much to do with the Blitz, and the drastically altered urban landscape that it created, but reading Richards' *Bombed Buildings of Britain* now, what is striking is the way in which the war seems to have legitimised an unequivocally picturesque world-view. Over 138 pages, Richards and the architectural historian John Summerson surveyed the major buildings damaged in August 1940 and May 1941. The majority were in London, but included other bombed cities including Liverpool and, most dramatically, Coventry. In Richards' words it was partly a record, partly an 'obituary notice' – but partly also an aestheticisation of the war damage, to be appreciated by a 'connoisseur of ruins'. 'The architecture of destruction not only possessed an aesthetic peculiar to itself', wrote Richards, but

> it contrives its effects out of its own range of raw materials. Among its most familiar are the sacrificed surface of blasted walls, the chalky substance of calcined masonry, the surprising sagging contours of once rigid girders and the clear sienna colouring of burnt out brick buildings, their rugged crosswalls receding plane by plane, on sunny mornings in the City. Moreover the aesthetic of destruction bears no relation to any architectural merit the building may once have possessed in life. In death merit is of a different order, and some of the most dramatic and evocative ruins have flowered suddenly out of a structure no one would have looked at twice.

> (Richards 1942: 3)

Richards appreciated that the conversion of military action into aesthetic spectacle might appear 'unfeeling'. But, he argued, it was

> surely the very intensity of the symbolism they are charged with that justifies the claim of ruined buildings to be looked at for the sake of what they are at the moment. It has always been the role of the ruin to compress into the same picture both the embodiment of historical experience and the form and colour of architecture itself. Hence its romantic appeal.
>
> (Richards 1942: 2)

More grandly, he wrote that 'to posterity they will as effectually represent the dissolution of our pre-war civilisation as Fountains Abbey does the dissolution of the monasteries' (Richards 1942: 2).[22]

The Bombed Buildings of Britain was a response to exceptional circumstances, but the aesthetic it advocated had lasting influence, and was propagated by many others beyond Richards and his colleagues. For another important example, I would cite the artist John Piper's 1947 article 'Pleasing Decay' which argued that the natural post-war desire for the new should not obscure the aesthetic possibilities of decay. For the town planner 'decay – *present* decay as well as possible future decay – should be one of the tricks in his box of tricks to be used, as the country gentleman used it in the eighteenth and early nineteenth centuries for certain specific purposes' (Piper 1947: 93).

Piper assumed that almost everything could and would decay, including Victorian and Edwardian buildings, which he now saw taking picturesque forms as they fell into ruin.[23] He was unambiguous about his aesthetic position, and that of his readership: the cultivation of decay was a game to be played by a privileged outsider, who enjoyed the spectacle of decay without, implicitly, having to inhabit it.

Besides 'Townscape' and Piper's advocacy of decay, the *Review* also began to promote industrial architecture through what Richards called 'the Functional Tradition'. Richards had already made use of this idea in his *Introduction to Modern Architecture*, and his views on the subject were in large part shared by his colleague Pevsner. The book, *The Functional Tradition* was published in 1958, with photographs by Eric de Maré. In it, Richards restated the argument that the Modern movement did not simply super-impose itself on pre-existing built forms, but developed out of industrial traditions. The Crystal Palace and the dock warehouses of Telford were precursors of the Modern movement. This teleology had the effect of less-ening the revolutionary potential of Modernism, making it more acceptable to an English readership. The English, he wrote, could already happily accept railways in pastoral valleys, or textile mills on the 'grey north country hillsides' and even regard them with a certain nostalgia – so perhaps they would one day come to appreciate power stations, airports and other modern industrial structures (Richards 1958: 21). Richards made clear that the world-view that would permit this was picturesque, and therefore one predicated in an aesthetic detachment from the scene. *The Functional Tradition* expanded the canon of architecture to include what were previously only regarded as engineering structures, but it did so through the frame of the picturesque. It was therefore vital that the structures assimilated into 'architecture' through the picturesque be old, and preferably disused. Where a building could not easily be assimilated to the picturesque, it was dismissed as 'grim' or (very curiously) 'industrial' (Richards 1958: 40).

Among the buildings treated by Richards is the Albert Dock at Liverpool, with extensive photography by de Maré. All the photographs show the Dock in a state of inactivity, underlined by choice details: a broken ladder, broken windows, iron columns stained and dirty, debris of all kinds. All of these images, whether the general views or the details, demonstrate a picturesque mode of composition, where any need to describe function is subordinated to the desire for visual pleasure. After de Maré, the picturesque mode became the standard for photographing the Dock. Quentin Hughes' *Seaport* is if anything more picturesque, although the Dock had perhaps reached perhaps a more advanced stage of decline by 1964 (Figures 5.3 to 5.5). Hughes, in his text, was unapologetic about the book's mode of representation. Liverpool's slums, he wrote,

> have pictorial qualities – the harsh contrast of blackened brick and sharp silhouette against those iridescent skies which so characterise the city. Rumpled newsprint lies like a giant white rose on city pavement. The serrated skyline of windowless façades and wet slate roofs in the fleeting light of early morning conjures up a poetry which can be appreciated only by those who do not have to live in these conditions.
>
> (Hughes 1964: 121)

Hughes' description of Liverpool is the apogee of the picturesque in relation to Liverpool, and it is critical in forming the Albert Dock as a discursive ruin. As I hope is clear by now, the Dock may have been tidied up and renovated, but it cannot escape the idea of the ruin; it remains caught up in this classic picturesque trope. Not only that, but I would argue that its practical existence affirms a fundamentally picturesque character. Take, for example its

5.3
Photograph
of Albert Dock,
Liverpool, from
Hughes, *Seaport*
(1964)

5.4
Photograph of Albert Dock,
Liverpool, from Hughes,
Seaport (1964)

5.5
**Photograph of
Albert Dock,
Liverpool, from
Hughes, *Seaport*
(1964)**

5.5
**Photograph of
Albert Dock,
Liverpool, from
Hughes, *Seaport*
(1964)**

setting. One senses that it has always been particularly, first, valued because it exists as a discrete structure in a landscape; it can be both perceived as a single object, and from it a landscape can be seen. It is not a conventional picturesque setting, I admit, but nevertheless, the relationship between figure and ground is of the picturesque type; it is the same as the relationship between the country house and the landscape. To put this a different way: this is not a building in a real urban setting, but isolated from it. Its visual relationships are to the sea (now only occasionally marked by the urban, i.e. ships), and to a distant cityscape. Second, the setting imposes the same discipline on the visitor as that involved in visiting a country house. Access by car is positively encouraged – the complex is surrounded by acres of car and coach parking, so the visitor arrives and departs in the same way as they might approach Fountains Abbey. Third, is the architecture. The grandness of the Doric used here speaks inescapably of empire, and of its passing. Fourth, is the debris of the business of the docks, the cranes, bollards, derricks and so on, all restored to within an inch of their lives, but all quite useless. These are indubitably ruins, and speak of the passing of an entire mode of existence. Overall, it is the legibility of the business of the Dock, the fact that what it was is so inescapably still present, yet at the same time so obviously of the past, that makes it ruinous. It is as grand as Fountains Abbey; and it is equally finished as a mode of being.

Nowhere is it stated officially that the ruinous character of the Albert Dock was an attraction for the Tate trustees.[24] However, their Millbank Gallery contains some of the classic painted images of ruins in the English landscape, of which the full-size sketch for *Hadleigh Castle* by John Constable is one of the best, and most appropriate, examples (Figure 5.6). A large-scale meditation on loss, it places the ruin of an exhausted civilisation against the sea, the mouth of the Thames, at a point that, as with the Mersey, ought to be busy with shipping linking the ports of empire. Conventionally read as an image of personal grief (it was painted shortly after the death of the artist's wife), it is also one of the key images in the English romantic imagination, in which modern civilisation is depicted as temporary and fragile. That the new gallery at Liverpool so clearly confirms this view is not coincidental; the certainty with which the gallery reports the finding of the building in 1986 ('we knew we had found the right place') suggests as much.

Conclusions

The Albert Dock, I suggest, is better seen as a picturesque ruin than a displaced New York loft. This is worth saying, it seems to me, because of the ideological baggage these concepts carry. The loft, as we have seen, is a nimble operation in the interstices of capital, a means of negotiating the material changes brought be de-industrialisation. The ruin is quite different.

It speaks of a desire to make monuments, to admonish, and to warn: it shows a preoccupation with the past rather than the future.

If I were to make a value judgement about this image making, I would say, perhaps, that it is ultimately authoritarian, about the imposition of a view of the centre on the periphery in a way that in retrospect seems almost colonial.[25] The processes by which the Tate Gallery was realised in Liverpool were certainly neo-colonial, involving the operation of governmental and quasi-governmental agencies over the local. Local government, as we saw, was suppressed, and several of its functions taken up by the centre; at the most critical stage of the conflict between centre and periphery, in 1986, central government began to consider the possibility of direct rule of Merseyside, in an explicitly colonial sense. One administrative legacy of this period was the creation in 1986 of the National Museums and Galleries on Merseyside (NMGM), in which important local collections were taken out of local control.[26]

Specifically about the Tate, its director, and many of the original staff came from London, and retained strong ties there. And the mission of the gallery was in effect to civilise the north through art, an idea clearly expressed in the 1986 biennial report (Tate 1986: 21). The policy was materialised not only in the presence of the gallery in Liverpool, but in two unique strategies under the guise of 'education': gallery attendants, for example, were not only expected to maintain security, but to interpret artworks for visitors when requested, an unprecedented policy.[27] And a Volkswagen 'art van', decorated by David Hockney, was acquired for outreach work in the 'community', through which the Tate 'product' would be explained to the natives (Tate 1988: 33). As with all colonial relationships, that between London Tate and Liverpool Tate was never entirely straightforward, marked by tension and indifference, as much as authority by the former over the latter.[28] But there is no question that the model was a colonial one, and attempts to ameliorate this fact tended only to draw attention to it.

The colonial nature of the enterprise is indicated too in the distancing of relations between centre and periphery: the hostility to some in London to both the outpost and its location; the feeling that Liverpool was at the end of the earth; the worries about the security of art objects in such wild territory. The relationship between London and the Liverpool outpost increasingly became one of 'benign disinterest'.[29] It is in many respects a classic colonial scenario. Now I suggest, finally, that the architecture of the Albert Dock is in fact integral to this scenario. Its legibility as ruin, and through that its accession to the picturesque, invokes a way of looking that is inherently privileged. The Albert Dock makes a picturesque spectacle for the visitor to enjoy, rather than inhabit; its ruinous qualities generate aesthetic thrills, without offering solutions; its staging of elegiac decline is entirely consistent with a picturesque English world-view. It is not a world-view that much aids Liverpool's plight. Rather, it could be said to entrench it further for the morbid pleasure of the visitor, using Liverpool's anxiety about the urban to draw attention away from his own.

Chapter 6

The architecture
of civility

> Most if not all capital cities of Western Europe have a place that
> could be described as their 'front room'. This place attempts to
> give palpable expression to its host's social and political aspirations.
> It is most usually a place to be looked at, and only occasionally
> used; somewhere that will impress the neighbours and overawe
> the country cousins [. . .] in all their manifestations they are the sole
> and absolute province of the ruling class, who of course decide
> what will be recorded and how. The mass of the population gain,
> or have gained admission, both metaphorically and actually, to such
> places on sufferance only.
>
> (Mace 1976: 15).

This chapter deals with Trafalgar Square in London, and its reconstruction
from 1998 to 2003 as part of the 'World Squares for All' project designed
by Foster and Partners. It is a central case for this book: there is no more
symbolically charged public space in England, none more redolent of its
imperial past.[1] And there is perhaps no space more eloquent than this one
with regard to current anxieties about the urban. In his Marxist account of the
square, still the most detailed book on the subject, the historian Rodney Mace
outlines three established roles for it. First, he describes an official role as a
place that is to be looked at rather than inhabited, a place that through the
grandeur of its buildings, and the narrative quality of its monuments,
impresses the authority of the state on those who gaze upon it. Designed to
'impress the neighbours and overawe the country cousins', it is 'the sole and

absolute province of the ruling class' (Mace 1976: 15). Second, Mace describes the square as a site of dissent, a tradition that has continued until the present day. Third, he describes the square's related role as a place of gathering for the dispossessed. This role has been policed to varying degrees over the years, but it has likewise long been a part of Trafalgar Square's character.

My account of Trafalgar Square draws on Mace, but I am concerned with its contemporary situation more than its history. Specifically, I am concerned here to explain how its reformation aims define what might be called a secular purpose for the square, in other words a purpose which does not depend on belief in a grand historical narrative such as Empire, or the resistance to it. This purpose, which is in fact a liberal ideology, I call civility, bringing into play a term which has been much in use in contemporary political philosophy.[2] Civility supposes, for the first time, an official concern with the square from the viewpoint of the people inhabiting it, rather than gazing upon it from a distance. Its designers, and what might be called its principal shareholders – the galleries, Westminster City Council, the government – want a space that can be more easily negotiated and understood, a more civilised space for those who spend time in it. But as I argue here, the ideology of civility that underwrites the new square conflicts with its existing roles in highly problematical ways. Not only does civility abolish the old rhetoric about Empire and military conquest, but also the place of the square as place of dissent, the square as a refuge for the dispossessed, not to mention the square as bus station and traffic circle. Whatever physical changes have been made, ideologically speaking, the square has been remade as a site of bourgeois pleasure. Now replete with a permanent warden, an events programme and a list of new regulations specifying what is and what is not possible in it, Trafalgar Square no longer celebrates the past, nor offers any resistance to it (Figure 6.1). Rather, it is an old space assimilated to the shopping mall's paradigm of consumption and display.[3]

This ideological shift is, I argue, symbolic of wider English anxieties about the urban. As I have argued so far, English city spaces tend to be both literally uneasy – that is, apprehended anxiously by their beholders – and metaphorically uneasy, which is to say anxious in the symbolic role they play in the representation of city and nation. Trafalgar Square exemplifies these anxieties superbly. The reconstruction of the square, as we shall see, deals with them by trying to forget them. In the new square, the possibilities of the square as a symbolic space, and of it as a place of spontaneous action are both erased. The fourth plinth project, a series of artworks for an empty sculptural plinth in the square is, in a sense, emblematic of this anxiety.[4] Although critically acclaimed, it signifies a profound uneasiness with the traditional

6.1
**Trafalgar Square,
London, in 2003**
Nigel Young

values and role of the square. The result is a space that, as the sociologist Richard Sennett has suggested, may not even be urban at all.[5] Trafalgar Square remains at this point an ideological project, a project that may or may not have material results. At this point in its life, it can do little more than stage civility: how precisely it develops as a public space remains to be seen. But it is nevertheless worth interrogating the official discourse around it to see how it has been rethought.

Trafalgar Square: an introduction

Trafalgar Square is an untidy accumulation of buildings dating from the eighteenth to the twentieth centuries, built around a large, uncertain area that is more pentagonal than square in form. Significantly inclined to the south, busy with traffic and public monuments, it is no place for military parades. It lies at a strategically significant part of London, between the Mall, the Strand and Parliament, which is to say at a meeting point of the royal, commercial and political cities. This location was the heart of the eighteenth-century city, a place then as now 'disorderly, dirty, teeming with traffic' (Saumarez Smith 2001). Until the early nineteenth century, in the middle of it could be found the Great Stable, an attachment of the Royal Mews, which provided an open space, for royal, rather than public, use.

It was formalised as a public space in the early nineteenth century, when the architect of Regent St., John Nash, drew up plans for a radical remodelling, in which it would become a formal zone of culture. There were plans for a new National Gallery, a Royal Academy, a Royal Academy of Literature and the Athenaeum Club to be located along the north side of the square. These plans were partly realised when the new square was built between 1829 and 1841 to commemorate Admiral Nelson's 1805 victory at the Battle of Trafalgar, a battle at which the French fleet was suddenly and opportunistically defeated. In 1838, a new National Gallery on the north side was completed to the design of the architect William Wilkins; important later additions were Canada House to the west, South Africa House to the east, and, overlooking the square, the 1960s tower of New Zealand House.

The monuments that the square contains include Nelson's column, a single Corinthian column 185 feet high, supporting a 17-foot statue of Nelson himself. The base of the column was decorated with sculptural reliefs depicting four of the greatest of Nelson's military victories, St Vincent (1797), The Nile (1798), Copenhagen (1801) and finally Trafalgar (1805), the battle at which he was killed. Nelson's popularity at the time of his death was great: Britain's success in checking the imperial ambitions of the French, and, more broadly, revolutionary activity in Europe, were personified in him. But as Mace points out, Nelson is significant as a specifically *bourgeois* hero, emblematic of a transition of economic power from the landed gentry to the bourgeoisie. During the Napoleonic wars between 1793 and 1815, Mace argues that sculpture in England changed from being a 'private indulgence of the ruling class' to 'an object of more public display, often financed by the government with a direct didactic purpose' (Mace 1976: 49). William Railton was selected by a competition in 1839 to design the monument, which took the now familiar form, with a subsequent decision appointing Edmund Baily to design the statue of Nelson, and John Lough to make the lions at the base. Both had been runners up in the competition (Mace 1976: 65). The revival of the idea of a monument to Nelson thirty-five years after his death was an attempt to mitigate an economic downturn through the erection of chauvinistic symbols. The positioning of the column vis-à-vis the other monuments in the square would also seem to confirm the ascendancy of the bourgeois. As has often been pointed out, the statue of George IV on the south side of the square has the king gazing up towards Nelson's buttocks, an arrangement that apparently would have satisfied the admiral (Mace 1976: 111).

Nelson's column is by far the largest monument in the square, and dominates it both physically and ideologically. The battle it represents is a crucial moment in the consolidation of the British Empire, after a long period of ill fortune, when it seemed as if Napoleon could have moved to take India, the French threat was suddenly neutralised. The other two monuments built for the square proper similarly reinforce the imperial narrative. They depict

Major-General Charles Napier, whose statue was erected on the north side of the square in 1859; as commander of troops in the north of England he had been responsible for quelling disturbances by Chartists; he was later appointed as governor of Sind province in India, annexed after a successful, but bloody, battle over the native Amirs. He ruled Sind in a 'rude and vigorous manner' for four years (Mace 1976: 116). The second statue that needs to be mentioned here, of General Sir Henry Havelock, depicts the general who was chiefly responsible for putting down the Bengal mutinies of 1857; the brutality of his work in India, in particular the punishment meted out to mutineers was exceptional. Mace describes another statue of another general, Charles Gordon, who was responsible for the suppression of the Taiping rebellion of 1863, and later became governor of the Equatorial Provinces of Africa. His statue was removed from Trafalgar Square during the Second World War to allow the exhibition of a Lancaster bomber; it was later re-erected outside the Ministry of Defence.

These monumental public sculptures, along with the presence of the embassies of South Africa, New Zealand and Canada in, or overlooking, the square, place Trafalgar Square at the centre of an imperial narrative. The sculptures celebrate imperial conquests, in modern terms often bloody and racist, while the embassies of former white settler territories imply the continuing importance of empire in the definition of national identity.[6] The official role of the square, as what Mace terms the 'front room' of the nation, is therefore underwritten by an imperial text. What is meant to impress the beholder, to hold him in awe as he gazes upon the square, is this history of imperial conquest, a history that is reiterated aesthetically by its grandiose neoclassical architecture.

Around this official role might be said to pivot the two other traditional, though unofficial, roles of the square: the square as a place of dissent, and the square as a refuge for the dispossessed. I say pivot, because it is the square's position as the symbolic centre of empire that makes it attractive to these activities: in each case, the margins are calculatedly placed at the centre to draw the attention of authority.[7] Trafalgar Square attracted both dissent and refuge from the beginning of its existence, and both have frequently been the object of official censure, resulting in a long list of byelaws defining activities on the site[8] (Figure 6.2). The official response was sometimes extreme. In 1848, for example, with a revolutionary political climate affecting much of mainland Europe, all gatherings were prohibited, on pain of death. Its design has frequently been discussed in terms of the way it might inhibit assembly.[9] Lighting, for example, was installed both as a security measure, and a means of policing the dispossessed. When installed, Mace writes, it was 'to prevent footpads from lurking in the shadows, but also to make it more difficult for the

6.2
Trafalgar Square, London: list of byelaws relating to the use of the square

homeless to rest there unseen' (Mace 1976: 88).[10] But he describes how in the late 1880s, during a period of economic crisis, and high unemployment, several hundred people were to be found 'infesting' the square, as the vestry of St Martin-in-the-Fields complained (Mace 1976: 170–1). Trafalgar Square in its reformed state is no longer the site of dissent or the dispossessed in the same way – but the list of regulations posted around the square make clear the continued tension between official and unofficial roles.

The architecture of civility

But my subject here is not so much the square's place as a site of resistance to authority. Rather, I am concerned here with the way that, in recent years, authority has sought to recast the square in new terms. The reformed square no longer, I argue, stages an imperial narrative, and as a result, it no longer seems the natural place for dissent. In any case the new regulations for public assembly make meaningful dissent ever less likely.[11] The recent debate about the possibility of a statue of Nelson Mandela in the square, an idea supported by the Mayor of London, Ken Livingstone, could be said to memorialise dissent, to make it a thing of the past. The reformed square, I argue, makes a new ideology central to the square. Specifically, the old ideology of Empire is replaced by civility.

The term civility requires some discussion. A complex and fugitive term, its etymological roots lie in the Latin *civitas*, usually translated as 'citizenship', a system of rights with responsibilities.[12] It clearly also relates to the term 'civil society', the set of social institutions that Karl Marx understood to be essential to the functioning of the bourgeois state. Civility might usefully be said to be the social expression of civil society.[13] But what I am primarily concerned with here is the more or less contemporary discourse around civility, where it has had an impact on architectural thinking, and where specifically it might be said to underwrite the form of the new Trafalgar Square.

Although civility is a term that widely appears in architectural writing, its meaning is rarely discussed. For instance, Richard Rogers laments London's lost 'civility' in *Cities for a Small Planet*, where it seems a straightforward term, signifying something like good public manners (Rogers 1997: 105).[14] But in his thinking, and elsewhere in contemporary architectural discourse, civility's profound contradictions remain elusive. Especially elusive is the sense that civility necessarily involves the imposition of authority, achieved by means of the law, social convention or the police. Civility in architectural writing is rarely a state that has consequences, especially moral ones. This sense of civility as an essentially moral condition needs to be recovered here before I consider its application at Trafalgar Square.

As a moral condition, civility closely relates to *politeness*, the aestheticised manifestation of civic humanism that emerged in the eighteenth-century London coffee house.[15] As the art historian David Solkin has described, at the beginning of the eighteenth century, attempts were made to codify a moral public behaviour at a time when the development of a modern commercial sphere appeared to some, such as the critic Bernard Mandeville, to threaten the possibility of morality at all (Solkin 1993: 27–47).[16] For Anthony Ashley Cooper however, the seventh Earl of Shaftesbury, public morality certainly existed, and could be codified to be a check on commerce. His ideal imagined state was a hierarchical republic, ruled by a 'disinterested élite of male citizens, autonomous men of public virtue who stand above and apart from the interdependent world of corrupt and commercial modernity' (Solkin 1993: 4). Shaftesbury's state nevertheless recognised the necessity of commerce as his belief in politeness, a conflation of manners with morals, made clear. Unlike Roman *civitas*, politeness was not a privilege or birthright, but could be acquired through conversation or exposure to the correct things.

In other words, his state does not imagine aloofness from the world, but a sophisticated engagement with it. And it is, I stress, an aesthetic engagement with the world, in which human behaviour is modified for visual effect. Beauty and politeness are inherently bound in this scheme. For Shaftesbury, writes Solkin, 'beauty, truth and goodness are ultimately one and the same' (Solkin 1993: 11).

Now this aestheticised model of public behaviour, advocated as a means of ameliorating commerce's more barbaric tendencies, is very close to contemporary visions of civility. All versions of contemporary civility in one way or another accept the market, but seek to control its social manifestations, and it is no accident that they should appear during the 1980s when, in the anglophone world, capital had been freed to such dramatic and brutal effect.[17] I will concentrate here on two contemporary manifestations of civility, one British and the other American. The first is exemplified by the work of the conservative aesthetician Roger Scruton who has put forward a well-developed anti-Modernist position on architectural civility (Scruton 1994).[18] Principally a means of castigating Modernist architecture in favour of a return to the pattern-book classicism of the eighteenth century, it defines civility as that sense of public virtue that enables civil society to function, or to put it another way, a set of social conventions that permit the rule of law. Civility is, he writes 'respect for persons, as agents able freely to bind themselves to strangers, despite, and because of the fact that they owe no debt of gratitude or love'. Civility is not superficial, he continues,

> but the essential condition for the building of the public world [. . .] civility [. . .] consists in the ability to adjust to one's neighbour, to meet him on terms, even when the terms are unequal [. . .] without the virtue of civility we neither acquire the public existence which defines our field of action, nor the private life in which we are consoled.
>
> (Scruton 1994: 17–18)

In these terms, civility as applied to architecture has to do, broadly, with defining the public realm against the private. More precisely it is about how the mediation between the public and private realms may be made polite. For Scruton, this is done principally by means of the architectural façade, which he believes exactly equivalent to the human face, allowing the viewer an anthropomorphic means of communication with a building. The buildings that best exhibit civility are those that mediate this liminal dimension, the ones that 'refuse to outrage or defy', where openings are 'civil and friendly', the ones that through architectural 'conversation' politely discipline the citizen, encouraging him to linger where it is appropriate and to hurry where it is not (Scruton 1994: 39). The precise architectural form which best describes these characteristics is – not surprisingly to anyone familiar with Scruton's other writings – the Georgian terraced house, a built form that in his view achieves all of these tasks with a dignity and calm which cannot in his view be improved. Lasdun's Institute of Education is by contrast in his view a profoundly uncivil building, contrasting aggressively with its neoclassical Bloomsbury neighbours, turning its back on the street, keeping its entrance obscure, and, worst of all, being aggressively *horizontal*, an axis which Scruton associates with what he terms the most 'traumatic', and 'usually' most private experiences – 'birth, copulation, and death' (Scruton 1994: xiv)[19] (Figure 6.3). In summary, Scruton enlists the socially conservative philosophy of civility in an attack on architectural Modernism. He assumes that architecture creates the social conditions that it frames, and that consequently the Georgian vernacular he advocates will lead to civility. Although he states how and why this might occur – the Georgian street incorporates readily understood conventions which discipline the space – this is an architecturally determinist approach, which assumes that architecture and the behaviour of the building's users are linked in some essential way.[20]

My second reference to the term civility is broader, and consists of the work of a number of American writers in the field of political philosophy. Their impact on the Clinton adminstration was significant, and the process has been repeated in the UK under New Labour (J. Hall 2003).[21] The wealth of publications on the subject for both professional and popular readerships describes nothing less than a civility 'boom' (DeMott 1996: 11). The term has been much debated, and at different times captured by left and right alike. The desire for a self-policing order, a state of good manners, has been an aspect of both radical and conservative politics. Broadly speaking, this view can be found equally in the later work of Richard Sennett, and more socially conservative writers, such as Stephen Carter and Robert Putnam, the latter being law professors, both of whose work has been widely read in the US (Sennett 1986; Carter 1998; Putnam 2000).[22] All would broadly agree that civility is not simply a question of good manners, but morality. They would argue that civility is a product of conflict, and they assert that it is through the encounter with the other, and the accommodation of difference, that civilised behaviour results. And they are certain that civility is impossible without faith, or at least the appearance of faith. Without the belief, Sennett has written, that it is divinely ordained that there should be difference in the world, there is no implicit in centive to come to terms with it (Sennett 1986: 376). Carter, a leader writer for the *New York Times* and erstwhile advisor to the Clinton government, goes

6.3
**University of
London, Institute
of Education
(1970–6), architect:
Denys Lasdun**

further. His book *Civility* (1998) makes clear, like Sennett, that civility is pro-foundly moral, and that it involves sacrifice. He writes at length of 'sacrifice' and of 'sacrificial civility', arguing that civility is meaningless unless those who practise it give something up in order for it to function. But the difficulty of sacrifice in most cases will require belief (Carter 1998: 18).[23]

Carter concedes that secular civility is possible, he writes a little later, but qualifies it by stating that if it 'rests on the shifting sands of secular morality it might topple with the next stiff political wind' (Carter 1998: 31). Putnam's argument in the best-selling *Bowling Alone* is similar in that he links the decline of civility in America to the decline in religious faith, and he believes that the reverse in the latter will lead to an improvement in the former. But he admits that in the production of civility, the private belief system matters less than the look of belief. Believe what you will in private, Putnam seems to argue, but at least perform the social rituals of belief as doing so confers benefits on society (Putnam 2000: 66–9).

In summary, civility in these contemporary guises is about an ideal of disciplined public behaviour, an ideal that its proponents argue can be achieved through judicious use of architecture, or through the maintenance of existing social institutions. In Putnam's case, such institutions include organ-ised religion, and bowling clubs, the latter providing the book's leitmotif. Now, some or all of these things are legible in the Trafalgar Square project as we shall see, but before we can make a critique of that project, we need to high-light some of the problems of civility as an ideal. These can be structured around the question of authority.

Civility and authority are rarely thought of as in any way contermin-ous. Civility is usually presented as an ideal condition in which all may participate equally. When Richard Rogers laments the supposed decline in London's civility, he imagines, nostalgically perhaps, an old city of fine public spaces and a well-developed public culture, implicitly democratic, and open to all. This is the subtext to his opening remarks about London in *Cities for a Small Planet*. And when Foster and partners rethink London's public spaces in terms of civility, they call the results 'World Squares for All', invoking an ideal of liberty. Civility and freedom are conflated here, yet in many ways these terms are mutually exclusive. Civility may give the appearance of freedom in the urban realm, but it can only be brought about by authority, which is to say, unfreedom. In the case of Trafalgar Square, as we shall see, it is a highly complex system of regulation and surveillance that allows it to occur. In other cases, it may be a system of social institutions. Therefore the state of civility is inherently contradictory: a state of apparent freedom, it is in fact the social representation of a particular kind of authority.

Some of the inherent contradictions of civility were explored by Jürgen Habermas in his *Structural Transformation of the Public Sphere* (1961, translated 1989). Thinking about civil society as it developed in the west from the eighteenth century, he described it as much a form of discipline as a freedom.[24] He noted its assertion of basic rights of man, and yet at the same time, its restriction of participation in those rights to a certain class. To explain this he drew a distinction between the exclusive origins of the idea of civil society, and a more contemporary understanding of public building: 'As in the expression 'public building', the building does not even have to be open to public traffic. 'Public buildings' simply house state institutions and as such are 'public' (Habermas 1989: 2). Habermas went on to define the precise nature of the public imagined in the phrase 'civil society'. It was primarily a public that is educated, a 'reading public'. Writing of eighteenth-century Prussia, he noted that 'the authorities addressed their promulgations to the public, in principle to all subjects. Usually this did not reach the common man in this way, but at best the educated classes' (Habermas 1961: 22). Curiously, the social exclusion extended upwards as well as downwards: European court aristocracies of the period were not part of the reading public either. Later Habermas argued that the public also defined itself in terms of property ownership:

> The fully developed bourgeois public sphere was based on the ficti-
> tious identity of the two roles assumed by the privatised individuals
> who came together to form a public: the role of the property
> owners and the role of human beings pure and simple.
>
> (Habermas 1961: 56)

So bourgeois civility as defined in Habermas' terms assumes a highly exclusive public. A slightly different point is made by the journalist Benjamin
DeMott in his attack on the civility 'boom' in the US. There he argues that
civility not only defines the public in exclusively bourgeois terms, but it
occludes genuine class conflict. In fact, he writes, it dresses class conflict in
the clothes of morality. 'The incivility railed at by the élite should be seen as a
protest by Americans outside the ranks of the publicly articulate against the
conduct of the their presumed betters' (DeMott 1996: 12). The advocates of
civility simply refuse to take this protest seriously – until expressions of
dissent are couched in terms that are acceptable to the élite, there can be no
debate. He continues: 'sold as diagnosis or nostrum, civility is in fact a theater
of operations – the classless society's new class war zone' (DeMott 1996: 12).
Common ground, social capital, civic trust, communal participation are all
myths, he argues, a condition revealed when one considers the question of
race, where civility masks oppression.[25] He declares that at least some of
civility's advocates found the civil rights movement disturbing because it
involved a degree of violence to achieve its ends. 'But when you're in an argument with a thug,' DeMott writes 'there are things much more important than
civility' (DeMott 1996: 19).

Under these authoritarian conditions, I suggest that the only people
capable of enacting civility are those for whom its authority may be a positive
benefit: tourists. As the architectural critic Martin Pawley has argued in
Terminal Architecture (1998), many of the places cited with approval by the
advocates of civility – Covent Garden in London, the Paseo de las Ramblas
in Barcelona, SoHo in New York – are almost entirely inhabited by visitors
to the respective cities rather than inhabitants (Pawley 1998: 167–9). What
these 'phantom populations' therefore present is not an image of civilised
urban behaviour deriving from the character of a specific place, but a place*less*
behaviour giving an inaccurate sense of plenitude and life.

World squares for all

Now we know more about civility, let us return to Trafalgar Square in order to
pose some questions of the way it has been reformed. How does it, in its new

form, articulate the idea of civility? What precise strategies does it employ that show a change in the official imagination of the square? How does the reformed square treat the traces of the historical square? To answer these questions, I look first at the images of a reformed square produced by Richard Rogers and Norman Foster from 1986 onwards. I then briefly consider some non-visual sources for the new square, namely the way it exists in the rhetoric of the Greater London Authority (GLA), how they imagine it, and what it stands for in their rhetoric.

It should be said that the reconstruction of Trafalgar Square took place at a time when the Labour government, elected in 1997, had taken an unusual interest in the whole question of public space, elaborating developments that had occurred towards the end of the previous Conservative government.[26] In 1998, it set up the Urban Task Force under Lord Rogers, which reported in 1999; it published the resulting Urban White Paper in 2000; it replaced the architecture-focused Royal Fine Arts Commission with the Commission for Architecture and the Built Environment (CABE), a body with declared interests in the public realm as well as architecture; in 2001, Tony Blair made a campaigning speech in Croydon ('Improving Your Local Environment') that was focused on crime reduction, but showed interest in design issues and their relationship with public behaviour (Blair 2001). At the time of the reconstruction of Trafalgar Square, public space was a therefore political issue, and through this, civility was on the political agenda.[27] In this political climate, the reform of Trafalgar Square fits well the logic of civility. At the same time as a government takes an interest in public space, specifically the way it is used and inhabited, a national space is reinvented in these terms: specifically, a place that was built originally to monumentalise the past, to celebrate the achievements of Empire, in particular its military prowess, has been reinterpreted as a site of bourgeois pleasure, with its promenades, its café, its 24-hour security presence, and one of its monuments, the empty fourth plinth, reinvented as an entertainment for gallery-goers. The logic of empire, in summary, is replaced with the logic of civility.

The architectural attempts to rethink the square, by Rogers and then Foster, take as their starting point the everyday experience of the square. The square, they noted, had long been uneasy, caught between its actual, highly disparate functions, of bus station, memorial and dissent. It was scruffy and down at heel. The official body responsible for its upkeep, the Department of National Heritage, was happy to sell licences for ice cream vans, and the sale of pigeon-feed, regardless of their impact on the overall conception of the square. It was widely perceived as dangerous and dirty. The director of the National Gallery, the main tenant of the north side of the square, described its condition prior to refurbishment as 'particularly disgusting' quite apart from the fact that the traffic and the road layout made it 'quite inaccessible'. At night its rough edges made it a dangerous place, the threat of violence clashing with the grandeur of the surrounding architecture.[28] Norman Foster summarised the square's problems as follows. It had

> all the potential to be an appropriate urban setting for the civic heart of the nation. Yet today it fails on almost every count. Despite the grandeur of its buildings and the significance of its heritage, it is a dirty and unfriendly environment, dominated by asphalt and the car [. . .] it is moreover, incoherently presented: it is hard to find your way around. It contains the vocabulary of city spaces, but lacks the grammar to make sense of those spaces and facilitate communication.
>
> (Jenkins 2000: 704)

The square as an architectural space has never been completely resolved. It is very large, very exposed, a strange shape, and its sense of enclosure leaks away southwards along Whitehall. It has not, since Nash, been planned as a whole. Architectural interventions have happened, but in an informal way, sometimes as the result of bizarre phenomena.[29] The square's history might therefore be said to be more the result of accident, accretion and history, in other words the usual ways of building in London.

The modern attempts to reimagine the square therefore take as their starting point the anxious experience of being in it. The first of these occurred in the competition for the National Gallery extension on the so-called Hampton site at the north western corner of the square, a vacant lot left by the bombing of the former Hampton department store during the Second World War (Hillier *et al.* 1982). The 1982 competition included several entries which integrated the new building with the space around it, most spectacularly Rogers' scheme, which used the gallery as a pretext for a much larger rethinking of central London (Rogers 1988). The gallery was merely a mid-point in a pedestrian way that would stretch from Leicester Square to the Thames and beyond. Neither the winning scheme, by Ahrends Burton Koralek (notoriously dismissed by HRH Prince Charles as a 'carbuncle'), nor the one which was actually built, by Venturi and Scott-Brown, made anything of Trafalgar Square (HRH the Prince of Wales 1984).

Rogers further developed these proposals for the square in 1986. That year, he took part in an exhibition at the Royal Academy, London, entitled *New British Architecture*, along with Norman Foster and James Stirling (Rogers 1988: 132–7; *Architect's Journal* 1986; Jenkins 1986; Cruickshank 1986a, 1986b). Rogers' precise contribution was 'London as it Could Be', a research proposal for the comprehensive redevelopment of the area between Leicester and Square and the South Bank centre, via Charing Cross, structured around a pedestrian boulevard between the two points.[30] The scheme proposed drastic measures: the abolition of Charing Cross station, with its trains diverted to Waterloo on the south side of the river; the replacement of Hungerford Bridge with a high-tech structure combining a pedestrian walkway with a monorail connecting Waterloo station and the north bank (Figure 6.4). The Embankment, the road along the north bank of the Thames, would be buried in a tunnel and overlaid with a pedestrian boulevard (Figure 6.5). As imagined by Canaletto in the eighteenth century, a set of steps would lead down to the Thames.

By comparison, the Trafalgar Square portion of the scheme was restrained: Rogers proposed removing the traffic from the north side in front of the National Gallery, creating a new pedestrian plaza as 'a new open-air sculpture space for London' – a space which would spill over towards the Strand, taking over Duncannon St.[31] With pavement cafés occupying an arcade below the terrace, Trafalgar Square itself could become 'a vibrant meeting place for Londoners and a place to enjoy outstanding views [. . .]' (Rogers 1997: 128). In other words, it is no longer a transit hub, a traffic roundabout, a place of passage, but a leisure destination.

I say this is a restrained scheme, because apart from this limited pedestrianisation, the scheme does not propose any great architectural changes. Indeed, in the widely published perspective drawings of the scheme (drawn by Rogers' talented colleague, Laurie Abbott) the modern is conspicuously repressed (Figures 6.6 and 6.7).[32] The image of the square as seen from the east, its right hand corner framed by the National Gallery, occludes both the new extension for the gallery, and the high Modernist tower of New Zealand House beyond. The square is imagined here as an architecturally traditional space, with the new proposals meant to foreground the most historically significant buildings. About a hundred human figures (and a dog) dot the scene, in silhouette, weakly defined in terms of age, althoughthey appear as small family groups. Some figures are legible as children, and there is the suggestion of prams and pushchairs. No cars or buses appear in this scheme, nothing in fact to indicate that it is a modern scheme. Its imagery belongs to the early nineteenth century as much as it does to the present day.

This repression of the modern is significant for the imagination of the square's function. Its modern functions, besides those of monument and protest already described, have been mostly those of a traffic roundabout and transit hub; the majority of the people in the square were passing through on the way to somewhere else. It was less a place than a zone of passage. Rogers reinvents it here as a transplanted Italian piazza with its neoclassical

6.4
Plan for Hungerford Bridge, London, from *London as it Could Be* (1986), architect: Richard Rogers Partnership

6.5
Sketch of the proposed pedestrianisation of the Embankment in front of Somerset House, from *London as it Could Be* (1986), architect: Laurie Abbott/ Richard Rogers Partnership

6.6
Sketch view of the proposed 'reclaimed' terrace fronting the National Gallery: a new open-air sculpture space for London, architect: Laurie Abbott/Richard Rogers Partnership

6.7
Sketch view of the proposed pedestrianisation of Trafalgar Square showing traffic re-routed to the south, from *London as it Could Be* **(1986), architect: Richard Rogers Partnership**

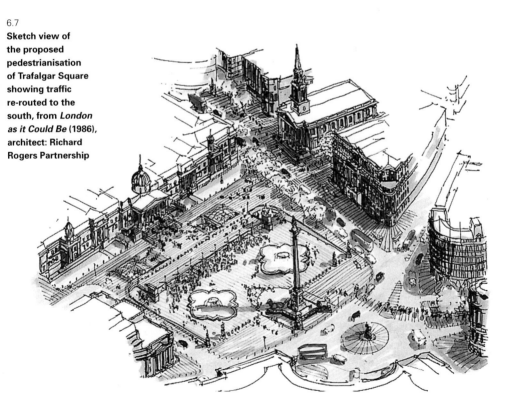

architecture and strolling family groups. Urban life is imagined here in specifically bourgeois terms, the fantasy of urban Italy calculated to appeal to a certain
class of English tourist. In the statement about the square quoted above,
Rogers entrenches the plans even more firmly in the bourgeois realm,
planning a sculpture terrace for promenading, outdoor cafés, viewpoints,
(shopping) arcades. The polite strollers enact a fantasy of civil society in which
all is order, moderation and politeness.[33] In these plans, Trafalgar Square
moves from a scruffy place of popular dissent, to the quintessential site of
bourgeois pleasure.

All this, I suggest, is problematical with regard to the imagination
of public life. Let me sketch out two problem areas. First is what might be
called the Italianate quality of the image. In style it belongs in exactly the
same category as the imagery described in Chapter 2, namely a bourgeois
fantasy of Italy produced for English consumption. Its picturesque composition, its viewpoint, its treatment of figures, its appeal to tradition all situate it
in this category. However this agreeable scene has no social basis. The
passeggiata (for that is what it seems to describe) cannot take place here
because Trafalgar Square lacks the social structures that make such behaviour
possible: the dense habitation of surrounding areas, the rituals of family life
and the church, the tradition of the performance of public realm, the existence
of a certain form of street café with which to punctuate the strolling. Even
with the removal of the traffic from the northern part of the square, the square
must still by its nature be a place of transit or passage. The image of civility
that is presented here cannot will into being an Italianate style of life.

The second issue these images raise concerns dissent: specifically,
what happens to the square's historical status as a place of protest when
these images of civility are superimposed on it. Civility may illustrate a certain
idea of freedom in a liberal society, but as Patrick Joyce has argued, it is
a freedom that has to be performed according to certain rules for it to be
understood (Joyce 2003: 9–11). Not only does it involve the cultivation of a
new kind of self, in which self-discipline and restraint are the key terms, but it
also imagines public life as a performed ritual, which he calls 'the only fully
meaningful display of the self'. Such an idea, whereby the public is no more
than a theatrical performance, is essentially bound up with power. It is through
the performance of this image of public freedom that power is exercised in a
liberal society, not as it were by coercion, but with the consent of its subjects
– individuals willing to perform the rituals that maintain authority (Joyce
2003: 119).

In the 1997 book, *Cities for a Small Planet*, there is an image of a
'Stop the City' demonstration reproduced in a same section of the book as the
proposals for Trafalgar Square (Rogers 1997: 127). It depicts one of a series

of environmental protests carried out in the 1980s and 1990s, in which cyclists would congregate in Trafalgar Square on summer Fridays to cycle slowly around it, bringing vehicular traffic to a standstill. The position of the image in the book is highly ambiguous. On the one hand, it seems to underline or emphasise the environmentalist stance of the book: the image is a positive one, representing the protestors as a heterogeneous collection of individuals, clearly enjoying themselves.[34] Their action creates a form of liberty to which Rogers is sympathetic. This is not an image of civility as such, yet it might be said to be a quite idealistic, even Utopian, image in which protest is seen to create a powerful sense of group identity, entirely consistent with Rogers' advocacy of urban living. Yet oddly the image appears not so much to confirm the value of urban life, but to condemn it in its current condition. Trafalgar Square in this image does not celebrate the value of protest, but represents the degraded quality of the existing built environment, and environment which will be improved by Rogers' proposals. But 'London as it Could Be' as far as we can tell from the images with which we are presented, has no place for dissent. It represents, in the form in which we see it, an exercise in civility imposed on the square, whose superficial freedoms represent an increased degree of social control, with architecture to match. I do not imagine that Rogers or Abbott imagined that their proposals might be understood in this way, but what my critique points up is the fact that they are built on contradictions (Rogers 1997: 127).

'London as it Could Be' was never built, although its images were published widely in various sources over a ten-year period – there is no question that it informed a wider debate about the appearance of a reformed Trafalgar Square. The second of the schemes to remake Trafalgar Square, and the one actually realised, was the superficially similar 'World Squares for All' project by Foster and Partners, designed principally by Spencer de Grey (Figures 6.8 and 6.9). Like Rogers' project this was part of a wider pedestrian scheme designed to facilitate free movement along newly created pedestrian boulevards. It was similarly preoccupied with the use of the space as it actually existed, rather than the existing traditional functions of the square. And it envisaged replacing these functions of monument, dissent and transit with civility. Formally, the two schemes were superficially similar. Both had as their major formal element the removal of traffic from in front of the National Gallery to create an extension to the public realm. Both included a café, a late addition in the Foster case. Both envisaged the square as a place where, principally, civility would be enacted, and both were underwritten by a belief in the redemptive value of public space, in other words the capacity of public space to establish a moral place in a city otherwise driven by (supposedly amoral) commercial interests.

6.8
'World Squares
for All', image
on hoarding
illustrating works
at Trafalgar
Square in 2003,
architect: Foster
and Partners

However, 'World Squares for All' was not a speculative research project generated by the practice (as Rogers' scheme had been) but a project that was meant to be realised. Unlike Rogers' scheme, it had political support from the beginning. The remodelling was, its architects hoped, 'a sort of blue-print for the importance of public space', an idea that they claimed was 'firmly ingrained' in the ideology of the Labour government of the time (de Grey 2001). Its origins lie in the mid-1990s when a committee of those with a direct interest in Trafalgar Square was convened by John Gummer, the Secretary of State for the Environment in the 1992–7 Conservative government.[35] There was representation from the city of Westminster, the Government Office for London, English Heritage, London Transport, the Royal Parks and the Department of Culture Media and Sport, all of whom had an interest in any

6.9
'World Squares for All', (1996–2003), visualisation of the remodelling of Trafalgar Square, architect: Foster and Partners

changes. The government advertised for expressions of interest, out of which a shortlist of Rogers and Foster was drawn up, with the commission being given to the latter. The beginning of the design process, in 1998, was a public consultation exercise, in which Foster laid out eight options for change to the square, ranging from no change at all, to complete pedestrianisation. Much work was done by observing and modelling pedestrian flows, partly using the theoretical model of space syntax developed by Bill Hillier at the Bartlett School of Architecture, London (see Hillier 1996). The extensive public consultation on the scheme, resulting in a document known as the Grey Book, and the emphasis on the quasi-scientific analysis of site to establish form, identify significant methodological differences between the Rogers and Foster schemes. Whereas the former began with an image of bourgeois pleasure, which it presented uncritically as an ideal, the latter proposed that form ought to emerge rationally from observed patterns of human behaviour.[36]

These differences in approach did produce differences in the actual schemes. Rogers, as we have seen, tended to describe the square in picturesque terms, despite the relative formality of the architecture. None of Abbott's drawings present a long axial view; the principal view of the square uses the east side of the National Gallery as a frame, rather than look at it frontally. As a result, the square appears as an irregular composition that has grown organically over the years, in a typically English manner (see Rasmussen 1937 for an account of London in these terms). Foster's plan, by contrast, presents a more formal, austere and restrained version of the square, which emphasises its monumental characteristics. The detailed work involves the tidying and simplification of the square, and the removal of residual picturesque aspects and their replacement with hard surfaces. It is at heart an inorganic, clear and formal solution, Consistent with this, Foster initially rejected – after some debate – the idea of any retail outlets or cafés, given that these were available close to the square.[37] The Square, they argued, ought to have a distinctly formal character, separable from the everyday, commercial city (de Grey 2001).

In the Foster image, the improved square is depicted from Canada House on the west. Nelson's column, the South African embassy, the church of St Martin-in-the-Fields, the Grand Buildings and the National Gallery are all in their usual positions, but the road in front of the Gallery has been reclaimed for pedestrians, and now forms a terrace from which one may observe the main part of the square. There are some minor alterations to the traffic flow at the southern end of the square, and the image suggests the introduction of some new, but restrained paved surfaces and street furniture. Apart from the drawing technique (this is a computer generated image, as opposed to a pen-and-wash sketch) what is striking is the choice of viewpoint. Rogers presents the square as a picturesque composition, framed by the architecture of the National Gallery; Foster depicts it from above, so that an axial view is implied from the steps of the gallery across the square through the two fountains. The formality is further emphasised by the depiction of Northumberland Avenue, seen just to the right of Nelson's Column. Tree-lined and dead straight, visually completed by the smaller of the Shell buildings at its apex, it appears as a Haussman boulevard transplanted from Second Empire Paris. The work of these images is extremely subtle. There are few dramatic changes, but their emphases – the revelation of the National Gallery façade and the symmetry of the central part of the square, subtly exaggerating a long axial view towards the Thames – make possible a non-picturesque reading of the square. Saumarez Smith confirms this view in a Paul Mellon lecture, when he describes the potential impact of the Foster scheme:

> It is, I think, inescapable that the mood of the Square will change quite dramatically and become not merely much more pedestrianised, more open, and more civic, but also more axial, read as a series of formal vistas from the south, so that the National Gallery will be viewed more formally, not framed from the west as part of a picturesque composition including St Martin-in-the-Fields, but from the south as part of an urban composition which one might more normally expect to find in Hanover or Copenhagen.
>
> (Saumarez Smith 2003)

What Saumarez Smith identifies in the Foster plans is therefore the possibility of reading the square as a formal *composition*. He would like to see an extension of this formality through a proposal of the architects Dixon:Jones; their masterplan for the National Gallery involved the creation of a monumental stair for the gallery to replace the existing stairs, which would lead down directly to the foot of the square, therefore cutting through the new terrace.[38] It would make the Gallery a more monumental building than it actually is, evoking the plinth-like quality of such buildings as the Metropolitan Museum of Art or the New York Public Library (Saumarez Smith 2003).

Yet if 'World Squares' seems in this way to return Trafalgar Square to the monumental character of its traditional role – the 'front room' function as Rodney Mace describes it – it lacks the one essential characteristic of belief that the monumental square had. The monuments affirmed belief in the Empire. There was no question about what they and the square stood for, and the manner in which they were to be apprehended. The square was a backdrop for the celebration of Imperial success, or – through dissent – its critique.

6.10
'World Squares for
All', (1996–2003),
proposed
pedestrianisation
of Parliament
Square, architect:
Foster and
Partners

Its symbolic place was assured in both cases, and its scruffiness, its lack of creature comforts, and its urbanistic illegibility were of little import. 'World Squares' ostensibly underlines this residually monumental character, and it may, as Saumarez Smith argues, lead to different ways of perceiving the square. But like the earlier scheme by Rogers, 'World Squares' is underwritten by the rhetoric of civility. Foster's image is populated, it might be said, with the same figures who appear in the Rogers scheme.[39] It is a scene of polite strolling, of bourgeois pleasure, an area where 'visitors to the gallery can recuperate and promenade [. . .]' (Saumarez Smith 2003). In both images, Trafalgar Square, a site of immense civic and national importance, of conflict and of dissent, is made polite, and through that, its traditional functions, both official and unofficial, are occluded.

Both speak of an embarrassment about the imperial narrative that underpins the square; both elevate the pleasure of the bourgeois above the monument; both speak of the contemporary world of leisure, particularly the appreciation of art, rather than of history.

In this account of the reformed Trafalgar Square, I have made architects' perspective drawings carry a lot of weight. There have been good reasons for doing this, principally that here as elsewhere in the book, because they were made with the desires of a client in mind, they articulate precisely a matrix of interests and desires about the city, and not just those of the architect. However they remain a partial source, and they do not describe all the details of the ways in which the reformed space has changed. One in particular – the decision as to whether the reformed square should contain a café – pointed up differences of approach between the architects, and the square's de facto owners, the GLA. Foster imagined the square as a formal space that would punctuate the commercial life that surrounded it – they therefore planned no café. But pressure from the GLA, particularly from the mayor, Ken Livingstone, saw one included at a late stage in the plans – he said that he could not imagine a major public space without a place to drink coffee.[40] Livingstone's approach, if anything, signalled a greater desire to assimilate the square to the idea of civility, introducing a further element into its fabric that imposed and regulated behaviour. And Livingstone's remarks about the role of the square and its future indicate a further embedding of the rhetoric of civility. The square, besides the café, now has space for a warden, permanently present on the site, whose presence along with that of closed-circuit television puts the square under constant surveillance. The square, the GLA recognises, has a tradition of free speech that must be preserved, but this is now to be maintained in conjunction with a substantial programme of cultural events, managed by the GLA: all activity must now conform to that of a tourist programme. And finally, the ideologically awkward aspects of the square's history, namely the imperial narrative that underwrites it, is ameliorated by the GLA's staging of it as a multicultural space. Livingstone's support for a statue of Nelson Mandela in the square not only recalls his support (and that of other members of the GLA) for the campaign against the South African government in Trafalgar Square during the 1980s, but it memorialises a form of dissent, and in doing so, institutionalises it. Further, Livingstone suggests that the square should be programmed in a way that celebrates London's cultural multiculturalism. He describes its 'innovative events programme that celebrates London's cultural and social diversity' (Greater London Authority 2002b). Now this cultural activity means well, and it may lead to the square becoming better used, and more central to the life of the actual city, as Livingstone and the GLA would like. But it needs to be made clear the extent to which these things mark an ideological shift in the way the space is officially regarded. The cultural programming and the advocacy of a Mandela statue, suggest the extent to which the square now reiterates the agenda of civility. These gestures are part of a larger pattern of imposing an appearance of freedom on the place. As Joyce described in relation to liberalism in the nineteenth-century city, a sense of freedom must be publicly contrived by means of rules and social conventions, performed as it were. Here it is performed too.

Civility is a response to quite realistic anxieties about Trafalgar Square. With good reason, it was understood by bourgeois London as an insecure space, both in terms of actual inhabitation, and symbolic meaning. The processes of civilisation, both architectural and political, have created something quite new – no longer is it the imperial space, although the monuments remain. No longer can it be the space either of dissent or of the dispossessed. It remains to be seen, in conclusion, to be seen precisely how the reformed space, which opened in July 2003, mediates the desire for civility, and the pressures generated by its actual use.[41]

Chapter 7

'America, E14'

Introduction

One of the more peculiar contradictions of the English city of the 1980s is manifest in Canary Wharf. At the same time as English culture might be said to have reached the apogee of anti-urbanism, it engaged on the biggest urban construction project in Europe, a job that has only recently been exceeded in scale by the reconstruction of Berlin. My questions here are not so much how this immense piece of city came about (for that may be explained by the immense changes to the flows of capital at the same time) but rather how it could be imagined at a time when positive urban images were rare, when urban infrastructural and cultural projects were stalled or cancelled, and when cities themselves were shrinking. How could this vast extension to London be imaged? What images might it invoke to give it form? How, more generally, would it have to stage itself in order to assuage, or negotiate, English anxieties about the city?

Canary Wharf has much in common with city developments in other global financial capitals, and as a result, it tends to appear in urban discourse as an exemplar of global urban trends, the implication being that it could be anywhere, but just happens to be in London (see Zukin 1992). Such accounts have, rightly, focused on the deregulation of the City's financial markets in the 1980s and the sudden and unprecedented influx of foreign capital into London, accompanied by trading in what has been termed 'fictitious' capital in 1980s through deregulation: futures, securities, options, leveraged buy-outs (Merrifield 1992: 1250). The expansion of the financial sector produced new opportunities for consumption, including, as Merrifield (1992) has pointed out, the 'production of new urban spaces' of which Canary Wharf was by far the biggest. The inherent instability in the financial markets had one spectacular victim, namely Canary Wharf's developers, Olympia and York, which collapsed in 1992 with debts of US$20 billion, having absorbed public subsidies estimated at US$1.5 billion.[1] It was a classic case of over-supply. Only 45 per cent of the offices at Canary Wharf had been let at the time of the collapse, the majority of them on lengthy rent holidays, offered as inducements to take leases.

Justly or not, Canary Wharf has now recovered from this disaster, and I do not propose to say anything more about this part of its history. My focus here is the architectural meaning of it as a space, a question that is somewhat more complex than has been so far described. It is, as has gener-ally been implied to date, a space that may be written about simply as a function of global capital (see Zukin 1992).[2] But as I argue in this chapter, Canary Wharf also displays a number of profoundly English anxieties about the urban. As much as it represents a global phenomenon, it represents an English negotiation of it. Urban in scale and architectural reference, it nevertheless displays deep, and culturally specific unease.

This anxiety has many locations. Some of it is located in the official presentation of the project to clients and the general public; some of it is found in the professional architectural discourse around the buildings; some of it in reports in the mass media; some of it in the literary representations of the docks. The authors of the scheme (its American architects and devel-opers) fear the immediate environment, namely London: through the propa-gandist means of the perspective drawing, and the co-option of establishment consultants, they seek to establish English credentials for a foreign-financed and foreign-designed imposition. The British architects (represented by the discourse in the professional journals) fear, above all, the loss of control over the built environment that Canary Wharf seems to imply; it operates within a regime of minimal control, in which traditional notions of planning seem to have been abolished. They fear also the domination by the other, namely the Americans. Early visitors, especially academics, fear the place itself: eerie and depopulated, yet the subject of a major property boom, it seems to repre-sent everything that is inhumane about the relationship between capital and the urban. The place seems to represent both a model future and also a dystopia, a form of urbanism that threatens traditional forms of city life. Everybody, finally, fears terrorism. Canary Wharf itself was the subject of a very large terrorist bomb in 1993. As discussed in due course, the project is now ever more circumscribed by security measures. There is no traffic, because none is permitted to circulate freely; access to all the build-ings is restricted to those with a clear purpose for being in them; each and every part of the development imposes what the anthropologist Marc Augé has called 'contractual' relations between an individual and space, in which behaviour is subject to legal definition, and transgression expressly forbidden (Augé 1995: 101).

If this is right, then Canary Wharf has become the archetype of non-place, a definition that is more normally applied to spaces of transit, airports especially. My account of Canary Wharf is therefore preoccupied less with it as an English response to some peculiar anxieties about the city – but as an anxious space that happens to be in an English context, and produces its own anxieties as a result. Its peculiar situation, and the weird ambience it undoubtedly has, are not without their attractions, as my conclusion shows.

An introduction to Canary Wharf

Canary Wharf lies three miles to the east of the City of London on the Isle of Dogs. It occupies a space that was once the East and West India Docks, the heart of what was once the world's largest port. Its decline from the 1950s saw the transferral of port functions to the edge of the Thames estuary, and Felixstowe, where larger vessels, and containers, could be handled. London exemplifies on the grandest scale the processes that affected other English ports, especially Liverpool (see Chapter 5). The loss of dock business led to the progressive closure of most of the docks by 1970. After a number of false starts, the reinvention of the Docklands from 1981 was charged to an agency appointed by the then Conservative government, the London Docklands Development Corporation (LDDC). The developmental model derived from the 'freeport' solution envisaged by the academic and planner Peter Hall.[3] In this model of inner city development, within a restricted area, the normal controls on development (taxation, planning, immigration) would be lifted in order to create the competitive environment of 'Hong Kong of the 1950s and 1960s' (Hall 1996: 356). The LDDC's plan was a weak version of this idea, an Enterprise Zone, exactly parallel to that created in Merseyside at the same time, in which prospective developers would be free of the normal planning restrictions and corporation tax for ten years.[4] Its results by the mid-1980s were modest, such as the small-scale speculative housing schemes along the river, some single-storey warehouses, and a little-used airport subject to severe controls (passenger flights could only be made using a single aircraft type, the unusually quiet de Havilland Dash 7).[5] A printing works for the *Financial Times* by Nicholas Grimshaw, and a high-rise block of flats called 'Cascades' by CZWG were the only schemes that were urban in scale, or aspiration.[6]

To build a megastructure on a world city scale was not part of the plan. But in 1985, the chairman of Credit Suisse, who was lunching with LDDC, informally proposed building a 200,000-square-foot back office in a vacant warehouse, based on the example of warehouse-to-office conversions he had seen in Boston. Out of this informal interest, a consortium was assembled which included Credit Suisse, First Boston and Morgan Stanley, headed by Gooch Ware Travelstead of First Boston Real Estate (London Docklands Development Corporation 1990: 29). Travelstead had a masterplan drawn up by the American architects Skidmore Owings Merrill (SOM), which quickly established the scheme's imagery. Unlike the ad hoc style of the development until 1985, SOM proposed a grid as formal as Baron Haussman's Paris.[7] There would be a cluster of three fifty-storey towers, and a formal, tree-lined boulevard, lined with bulky large-floorplate office buildings in a mix of Edwardian and neoclassical styles. In the American fashion of the time, SOM envisaged a raised pedestrian mall linking the different parts of the development, with road traffic directed underneath (this was later substituted by a conventional boulevard with a subterranean service road). The total effect resembled early twentieth-century Chicago, the city in which, at SOM's head office, much of the detailed design was in fact done.

Travelstead's failure to close the deal led to the scheme's takeover in 1987 by a group of Canadian developers, Olympia and York, headed by the Reichman brothers, who were simultaneously developing the comparable World Financial Center close to the World Trade Center in lower Manhattan.[8] The Reichmans kept the SOM masterplan for the most part, and the architectural imagery.

Canary Wharf in 1991 consisted of a half-mile tree-lined boulevard linking Westferry Circus with East India Circus. At the eastern end was one of the three towers originally proposed by SOM, No. 1 Canada Place, designed by the Argentinean-born, New Haven-based architect César Pelli (Figure 7.1). It was the only one of the three original towers to be realised, and at 245 m and 46 storeys was slightly shorter than first envisaged.[9] Nevertheless, its scale exceeded anything yet built in London. The tower alone was four times the size by floor area of the former NatWest tower in the City, and six times the size of Centrepoint, the landmark 1960s tower built by Richard Seifert in the West End. Its design adopted the discontinuous lift shafts and sky-lobbies that were standard American practice. Its construction also brought new practices to the English building site. There was much prefabrication. Virtually all materials were sourced from abroad: semi-mature trees from Germany, marble from Guatemala, stone from Italy, cladding from Belgium, toilet pods from the Netherlands (Edwards 1992: 76). Labour was also imported, from Ireland, Germany and the US. These innovations, it was claimed, enabled a much faster construction than usual in Britain, permitting the whole building to be finished in three years instead of the ten it had taken the NatWest tower (Glancey 1989: 36).

The building's size and technical innovation were unfamiliar in London. But it concealed its novelty behind an exceedingly restrained façade, its square plan, symmetry, and its window proportions recalling American municipal neoclassicism of the 1920s. Los Angeles City Hall was thought by one critic to be a good comparison (see Sudjic 1991: 34).[10] Clad in stainless steel, it has a highly mutable appearance, some days appearing as solid as marble, others translucent and shimmering. Topped by a huge pyramid which conceals the ventilation outlets for the building, on cold days steam pours from the tip, leading to false alarm calls to the local fire service (Martin 2003: 4).

Moving southwards is the self-effacing Cabot Square shopping centre, a vaguely neoclassical structure rising to four storeys, but formally the pedestal of the Pelli tower. To the right of the mall is No. 25 North Colonnade, by Troughton McAslan, the only British firm involved on the original scheme. A squat fifteen-story steel-frame building with two projecting bays, its bland exterior makes no overt reference to the architecture of the historical past, although the curved treatment of the corners invites comparison with Frank Lloyd Wright. Sudjic thought that 'buttoned-down, Brooks-Brothers quality makes it feel almost as American as its neighbours' (Sudjic 1991: 34).[11] Passing along the North Colonnade by the water, under the Docklands Light Railway tracks, the visitor comes to the most overtly historicist building on the site, 10 Cabot Square by SOM, an Edwardian fantasy in yellowish terracotta and stone (Figure 7.2).[12] At ground level it has a baroque colonnade containing shops, bars and restaurants, some of which, such as a traditional gentleman's outfitters on the south side, help complete the historical theme. The south façade is symmetrical, with cylindrical towers at each end, and a raised pediment in the middle, enclosing a short recessed vault. Here the fantasy of early twentieth-century Chicago is most strongly materialised.

Opposite these two bulky constructions, on the other side of Cabot Square is a matching pair of buildings by Kohn Pedersen Fox, separated by the DLR tracks (the north-bound train makes a dramatic entrance to Canary Wharf through them, as if cleaving them in two). Steel-framed, but clad this time in white marble, they allude to the art deco of Miami Beach. Each block has a spectacular curved façade, a signifier of a now nostalgic idea of modernity. The middle storeys of these façades are faced mainly in glass, the combined glazing reading as a single unit, a huge dark window criss-crossed with mullions, slightly inset in the stone. The upper storeys, with their windows recessed deep into the façade suggest an aerial colonnade, or, possibly, battlements. At ground level, generous windows are provided for the bars that occupy the base of the building, allowing views out over the water. The lobby,

7.1
No. 1 Canada Square, Canary Wharf, London (1992), architect: César Pelli

as Sudjic observes, carefully contrives the feeling of jazz-age America, and the wave-like ceiling completes the effect (Sudjic 1991: 34). The building's corners on Cabot place are marked by small octagonal towers.

7.2
10 Cabot Square, Canary Wharf, London (1992), architect: SOM

Moving west along the main axis, there are two rather nondescript office buildings, 25 Cabot Square, and 1 Cabot Square, by SOM and Pei Cobb Freed and partners respectively, both steel-framed and stone-faced, the latter in limestone. In appearance both are informal, and asymmetrical in plan. Each rises to twenty storeys and each has a bulky central tower that is only weakly differentiated from the rest of the building. The SOM building is the more overtly historicist, the ground level consisting of a restrained classical colonnade, and the top a vague loggia. The Pei Cobb Freed building has a complex shape but a notably undifferentiated skin, in which different aspects are signified only by bulk. The original development was completed by the final large building at the western end, 1–11 Westferry Circus, by a consortium including SOM and Koetter, Kim Associates. Faced in limestone, this structure curves gently around the traffic circle, defining the northern half. Classically proportioned, it has a clearly defined baroque colonnade at ground level, and five floors of offices above, surmounted by a heavy cornice, above which there are several more storeys in the form of a loggia. It is the building that makes the strongest appeal to classicism, and it makes a dignified and restrained entrance to the development from the City (Figure 7.4).

7.3
**Canary Wharf DLR
station; London
(1992); architect:
SOM**

7.4 (below)
**1–11 Westferry
Circus, Canary
Wharf, London
(1992), architect:
SOM and Koetter,
Kim Associates**

The architects' fears

I give over much space to the form of Canary Wharf in order to provide a context for the violent reactions it provoked. Described in this way, Canary Wharf appears a harmless historical fantasy, something of an architectural zoo, perhaps, but corralled by the most formal plan seen in London since Wren's scheme for rebuilding after the Great Fire. It is worth adding that the quality of surfaces was extremely high. Much attention to detail was paid in the treatment of the public realm; street furniture and planting were of high quality. Yet despite the (in some ways unprecedented) investment in the quality of the public realm, and the inoffensive quality of most of the architecture, it was the object of contempt from the British architectural establishment and its allies. It was an 'unsustainable development without real civic quality or lasting community benefit' (Rogers 1997: 109); 'an urban and architectural disaster [. . .] each building – except in its gimcrack gimmickry – dismally indifferent in its indifference to its neighbours' (Buchanan 1989: 39); it produced 'a rash of quite unsuitable buildings' (Powell 1993: 47); it contained 'some of the very worst new buildings in Europe' (Davey 1989: 46); '[i]n their vulgarity, their insensitivity to place and to each other, the buildings of the enterprise zone epitomise Thatcher's Britain in all its philistinism and selfishness' (Davey 1989: 46); it has been 'an appalling mistake' (Bor in Middleton 1991: 58); its 'architecture is horrible and the planning is horrible' (Bohigas in Davies 1990: 24–5); '[a]s a piece of urban design is simply abysmal' (*Architectural Review* 1988: 9). A Labour politician, Allan Roberts, elaborating these views thought it better if the area 'were still derelict than what has happened' (Middleton 1991: 58).

In these critiques from the architects Richard Rogers and Oriol Bohigas, the architectural critics Peter Buchanan, Peter Davey and Kenneth Powell, and the planner Walter Bor, there is a sense of horror, or even disgust, at the development. Their disgust is predictable, perhaps – Bor's work as a planner was threatened by this form of urbanisation – but it is so extreme that it requires examination. What is the nature of this criticism? Why did they find Canary Wharf so repellent? What did they fear?

It might be said that the architects' greatest fear was of their own erasure. To begin with, this vocal part of the profession was mostly identified with the left, and those in Britain had been involved in its material representation in the form of the welfare state: they built its schools, hospitals and universities, and, broadly speaking, they believed in the construction of these things. Canary Wharf represented an entirely different set of political beliefs; its construction was supported by a Conservative government, and it quickly became a symbol of that government. Second, it represented a challenge to another ideology, that of Modernism. It revived historical styles; it concealed functions behind thin historical façades. Third, Canary Wharf represented in the most brutal way the exclusion of the English architectural profession from the most visible public project of the time. Largely American-designed for American tenants, it was also built with American materials and using American construction techniques, and underwritten by American capital. Hence one journalist's neat description of it as 'America, E14' (Treanor 1999).[13] Fourth, this exclusion underlined the shift in architectural patronage that occurred in the first term of the Conservative government. Architects until 1979 expected most of their work to come from the state, and perhaps to work for state architects such as the GLC's enormous department of architecture, or one of the new town corporations. Canary Wharf might be said to symbolise the end of such an architectural world: it signified, in the grandest possible way, that the English profession was dispensable. Fifth, and no less dramatic, Canary Wharf signified the end of planning as it had been understood up till that point: it existed in the context of Docklands, an area in which, as described above, normal planning controls had been suspended, while the formal plan for the layout of Canary Wharf per se was made by the architects SOM.[14] The dissolution of planning evidenced at Canary Wharf perhaps explains Walter Bor's reaction.[15]

The English architectural profession therefore had much to fear from Canary Wharf. The project, as I suggest above, seemed to threaten its erasure, or at least provide an image of that erasure. This development imaged, to put it another way, an urban scene without English architects. Perhaps erasure is the wrong word here: perhaps the most primitive, albeit at the same time most profound, fear was that of the *other*, which here is named America. The America that is feared may not have had a great deal to do with the actually existing nation, but it is no less powerful for that. The fear was given intellectual justification by Kenneth Frampton in particular. You will recall (Chapter 3) Frampton's call at the end of *Modern Architecture: A Critical History* in which he argues that the role of architecture is to resist such modernisation as 'other' (Frampton 1992: 343). America is not named here, but it is undoubtedly the source of such a pervasive culture of modernisation.

The architects feared America in this way. The actual development is frequently described as 'mid-Atlantic', which is to say it is of an impure England, contaminated by American influence ('mid-Atlantic' is *always* a pejorative term when used by the English professional classes). Or it is located vaguely in the 'mid-west', an English journalistic shorthand to signify the part of America that no civilised European can, supposedly, bear. Or it is located in some place of the near historical past, such as early twentieth-century Chicago, or the Los Angeles of the thirties, where in Sudjic's view it – particularly the Pelli tower – resembles the neoclassical municipal architecture of the city hall. When Lord St John of Fawsley, head of the Royal Fine Art Commission, the government-appointed body then responsible for overseeing urban design, spoke at the RIBA of London being 'invaded' by a 'rash of quite unsuitable buildings', he articulated a widely held fear of cultural domination by the US (Fawsley in Powell 1993: 47).[16] It had, as one American architect noted, unpleasantly racist overtones, but was nevertheless a view widely supported in the profession.

Of course the fear of the other could not be articulated publicly as simple prejudice, but had to be mediated; the key word in Lord Fawsley's attack was 'unsuitable', by which he meant that they were stylistically incompatible with their surroundings. In this he was largely supported by the architects. By 'unsuitable' he meant partly their height (about which there was, and is still, disagreement) but rather more about the treatment of surface. All the buildings are Canary Wharf were modern in construction, making use of steel frames, lifts, mechanical ventilation and modern cladding. Yet they contrived, in the postmodern manner, a historical surface, seen most clearly in the Edwardian pastiche at 10 Cabot Square: the panelling gives the impression of much greater solidity than is actually the case. SOM's Edwardian pastiche at Cabot Square was a prime offender: outwardly a masterpiece of solidity, its fat columns and heavy terracotta dress giving the impression of indestructible bourgeois respectability, it was in actual fact a steel-framed modern building whose surface was a prefabricated skin no more than a couple of centimetres thick. As Deyan Sudjic puts it, 'its apparently massive walls (were) no more solid than the icing on the cake' (Sudjic 1992: 33). Otherwise generally approving, Charles Jencks wrote that it was 'urban wallpaper applied to big, ten-storey slabs' (Jencks 1991: 44). Brian Edwards wrote that it looked like an 'instant city' whose prefabricated neoclassicism gave it less, not more of an urban air (Edwards 1992: 74).

What these critics complain of is an exaggerated superficiality. This indicates a fear not only of the other, specifically America, but also of moral decay. In English architectural terms, surface has a moral dimension; it refers back to the Arts and Crafts tradition, in which craft and truth to materials were valued above all else, on the grounds that ornament was excess, and the product of an inherently unfair society. In a future socialist civilisation, William Morris argued we will 'produce to live, and not live to produce'.[17] These values, which, as Pevsner argued later, were central to the development of architectural Modernism, continue in the present day versions of Modernism. Frampton's work has continually emphasised the tectonic over the superficial. To emphasise surface in the American way did was to demonstrate a lack of moral fibre. This aspect of Canary Wharf, which to architects brought up with *Learning from Las Vegas* seemed to be especially American, was 'what most irritated British architects brought up in the moralistic Arts and Crafts tradition' (Davies 1991: 60).

This point was sharply visualised by the cartoonist Louis Hellman, in rare agreement with the English establishment (Figure 7.5). In a full-page cartoon for the *Architectural Review* in 1989, he depicts Canary Wharf as 'Doglands', a preposterous skyscraper zone populated by scrapping canine bankers. In the background a couple of unappetisingly named eateries advertise their pleasures. In the foreground, a privatised 'securidog' attempts to keep order. The caption reads: 'our greatest achievement, the sale of Canine

7.5
'Doglands',
Architectural
Review **(1989)**

Wharf on the Isle of Humans to our transatlantic coyote cousins . . . a dynamic development . . . a new business centre which respects the character of the old city.' Rising above the mêlée are Dogland's towers, whose form satirises SOM's vision of Canary Wharf as an integral part of 'London'. They are generic Miesian towers incongruously topped with a series of baroque and gothic monuments, which include St Paul's cathedral, the tower of the church of St Martin-in-the-Fields and Big Ben. The message is frank: the attempt at contextualisation is mere window dressing for a brutalising (American) capitalism. The emphasis on the façade connotes immorality.

Now this fear of the other was not common to all the profession, merely its most vocal part. The *Architect's Journal*, speaking for a wider public than either the RIBA or the *Architectural Review*, recognised that the criticism of Canary Wharf contained a good deal of 'envy mixed with shame'. While British architects had mostly failed to build anything of significance in the 1980s, the Americans had built the grandest project of all, 'with hardly a hitch'. Worse, they noted, ordinary Londoners seemed to like it (Davies 1991: 56). That said, what the *Architect's Journal* recognised was the extent to which the professional understanding of Canary Wharf was underwritten by the fear of the other. That 'ordinary Londoners' (who implicitly lacked any stake in its success) seemed oblivious to such fear is an important point to which we will return.

The developers' fears

The architectural opposition to Canary Wharf signified the possibility of wider cultural opposition to it, and the original developers, Olympia and York were sensitive enough to attempt to assuage local opinion.[18] Through the work of SOM, they tried to make Canary Wharf seem a part of London, specifically the City. This was in part a marketing strategy, as was widely acknowledged (Davies 1987: 34, 37). But it was also done out of a recognition of the need that Canary Wharf, for the sake of its success, should be perceived not as *other*, but as an integral part of the rest of the city. This was a conceptual challenge, given its peripheral location, and the alien quality of the architecture. Bruce Graham of SOM wrote that the selected architects 'have become aware of the need to collaborate not only with one another, but with Nash, Soane, Wren and Hawksmoor'. Whatever architecture they built needed to 'be subtle and sensitive to the overall composition of a great city' (Graham 1989). This attempt to locate the development in a historical context can be seen in a fascinating series of early perspective drawings, which both articulate the desire for continuity with London (and tradition), and the hopelessness of the attempt. These drawings are hence anxious in precisely the same way as the drawings of Milton Keynes, failing to absolutely confirm or deny their subject. They reveal, quite beautifully, the developer's fears for Canary Wharf.

Let me consider two images in particular, of Founder's Court, which later became, albeit much modified, Cabot Square. Canary Wharf is described by an axis which runs roughly East–West. Founder's Court lies roughly halfway along, between Westferry circus and East India Circle, in the shadow of the three monumental office. Founder's Court better resembles a traffic circle in central London. The image depicts the Court from the East, and shows a view down the main axis of the development towards Westferry Circus. The road axis has a tree-lined reservation at its centre, introduced at the Court end by a stone portico, approximately 20 feet in height and topped by a model of a three-masted clipper, a reference to the old business of the docks (in fact it is a reconstruction of the old portico at the entrance to West India Dock, and a version of it was made for a different location, by West India Quay) (Figure 7.6). In front of this portico, on the ground, lies what is un-mistakably a late Henry Moore sculpture of a reclining figure in two pieces, a ubiquitous signifier of corporate good taste in the public realm. The Court is defined by office buildings of five storeys, rising to eight on the square proper. Neoclassical on their ground and first levels, their upper levels are more restrained, but recall the Edwardian commercial buildings of the West End. At ground level, a classical colonnade provides shade. Pedestrian areas allow the inevitable café tables to spill out from underneath. A domed *tempietto*, containing an unidentified sculpted figure, defines the centre of each of these plazas. A six-storey octagonal rotunda dominates the centre of the Court, each of whose main façades is dominated by a large, vaguely Romanesque arched window. Just below cornice level there is a restaurant terrace. The whole structure is topped with a glass dome.

The main structures of the development are clearly imagined in neoclassical terms, as is the plan, which is rigidly formal. The formality of the design is not characteristic of London as a whole, a city whose character has been generally understood as a relatively informal and unplanned (see for example Rasmussen 1937). In plan, then, this is perhaps more of a 'gargan-tuised American version of Paris' as one critic put it (*Architectural Review* 1988: 4, 9).[19] The traffic and the figures say more about London. Our view from the rotunda terrace places us in the privileged position of the diners on the roof terrace. Fifteen figures are represented at the tables and they are with one exception male and middle-aged; all wear business suits of one kind or another. Two are three-piece outfits with the handkerchief correctly positioned in the breast pocket. Several figures sport fine moustaches; there is one pipe-smoker on the left hand side of the image; the figure sixth from the left in the pale three-piece with the sculpted beard is, it would seem, a caricature of a Jewish banker.

In view of the contemporaneous changes to the demography of the City's working population, such as the influx of young working-class men into a what was previously a preserve of the middle classes, this is a curious

7.6
Reconstruction of Victorian portico at the entrance to West India Dock, now at West India Quay

image for it reasserts the traditional look of the City. Indeed, so antiquated are the modes of dress and deportment that they appear to belong to the Edwardian age rather than the late twentieth century. This impression is reinforced by the nature of road traffic, which comprises only vehicles traditionally associated with London: black taxis, Daimler limousines with motorcycle escorts, a Routemaster double-decker bus. There are no ordinary private cars to be seen.[20] The road, with the exception of the bus, is the preserve of a privileged, and possibly even royal, élite.

The second image of Founder's Court reiterates these archaic themes. It depicts the Court from ground level from within the colonnade on the south side of the development. The big towers are clearly seen in the distance, while the middle-ground is occupied by the big rotunda. The foreground is well populated with the same besuited male bankers seen in the other image, with some additions; a man in a traditional Sikh costume on the far left, and another man in a cap and tweed sports jacket with leather elbow patches to his right, walking a terrier dog. This is a more heterogeneous scene than the first, but old-fashioned forms of dress are still much in evidence: tightly rolled umbrellas, trilby and bowler hats, neatly folded handkerchiefs, pinstripe trousers. The traffic again appears to have come from the 1950s: a Routemaster, two taxis, a Daimler limousine and, on the far left, what appears to be a Morris Oxford.

What is the purpose of this strangely archaic imagery? Barely anyone in these scenes appears to belong to the contemporary world, as if time had been frozen in the 1950s. It is of course a fantasy, verging on the architectural *capriccio*, albeit here without the artistic pretensions.[21] It would seem to derive from the developer's nervousness about presenting Canary Wharf for what it is, namely a colossal pile of offices, an irruption in the fabric of the docks, a facility for new and vaguely alarming kinds of financial business. It is all of these radical things, but cannot be presented as such; it must appear reassuring; it must invoke a 'myth of civitas', or a 'fantasy of community' (Bird in Miles *et al.* 2000: 306). The appeal to traditional notions of Englishness is clearly fantasy. But the tension between the polite fantasy and the vastness and modernity of the architecture makes for some very odd images indeed, and arguably only succeeds in highlighting the developer's fears rather than assuaging them.

The 'myth of civitas', is similarly invoked by Roy Strong, director of the Victoria and Albert Museum from 1974–87, latterly a garden designer. He was used by the LDDC as consultant on Canary Wharf on planting of semi-mature trees and landscaping. Strong claims in 1989 in an LDDC booklet that Canary Wharf's landscaping explicitly revives the London tradition of the residential square. In the booklet, Strong is photographed in a picturesque garden setting, surrounded by foliage, wearing a floppy broad-brimmed hat; his very appearance articulates an idea of bucolic leisure. His job at Docklands was to convince the public (insofar as it was aware of Canary Wharf at all at the time of writing) that the development was something it was palpably not, namely a quasi-rural idyll. The article was titled '*rus in urbe*'. Among the tactics Olympia and York had employed to produce this reassuring impression was to make a presentation at the deeply picturesque Chelsea Flower Show. Strong wrote that Canary Wharf was vaguely considered to be some kind of transposed 'Manhattan':

> What a pleasurable surprise therefore awaits the public in 1992, when the first phase is completed, for more than anything the visitor will be struck by this deliberate revival of the London square as the principal means of articulating urban space [. . .] the initial designs include a lake and an amphitheatre reminiscent of the eighteenth century garden at Claremont [. . .] Its presence at the Chelsea Flower Show should, therefore, come as no surprise to anyone who cherishes the revitalisation of the tradition of 'rus in urbe'.
>
> (Strong in LDDC 1990: 53)

The picturesque is bizarrely invoked here in a development that has precisely none of the picturesque's qualities. Its planning is exceedingly formal and rectilinear, its surfaces rigorously new and polished, its gardens well tended, its scale vast, its architectural reference points American rather than European. The invocation of the picturesque in this wholly inappropriate way speaks of the developers' own fear of the other, just as the perspective drawings they produced tried and failed to articulate a convincing sense of the old – which is to say, pre-deregulation – City of London. The anxiety about these representations points up the conceptual difficulty of what Canary Wharf achieved. It was a profoundly un-English development, yet had to pretend to be otherwise.

Fear and 'non-place'

My treatment of Canary Wharf so far has focused on it as it appears in architectural discourse, and the objections to it concern, unsurprisingly, the way it disturbs the English profession. It disturbs by ignoring them, by refusing their long-held moralistic position, and by refusing their (publicly stated, if not publicly materialised) commitment to the European, as opposed to the

American, city. I now move on to consider the space of Canary Wharf from the point of view of its users, and again I suggest that fear is a critical idea in understanding it.

Canary Wharf has since its inception been a place that critical visitors have explored in dystopian terms. It plays a minor, but important, role in novels by Salman Rushdie and Ian Sinclair; it appears as a backdrop in a James Bond film; it has been the subject of endless critiques by journalists, many of whom (in one of the letting successes of the 1990s) occupy space in 1 Canada Place. The tower building has become in effect a vertical Fleet St., home to the editorial offices of the The Daily Telegraph, Daily Mirror and The Independent.[22] As a place apprehended by non-professionals, Canary Wharf seems doomed to perform a place of fear. The weirdness of its atmosphere is what most seems to impress visitors. Unlike any other part of London, the visitor is not oppressed by traffic (there is none, for the security reasons discussed later). It is surrounded by huge open spaces; the vistas are gigantic, as are the buildings. Everything is clean and efficient (unlike, again, the rest of the city). And it is invariably presented as quite deserted, as if the scale of the buildings were in inverse proportion to the number of people they contained. 'The experience of visiting Docklands', wrote the cultural historian Jon Bird, shortly after the completion of the first phase

> is one of exclusion and alienation. The monumental scale over-powers the street; corporate architecture dominates and privatises every vista; the mirror-glass façades disorientate the relations of people, place and space whilst the physical combinations of height and mass create climatic conditions that, on anything other than the brightest and calmest day, threaten to sweep the unwary into the river.
>
> (Bird in Miles et al. 2000: 306)

A Guardian journalist, Janet Treanor, wrote later of 'the surreal, eerie atmosphere that is the area's hallmark' (Treanor 1999). The guards in the Pelli tower are, it is said, 'in the habit of enforcing a Tarkovsky-like no-go zone between the street doors and the lift core. [. . .] Don't misbehave' (Allinson and Thornton 1993: 18–19).[23]

Now the wind is a fact, a product of putting a set of very tall buildings in a mostly flat landscape near the sea, but the rest of the experience that these writers conjecture cannot be proved (although to the author, it seems more often lifeless and empty than it does busy). But as with the other cases discussed in this book, I am interested less in the experience of the place in terms of what may be observed, than I am in its discursive existence. Here specifically I am concerned with the way Canary Wharf is a rhetorically fearful place. Regardless of its actual existence, discursively it is always empty, peculiar, inhumane, alien, strange, utterly unlike the rest of London, a futuristic wasteland, in which everything is new, but appears to have been abandoned. Certain aspects of the development's history support this dystopian view: the collapse of Olympia and York in 1992, the initial failure to let No. 1 Canada Square, the long inadequacy of transport links to the rest of the city, meaning that it was effectively marooned from London.[24] But the way in which these roles continue to help define the place is curious.

To analyse what I mean by its fearfulness, I turn to a short theoretical text by the French anthropologist Marc Augé. *Non-Places: an Introduction to the Anthropology of Supermodernity*, published in French in 1991, translated into English in 1995, has become well known in architectural circles, and it is still useful in providing a vocabulary to describe new kinds of urban space. Its terminology provides, as I hope to show, a useful way of looking at Canary Wharf as a place that is used and inhabited in particular ways. *Non-Places* opens with a narrative, which illustrates the main parts of the argument. We are introduced to a generic business traveller, Pierre Dupont in the early stages of a journey to Bangkok. He appears first at an electronic cash dispenser, as he withdraws money for the trip, whereupon he drives to Paris along the A11 *autoroute*, paying the toll with a credit card. He checks in for his flight, passing the usual security controls, before passing 'with some relief' into the departure lounge to do a little duty-free shopping (cigars and cognac). He boards his flight uneventfully, and spends the few minutes before takeoff leafing through the in-flight magazine. He traces the route the flight will take, and notes the coincidence between the name of his type of airline seat ('Espace 2000') and a new type of Renault car advertised ('Espace'). Space is, it seems, a fashionable concept. The flight departs. Dupont notes a few more things in the magazine: that his Visa card is accepted worldwide, that globalisation has produced the need for the standardisation of products. He drifts into sleep – 'for a few hours [. . .] he would be alone at last' (Augé 1995: 6).

This little story is unremarkable in itself. Nothing happens, there is no character development, and no crisis, yet it tells the reader much about what Augé means by non-place. First, and most broadly it identifies non-place in connection with travel. This space is variable, and may include both moving vehicles temporarily inhabited by people (cars and aeroplanes) as well as built spaces inhabited as part of the act of travelling (*autoroutes*, departure lounges, duty-free stores). They are all spaces that are passed through, rather than inhabited. 'The traveller's space', he notes later on, 'may be the archetype of non-place' (Augé 1995: 86).

Second, Augé identifies the quintessential user of non-place as an *individual*. Crucially for Augé's argument, non-place dissolves the social realm. All the transactions Dupont makes involve him alone with an institution or authority. And yet when he enters the space of the departure lounge after all of these processes, he does not seek sociality by way of relief, but *solitude*, as if non-place not only enforces individualisation, but inculcates it as a discipline. The relationships between users and non-places cannot be 'organically social' as they are in what Augé calls 'anthropological place'. No, instead they must be conducted on an individual basis, given that the non-place forces individuals to identify themselves through credit cards, passports and other means.

Third, Augé describes the nature of the relationship between the individual and the non-place. The critical thing here is that the relationship is essentially contractual, in which an individual is identified, and permitted to be in the non-place *subject to conditions* (payment, holding the correct identification, holding an airline ticket). All of the transactions Augé describes are conditional in this way – the extraction of money from the ATM, the payment of the *autoroute* toll, the check in at the airport, the buying of duty free goods, the location of the airline seat – at each step of the process, Dupont's identity is subject to scrutiny, and his behaviour subject to surveillance. Augé writes, 'the user of the non-place is always required to prove his innocence' (Augé 1995: 102). It produces a relationship to space that is profoundly alienated, 'solitary contractuality' replacing the 'organically social' (Augé 1995: 94).

Fourth, and central to my overall argument here, is that all this security and surveillance speaks of fear. It is fear of violence, particularly terrorist violence that drives the urge to surveil. And indeed the history of non-places is such that they have often been the subjects of terrorist attacks. It could be said in fact that these anonymous places of consumption, are in fact the principal targets. The spaces that could be anywhere at all are the ones that seem to attract violence. This may, as Augé writes later on, be for reasons of 'efficiency'. 'But another reason might be that, in a more or less confused way, those pursuing new socialisations and localisations can only see non-places as a negation of their ideal' (Augé 1995: 11). Their ideal, of course, invariably makes a strong appeal to anthropological place. Palestine, Ireland and Euskadi are places (in theory, if not in practice) formed by 'individual identities, through complicities of language, local references, the unformulated rules of living know-how'.

Now, Canary Wharf is not a space of transit, but it functions marvellously in the terms described by Augé. Entering the development, one is subject to the same disciplinary régime as required by an airport. By road, approaching from the City, one enters the development at Westferry Circus, the western end of the axial boulevard that defines the centre. This traffic roundabout was built in the normal way but is cut by a half-barrier and a security post where guards check one's credentials and let one pass – or not. Only those with legitimate employment or a parking space are allowed through. There is no informal place to park a car, regulated with unusually specific signs regarding what will happen to unattended vehicles (Figure 7.7). There are checkpoints at the entrance to major developments and security guards prominent at the entrances to all major buildings. Arriving by tube or the Docklands Light Railway, one alights at one or another vast space. Foster and Partner's Canary Wharf underground station, opened in 2000 as part of the Jubilee Line extension, is a vast underground cavern topped by a half dome (Figure 7.8). The huge ticket hall, larger than the check-in halls at many regional airports, is, unlike virtually all other underground stations a panoptical space in which all points are visible from the centre. Here everything and everyone can be seen. Everywhere security guards are much in evidence, and the extent of activities that can be carried out without some licence (ticket, credit card, identification) is strictly limited. The promenading that has recently become a feature of weekends at the development, takes place under the eyes of security guards and CCTV cameras, along selected paths built for the purpose.

Now the justification for such surveillance, and the reason for the public's complicity with it, is the fear of terrorism. Canary Wharf's realisation coincides with the intensification of what Martin Pawley has described as

Figure 7.7
Parking sign, Canary Wharf, London, in 2003

7.8
Canary Wharf Underground station, London (2000), architect: Foster and Partners

'a continuous, low-intensity war, waged anywhere between the upper limits of vandalism, and the lower limits of outright armed conflict' (Pawley 1998: 149). Pawley is preoccupied with the effect of terrorism of London, describing how Canary Wharf itself was badly bombed in February 1996 when an IRA device exploded on South Quay, killing one man and destroying the façade of a Richard Seifert-designed office complex. Terrorism had already long informed London's urbanism, however. As Pawley argues, this 'low intensity war' determines the alignment and positioning of roads and the siting of buildings to make attack difficult, and imposes secret measures designed to make post-attack escape impossible (Pawley 1998: 149). Describing a series of measures imposed on the City in the 1990s (the so-called 'ring of steel'), he refers to 'road blocks', 'armed police' and other measures that were subsequently incorporated into the urban design of the place at all the main entry points to the City. This was, he continues, 'only one of a number of restrictions imposed on the use of urban space in London [. . .]' which collectively had the aim of creating a no-go government citadel surrounded by a traffic-free *cordon sanitaire*' (Pawley 1999: 150–1).

Without over-dramatising the experience of Canary Wharf, we can nevertheless easily locate the place in this context. Part of the fear that surrounds it concerns the fear that it represents not a piece of real city, but a place of surveillance and control that limits ordinary urbanity. It has no places for gathering; it contractually binds its users; it presupposes violence until proven otherwise. Hence the fear that it represents something profoundly alien and alienating; hence too the hope of those on the left that the place might literally implode after the financial collapse of Olympia and York in 1992. For writers, among them Jon Bird and Sharon Zukin, non-place is the antithesis of the city, something to be feared, and if possible, resisted. A collection of idealised façades standing in for anthropological place, it is no more a real city than Disneyland's Main Street USA (Zukin 1992: 222).

Now it would be misleading to end the story here, because non-place is eminently consumable. Augé's formulation of non-place does not deny the possibility that it may produce pleasure. Non-place's anonymity, its contractual relationship with its users, indeed its emphasis on security, could even be strangely liberatory: Pierre Dupont, the generic business traveller who introduces the book, feels a sense of 'freedom' at the point at which he deposits his luggage. The feeling of weightlessness leads to a pleasurable, aimless floating around the duty-free stores and business class lounges. But further, argues Augé, it is not just the loss of encumbrances that may generate a sense of freedom but (paradoxically) the strict limits imposed on behaviour that generate a sense of liberation. After all, having passed through all the controls, having checked in your luggage, having passed security and passport controls, all the passenger has to do for a time is

> keep in line, go where they are told, check their appearance. As soon as his passport or identity card has been checked, the passenger for the next flight, freed from the weight of his luggage and everyday responsibilities, rushes into the 'duty-free' space; not so much, perhaps, in order to buy at the best prices as to experience the reality of his momentary availability, his unchallengeable position as a passenger in the process of departing.
>
> (Augé 1995: 101)

I want to suggest, finally, that Canary Wharf now offers this kind of experience in abundance. Quite unlike the rest of London, Canary Wharf has a formal plan, skyscrapers, clean streets and squares, and an air of unhurried efficiency that almost exactly duplicates that of an upmarket American shopping mall. In London these are unusual characteristics, and they make for the condition of spectacle. Its weekday inhabitants are all gone after the early evening, and they would not, one imagines, dream of visiting outside of work time. But at weekends the place is busy with young tourists and visitors from other parts of London. They arrive in the cathedral-like spaces of the tube and DLR stations and take photographs of them. They crane their necks upwards to the three towers that now grace Canada Square, to the emerging slabs on

Bank St., and at Churchill Place. They stroll along the riverside walks below Westferry Circus, under the eye of the CCTV cameras and security guards; they stop to gaze across the Thames to the increasingly spectacular City, and in the other direction to the vast but useless Dome[25]; they drink coffee in the generic bars of Mackenzie Walk; they eat Italian food in Carlucci's at the foot of No. 1. Canada Square, or drink proper American martinis in Smollensky's, or nibble Spanish tapas in the restored warehouses-turned-restaurants on West India Quay (Figure 7.9); they shop in the upmarket malls at Cabot and Canada squares. All the while the character of the space impresses them. Utterly unlike the rest of London, this is a clean, ordered, generously proportioned space that provides a simulacrum of city life in complete safety.

No longer does Canary Wharf, as it did in the beginning, offer the visitor a kind of architectural zoo, a mélange of historical styles to half-convince him that he is in fact in an established chunk of city. No longer the Docklands equivalent of Main Street USA, it has become EPCOT, a theme park of the future where each new building employs the architectural rhetoric of the supermodern.[26] The latest contributions by Norman Foster, his HSBC tower and his Tube station, do this superbly. Non-place therefore has huge power to impress. Its ostensibly negative qualities – its heavy surveillance, its sense of alienation and anomie – may even, under the right circumstances, be pleasurable. For the privileged visitor, which is to say, the person who does

7.9
Bars and restaurants at Canary Wharf, London, in 2003

not have to inhabit it, Canary Wharf's strangeness may be enjoyed in perhaps the way that a horror movie may be. This possibility was recognised by ostensibly unfavourable critics on its inauguration. The *Architects' Journal*'s gossip columnist 'Astragal' wrote of the Pelli tower that it could produce 'a feeling of awe, even a strange, not unpleasant terror, as its shimmering cladding gives it an unworldly appearance in certain light conditions' (Astragal 1991). For a critic of the *Architectural Review* in an otherwise deeply hostile account, it was 'sublime' and 'slightly scary', 'like one of Boullée's architectural fantasies' (Davies 1991: 62). For the *Building Design* critic on a river tour of London, Canary Wharf was an 'architectural Dracula' that nevertheless looked 'magnificent' (*Building Design* 1991).

Sharon Zukin has written of the 'power of the façade to lure the imagination'. Her reference points are geographically and culturally distinct, namely the burgeoning cities of the American sun-belt, but there is nonetheless still much in common between them and Canary Wharf (not least their architects). We are fascinated by these places, she writes,

> because we think they show us the future. These cities stun
> because of their unique ability to abstract an image of desire from
> the landscape and reflect it back through the vernacular.
>
> (Zukin 1992: 220–1)

Here Zukin identifies the close relationship between power and the architecture of non-place. She is critical of non-place, writing from the position of one who is, or feels, alienated by such power, and she regrets the brutal new phase that capitalism appears to have moved into. Non-place reveals a capitalism that appears to have no limits, unlike earlier variants, which, she writes, tempered 'financial gain by asceticism and moral restraint' (Zukin 1992: 255). Like Frampton, she favours an architecture of resistance, in which a concern for the local acts as a bulwark against powerful global interests (Zukin 1992: 275). Yet she does recognise the power of non-place to fascinate. As indicated by the architectural criticism above, Canary Wharf has precisely this capacity too, and there is ample evidence that it is a widely consumed space. Its visitors come for an experience of the sublime, which it amply provides. The English architectural hostility to it was based on its representation of global capital, its huge size, its prolific security. These things are arguably part of the experience. The visitors do not generally stay, for there is nowhere for them to stay exactly – but they go home again happy in having had a terrifying, but perfect experience of the future. To criticise the place for failing to be the traditional European city is to miss the point, for it is being consumed in ways that are perfectly adapted to its condition.

Chapter 8

The museum, the city and the space of flows

The Queen Elizabeth II Great Court of the British Museum was opened by the Queen on 6 December 2000 in the middle of a media controversy centred on the architects' substitution of French for English limestone on the new south portico. At its height, the controversy threatened the demolition of the portico itself. As it turned out, it merely drew attention to the latent xenophobia in sections of the news media about cultural matters: the French stone being presented, as it were, as a foreign body at the heart of empire. Although the story is not important here per se, it is significant in terms of describing the culture in which the Court was built. In many respects it was a culture of fear: fear of the other, fear of the urban, fear of the monumental, fear of the public, fear of the city. All of these things were, one way or another, described by the Great Court. This was after all, an urban culture that seemed intent on denying its urbanity: the British Museum, the greatest monument to imperial culture had long been allowed to drift and deteriorate, and nowhere in the museum was this more clearly exemplified than in the original Great Court. Once one of the grandest of all nineteenth-century public spaces, it had become the rubble room of the museum, a jumble of temporary buildings and book stacks huddled around the old British Library, a metonym for the mess of the museum proper.

The design for the Great Court by Foster and Partners offered a radical solution. By making a public space the heart of the museum, they attempted to solve both the circulation problems of the museum, and put the

Museum itself into public circulation. This second aspect of the Great Court project was highly rhetorical: it proposed spending £100 million of public money on a space that would not only turn a notoriously inward-looking institution to face outwards and engage with the public realm, but it would also provide an example of a modern, urban, public space for a culture that, as we have seen in the previous chapters, was particularly anxious about such things. In summary, it would address both the practical anxieties of the museum, and the metaphorical anxieties of the English about the urban. Foster wrote in anticipation:

> The courtyard is a major new social space. With two cafés and a restaurant it is possible to eat there from early in the morning until late at night. Newspapers and magazines are on sale at the new bookshop. And for the first time, the magnificent round reading room is open to all. To complement the Great Court, the Museum's forecourt has been freed from cars and restored to form a new public plaza. Together they represent a major new amenity for London and a new rendezvous for those who live or work in the area.
>
> (Foster and Partners 2001: 14)

This deceptively simple statement is, in fact, immensely ambitious. Foster's transformation of the museum proposes in effect that it dissolve as a discrete academic institution, and attain the spectacular quality of the contemporary public space. As I argue in the latter part of this chapter, what happens, to put it another way, is that it transforms the building from a museum to a space of circulation, rather like a modern airport. That Foster wished newspapers and magazines to be on sale, in addition to the Museum's academic publications, is one small indication of this desire.[1] My questions here primarily concern the rhetoric of circulation. This is so strongly stated, effecting such a transformation on the museum, that its conceptual basis needs interrogation. What specific anxieties about city life drive it? How does that rhetoric of circulation respond to larger changes in the English economy, or in the life of museums? How can it be theoretically situated? As I argue, the Great Court invokes an image of the city that is in no way picturesque, and therefore contradicts traditional English ways of imagining the urban realm. Specifically, it imagines the city as flow. This conception of the city has to do with professional anxiety about modernisation, or lack of it in Britain, namely that Britain's failure to modernise its infrastructure will lead to a decline on economic performance; an image of a modern economy and society is therefore vital to restore success.

The Great Court

The Great Court as it now stands, is a reformulation of an old space. The old Great Court occupied the centre of the main British Museum building, a large neoclassical structure built by Robert Smirke in 1847 in Bloomsbury, and one of the first European museums to adopt this architectural language (Sudjic 2001: 46). The Great Court was a very large square at its centre, with access from four porticoes. It was comparable in size to London's Georgian residential squares, Hanover Square being a good comparison. However it only existed as a square for seven years, for in 1854 the construction of the British Library, by Smirke's brother Sidney, began at the heart of the museum, producing the great round Reading Room. The south portico was demolished, and the Room's exterior was gradually encrusted with ancillary buildings and book stacks to service the library, none of which were meant to be seen. The square became inaccessible to the general public – in fact it became a positively repellent place. It was dismissed in the nineteenth century as 'a mere well of malaria, a pestilential congregation of vapours' (Sudjic 2001: 53). The removal of the British Library and the Kings Library to St Pancras in 1997 freed up the space again[2]; a 1993 competition to redesign the Great Court was won by Foster and Partners; construction began in 1998 and the project was completed at the end of 2000.

The reconstruction has four principal parts. First, is a spectacular toroidal glazed roof made of triangular panels, and, in design philosophy owing much to Buckminster Fuller, with whom Foster had collaborated in the 1970s.[3] The dome of the Reading Room projects through the roof, while the weight of the new structure rests on a new load-bearing casing around it. The Reading Room does not bear the weight of the new structure. Second, is the remodelling of the Reading Room itself, which is now encased in Spanish limestone and elongated to form an ellipse. It incorporates a restaurant at a high level, and shops at ground level, with washrooms below. With the Library's collection relocated to St Pancras, the Reading Room retains a small collection of books for display purposes, and a bank of computer terminals from which one can access information about the Museum collections. Access to the room, previously a privilege that had to be earned, is now open to all (access, one might say, is possible only now that it is of itself little value to the visitor: the library contain virtually nothing by comparison with the British Library). Third, is the addition of a variety of new educational and retail facilities, two auditoria, washrooms and exhibitions spaces below ground, a shop at ground level and a high-level restaurant close to the roof. Fourth, is the surface of the court, the floors and exterior of the Reading Room (which was never before intended to be seen from the outside) both done in soft polished French limestone.

Meanwhile the porticoes were refurbished, and, controversially, the south portico, which had been demolished to allow the construction of the library, was replaced. The portico was not a copy of the original but a Foster invention. There was no historical precedent for the deep central opening, or the square light high up. It also now had three doors instead of one (Sudjic 2001: 53). Spencer de Grey, the chief designer, stated: 'it's a new structure [. . .] and it looks new' (Powell 2000: 31). Both the experience of the building, and the controversy over the stone, inflamed by the *London Evening Standard*, were very widely reported. Its newly identified purpose as a public space was also much discussed

This is a highly rhetorical building. Its rhetoric responds to fears about the place of the museum in the nation, the place of the museum in the city, and about the nature of museums and museum-going in general. Specifically, its rhetoric concerns modernity. Its architects wish to both modernise the museum and make an image of a modern public space that may act as a model for London in general. Broadly, this desire is evidenced in two ways in the project: in the treatment of surfaces, and in the idea of circulation that the building represents.

The rhetoric of modernity is, I think, what underpins the strength of the reaction against the south portico (Figure 8.1). On the one hand, the controversy has to do with the way in which the contractors appeared to substitute, without the authority of the museum, the French Anstrude Roche Clair limestone for the English Portland.[4] Here was, in other words, a foreign body in the museum. But this otherness has to do with its visibility as other, and in particular its modern look. The stone was new and looked it; bright and unweathered it looked distinctly unlike the stone of the three older porticoes, each of which had spent a century and a half in the open. On top of that, the portico design itself was new rather than a reconstruction. Such modernity was upsetting because it challenged received notions of the museum's permanence and immutability, a representation not only of the Empire, but also of a certain set of unchanging moral values.

The controversy over the south portico was, in summary, a battle between modernisers and anti-modernisers, in which national stereotypes were enlisted on either side. For the modernisers, the completion of the Great Court represented a victory in a continuing battle for cultural domination between the English and the French. Sudjic wrote of it as a 'direct response' to the remaking of the Louvre in the 1980s, and referred to the way the history of Franco-British competition was embedded in the Museum itself: the Museum's possession of the Rosetta Stone, for example, is the result of Napoleon Bonaparte's surrender at Alexandria. Hugh Pearman wrote in the *Sunday Times* of the Great Court as a 'riposte' to the Louvre (Pearman 2000).

8.1
South portico of the Great Court of the British Museum, London (2000), architect: Foster and Partners

For the anti-modernisers, the Great Court was a threat to the integrity of the museum itself. English Heritage, the government-appointed, but ostensibly independent, body charged with maintaining the historical built environment, accused the museum trustees of an unprecedented 'dereliction of duty towards the building'; their outgoing director Jocelyn Stevens repeatedly called for the board of trustees and the museum director Graham Greene to resign, and for the portico to be demolished. The building was one of the most important in the country, he declared: 'they cannot be allowed to get away with it' (Kennedy 2000a: 6). With the support of English Heritage, Camden, the local council who had granted the original planning permission, entered the debate: the museum had contravened the planning outline, they claimed, and enforcement of the regulations or legal action was required. A Tory councillor, Stephen Hocking, said 'we gave permission for one kind of stone and something else has been built [. . .] a closer colour match could surely have been achieved' (Alberge 2000: 2). Besides the colour of the stone, there were concerns over the quality of the workmanship, in particular the depth and clarity of the carving, concerns articulated by the then Culture Secretary Chris Smith: there were 'serious questions to be answered about the specifics of the south portico' (Kennedy 2000a: 2). Even those who had little problem with the aesthetics of the Great Court found something inherently disturbing about the situation. A *Guardian* journalist reported a conservator who had worked on the Reading Room as saying that the substitution of the stone was: 'appalling. Having said that, new Portland would still look new, and very white. I think it will tone down in time. Aesthetically, I think it is fine. But I do think it is something of a national embarrassment that it is not Portland stone' (Kennedy 7 December 2000). A solution to the dispute was found in late November, when English Heritage drew its conclusions. In spite of the combative remarks by its former director, it decided that the portico should stay. However, the museum had been guilty of 'dereliction of duty' and the situation at the Great Court ought to be monitored 'in perpetuity' (Kennedy 17 November 2000: 2).

In spite of these remarks, and that the Heritage Lottery Fund was advised to retain £1.3 million of funds as punishment for the mistake, the modernisers could be said to have won. But in terms of the idea of modernity, the look of the south portico is a small issue. Modernity is represented at the Great Court much more clearly in the way it images circulation. This amounts to more than making an image of a modern building (using modern materials and modern forms) and it concerns the imagination of a modern public. We have seen how in certain schemes, the modernity of a public place does not necessarily correspond to a modernity of use, Canary Wharf being a good example. There, the developers presented an image of it as an established part of London with unbroken traditions, the images of its new inhabitants exhibiting more or less Edwardian traits. By contrast, the architects of the Great Court saw their project as a means of making a new kind of public life, in which freedom of movement and freedom of consumption were rhetorically emphasised.

The space of flows

I argue that the Great Court represents circulation in three ways. First, it puts the objects of the museum in circulation within the museum itself, disrupting the processional narrative that previously existed. Second, it puts the circulation of the visitors on show so that they become a point of interest as much as the objects on display. Third, it puts the museum in circulation in the city. By making the Great Court the mid-point on a putative public route through London from St Pancras to the South Bank, the Museum becomes integrated with the city instead of resisting it. The desire to represent circulation is, arguably, a modern one. It is evidenced very clearly, for example, in Le Corbusier's work on the city, in which decongestion is a key term (Le Corbusier 1929: 163–77). Replacing old Paris with the Plan Voisin, he foresaw the city abolished to leave areas of empty open space. Crowds were replaced by images of people in transit, particularly in aeroplanes and cars. To explain better what I mean by circulation, however, I turn to a more contemporary theory, namely the 'network society' described by the Catalan sociologist Manuel Castells.[5] Castells' *Rise of the Network Society* (1996) provides a spatial representation of contemporary societies in the developed world. In economic and social terms, circulation is critical to these societies, which, he argues is represented as *flow*: it is no longer place that matters, but the space of flows. With the continuing development of global capital and information technology, economic and social life is no longer defined by geographical location, but by spaces in which the movement of 'capital, information, technology, organisational interaction, images, sounds and symbols' are in flow.[6]

The 'space of flows' has three layers, first being a layer of electronic communication, or essential practices based on electronic communications: 'microelectronics, telecommunications, computer processing, broadcasting systems, and high-speed transportation also based on information technologies' (Castells 1996: 412). The second layer is 'constituted by its nodes and hubs', which is to say places in which (principally) the transfer of information is effected. These places are organised 'hierarchically', argues Castells, depending on their relative importance in the network as a whole. Crucially, the 'node and hubs' tend to be cities. The third layer of the space of flows is the material space produced by the élites who themselves manage or produce or run the network. These élites are 'cosmopolitan' rather than local and they tend to reproduce certain kinds of spaces for residence, work and recreation, which may be located in actually existing 'real' cities but in another sense occupy an international space. Castells notes the tendency of the élites to operate in and produce 'secluded' space regardless of actual location – space the anthropologist Marc Augé elsewhere has called 'non-place' (Augé 1995):

> International hotels whose decoration from the design of the room to the colour of the towels is similar all over the world to create a sense of familiarity with the inner world while inducing abstraction from the surrounding world; airports' VIP lounges, designed to maintain the distance *vis-à-vis* society in the highways of the space of flows; mobile, personal, on-line access to telecommunications networks so that the traveler is never lost; and a system of travel arrangements, secretarial services and reciprocal hosting that maintains a close circle of the corporate élite together through the worshipping of similar rites in all countries.[7]
>
> (Castells 1996: 417)

The effects of this shift for cities are profound, but also unexpected. First, the city does not dissolve, as sociologists have often predicted in the past. If anything, existing cities – provided they are in this broad metaphorical sense networked – are re-centralised, for the network society demands ready access to a pool of labour and suppliers as and when it is required. Second, the city is re-centralised by the agglomeration of the poor. The space of flows tends to concentrate poverty along with wealth in mega-cities, concentrating those people who 'want to make visible their dereliction so that they will not die ignored in areas bypassed by communication networks' (Castells 1996: 404). Third, new 'nodes and hubs' in city form are constantly appearing (and disappearing). In a European context, Castells cites the experience of Madrid and Budapest, once-peripheral places now increasingly high in the network hierarchy as their economies develop, and capital increasingly flows through them. Fourth, the city also produces certain kinds of new architecture, such as those places mentioned above. None of these things are necessarily new taken in isolation, but the space of flows, Castells argues, accentuates them, concentrates them, and makes them more frequent and more important.

Castells goes on to provide a number of concrete examples of architectural projects, which, he thinks, represent the 'space of flows'. In each case, Castells argues, the space of flows is clearly represented as a critical aspect of the building; in other words these buildings do not simply enclose space, but operate at the level of morality, drawing attention to the contemporary human condition. Among these examples is Ricardo Bofill's El Prat airport at Barcelona, one of a number of remarkable public buildings erected in the Olympic year of 1992.[8] What Castells says about Barcelona is this: a vast, clear, mostly uninterrupted space of dark glass and marble, it reveals the space of flows by deliberately failing to conceal it. There is no attempt to hide the fact of the airport or turn it into something else. 'In the middle of the cold beauty' he writes

> passengers have to face their terrible truth: they are alone, in the middle of the space of flows, they may lose their connection, they are suspended in the emptiness of transition. They are literally in the hands of Iberia Airlines. And there is no escape.
>
> (Castells 1996: 421)

Whether this reading has anything to do with the architect's intention may be debated elsewhere. But three things are certain in Castells' thinking: that the space of flows has frequent, and important, architectural representation (architectural examples and metaphors are frequent throughout the book); that the architectural types that it refers to are usually spaces of transit such as airports and railway stations; and that they are designed in such a way as to stage the circulation that they contain. In other words, they do not seek to conceal their purpose, but instead, make it visible.

How is this a useful theory for explicating the Great Court? I should say that I am not drawn to it for Castells' success in reading architecture. In a footnote, Castells admits that Bofill (a fellow Catalan) is baffled by the explanation, regarding the airport instead as a more or less formal exercise, a witty amalgamation of classical and Modernist tropes; I am sure we should go along with the architect here. Castells' theory is nevertheless still worth pursuing, I think: he has just picked the wrong architectural example. Had he used Foster as an illustration, he might have found in the British architect's treatment of public spaces a quite unambiguous representation of the idea of flow. In his theory of flows, Castells is preoccupied with temporal and spatial indeterminacy. Flow implies something that exists in time; that has duration; that exists in more than one place; that is mutable; that has points of connection. All of these things are, it could be said, visible at the Great Court.

At the Great Court, flow is represented, first, by the way it puts the museum collections in circulation. The old conception of museum space, as described by Carol Duncan, is analogous to that of the temple or church. The architecture of the first public museums – which includes the British Museum – appropriated the neoclassical vocabulary of ceremonial architecture, and museum going, she argues, likewise soon developed a ritual aspect, which has been enforced over the years. As Duncan argues, the experience of visiting the museum has long been likened to that of going to church. William Hazlitt wrote that it was 'like going on a pilgrimage – it is an act of devotion performed at the shrine of art' (Hazlitt in Duncan 1995: 15). Duncan elaborates this substantially, comparing the museum specifically with the devotional rituals enacted by pilgrims in the visiting of the great cathedrals. Not just a single shrine is visited, but a series, with precise instructions for devotional behaviour at each point. Art museums, argues Duncan, 'resemble in some respects certain medieval cathedrals where pilgrims followed a structured narrative route through the interior, stopping a prescribed points for prayer or contemplation' (Duncan 1995: 12). The 'prescribed points' in the museum are individual works of art, singled out by their fame; the analogue to prayer or contemplation takes the form of reading a wall label, taking a photograph (if permitted), or, increasingly, listening to a description of the object on an audio guide. A knowledge of appropriate prayer ritual in the church equates in museum terms to a hierarchy of objects to be seen in a certain order, understood through certain special knowledge, while physical behaviour is carefully (self-)policed. In both places, one must move slowly and in relative silence, displaying reverence at the appropriate point.

The British Museum was a product of imperial history, and its collections – deriving from military or commercial conquest – were displayed in a narrative manner so that the visitor understood Western civilisation as the culmination of a glorious history. The ritual aspects of the visiting experience affirmed an imperial history, the reverential behaviour inculcated at each great object a means of impressing upon the visitor the power of the political system that facilitated it.[9] Making the Great Court the central space of the museum disrupts this narrative so that it is now possible to attain the realm of Ancient Greece without first passing though Korea. Previously, as the architectural critic Peter Buchanan noted,

> visitors were led through the antecedents to Western civilisation: oriental and pre-Columbian cultures were banished to the back of the building, and the ethnographic collections (from pre-civilised cultures) were housed entirely elsewhere [. . .] now the multi-level Great Court gives direct access to all parts of the museum.
>
> (Buchanan in Jenkins 2000: 429)

This architectural flattening challenges the previous hierarchy of the collections, so that Western civilisation is no longer accorded a uniquely privileged place.[10] In the same way as I. M. Pei's remodelling of the Louvre challenged that institution's exaltation of French art, the British Museum's Great Court appears to allow non-Western and Western cultures to co-exist with on more equal terms than before. The dismantling of the old narrative through architecture provides, for an increasingly diverse visiting public, a modernised way of understanding the museum's collections. No longer do they speak of colonial conquest, rather of consumption as de-historicised aesthetic objects by putatively free individual consumer-visitors. The invitation to Nelson Mandela, the first president of post-apartheid South Africa, to open the Court's BP lecture theatre underlined this message. Mandela said 'this great museum may have begun as the beneficiary of British imperial power but it has become a truly global institution' (Bailey 2000a: 1). In these ways the Great Court puts its collection in circulation, at least rhetorically, for the first time; the organisation of space, like the space of the reorganised Louvre, discourages the linear reading of the museum.

The second way flow is represented at the Great Court is in its staging of the circulation of visitors. The stage itself is extraordinary; it is vast in scale, one of the world's largest indoor public spaces, and in the fact of being such a space, the idea of circulation is made metaphorically spectacular. The most extraordinary, certainly most memorable part of the museum's architecture is now no longer the façade (a piece of two-dimensional sculpture, only truly appreciated by the art historian) but what Castells would term a node or hub (Figure 8.2). In terms of scale, the Great Court, a place of transit, now overpowers all other separable parts of the museum.

The Great Court is functionally a stage. It is in one account, 'not a place to linger': clearly the fact of the big drum of the library makes it useless as a place of assembly, for it blocks all sight lines, and occupies much of the available floor space. But other critics have noticed the transitory quality of the space manifest in the 'horizontality' of the roof (Pople 2001: 42). One might also note the quality of the surfaces – the very limited range of materials – limestone, marble, stainless steel – and the large expanses of white, polished stone; materials and surfaces, which, it could be said, by their hardness and reflectivity relate to the world of circulatory spaces rather than spaces of repose or contemplation. Added to this is the calculated incorporation of viewpoints in the space from which circulation may be seen (Figures 8.3 and 8.4). The viewpoints include various places from the stairs surrounding the library, and the upper level of the south portico, which as already noted, incorporates an aperture with no precedent in the language of classical architecture. Visitors are recognisable from these points as individuals, but only just. The

8.2
**South façade,
British Museum,
London (1823–47),
architect: Robert
Smirke**

8.3
Great Court of the British Museum, London (2000), architect: Foster and Partners

main impression is of unselfconscious bodies moving systematically through space, describing generalised patterns of circulation through the building.

The third way the Great Court represents flow is in its position in the city. It is clear from early sketches of the project that the new space was above all to be legible as public, an idea which was set against both the inward-looking traditions of the museum, and the English tendency towards the privatisation of space – the classic urban spaces have (see Chapter 1) always been semi-private or private interiors, which one attained though privilege of one kind or another – the gentleman's club, the House of Lords, most pubs.[11] Public life in England has generally meant a network of exclusive private spaces from where power is exercised on the mass of the population.

The clearest statement of this was the controversial reformulation of the British Library from an academic institution to which entry was barred to all those without good reason, to a space that was in theory open to all. Previously the British Library was one of these privileged spaces – to enter one needed to secure a reader's ticket, straightforward if one is already part of the semi-private academic world, much harder if one is not.[12] The public-ness of the space was also in theory articulated by situating the Great Court as an element of a new pedestrian route through London from the South Bank to Bloomsbury. Foster's advocates were effusive in their praise for this idea:

'The public takes full possession of the building' (Buchanan in Jenkins 2000: 429); 'It is a new kind of meeting place, apt for an age when with the prevalence of computer networking and working from home, the city becomes necessary again as a meeting space'; the Great Court in this scheme is 'a place of meeting, culture, and information exchange, at a prime juncture in intellectual and touristic London' (Buchanan in Jenkins 2000: 435); it was 'a radical extension to London's public domain' (Powell 2000: 26). The potential for the open public use of the space was always more rhetorical than real, as the opening hours of the Great Court, security measures, and the awkwardness of the linkage from the north entrance to the Court all mitigated against its coming into being. Especially the latter, it might be said, for the route narrows sharply to the north, climbs a flight of stairs and emerges onto Montague Place at what is very clearly a back entrance (Figure 8.5). But it is a clearly stated aim in the Foster plan for the Great Court, and it revisits proposals for such a cultural route through London by W. R. Lethaby in 1912 after the first extension to the Museum was created, and by Leslie Martin and Colin St John Wilson in the 1960s (Powell 2001: 31). In this way, the museum space is rhetorically returned to the city, and along with this symbolic return, there is the intrusion of experiences of consumption which were previously extraneous to that of the museum – eating, drinking and shopping. In some senses, the Great Court is a Food Court, albeit a sophisticated one.

8.4
Great Court of the British Museum, London (2000), architect: Foster and Partners

8.5
**North entrance
to the British
Museum,
London**

The Great Court and the airport

As Castells argues, the space of flows is best-represented at large transport hubs. The Great Court's rhetoric of flow has this museum space take the characteristics of such spaces, as was widely noted on its opening. A *Guardian* journalist reported a charity worker's reaction: 'It looks just like an airport' (Kennedy 2000b). The paper's architectural critic Jonathan Glancey wrote that 'with so many sandwiches being eaten there and so much shopping for second-rate souvenirs, it will always be in danger, on busy days, of feeling uncomfortably like an airport departure lounge' (Glancey 2001: 86). The novelist Howard Jacobson wrote of the peculiar experience the Great Court seemed to provoke in the visitor: 'the only thing we know for sure is that we're on holiday, gaping like tourists and itching to spend money' (Jacobson 2000). It is 'a duty free outlet for monumental sculpture' (unnamed critic quoted in Street-Porter 2001).

The material form of the Great Court could be said to justify this impression. Like the airport it is a hub, a central point from which one departs to somewhere else, a place that connects dispersed other places. It has a lot of circulation space. Its primary purpose is to facilitate passage, rather than public assembly. It is also, like an airport, a place of waiting, an ante-room before some other experience, and like the airport it has a lot of the same things to distract the visitor-passenger: the book and gift shops, the cafés, the sandwich bars, the washrooms, the information desks. In fact, one's movement through the Great Court almost exactly parallels that of the passage through an airport. One arrives at the main south entrance, deposits one's bags for the duration (answering security questions in the process), and passes what is in effect a ticket check, followed by a security check, before passing into the cultural departure lounge of the Great Court itself, where one has a drink and something to eat, visits the lavatory, and surveys the information boards to make sure of one's destination. And the remodelling of the circulation of the museum makes sure that it is now more than ever like a modern airport on the hub model: the destinations lie in distinct directions.[13] The remodelling of the Great Court turns the linear, narrative space of the museum into the networked space of air travel. Air terminals are among Foster's most significant projects, and there are formal similarities between Stansted (1990), Chek Lap Kok, Hong Kong (1998) and the Great Court. All share, for example, a spectacular roof, which helps make a collective image for what is in each case a very large, multifunctional covered space (Figure 8.6).

The comparison with airport design, however reasonable, raises some important issues or problems. First, in Foster's œuvre, there are great similarities between the typology of ostensibly different buildings, but to do this is not without problems of meaning. To build a museum space in the form of an airport is to disrupt the traditional meaning of the museum in several ways. Airports belong to the realm of what Augé calls 'non space', a geographically unspecific realm of spaces of transit.[14] There are a few cases of airports by well-known architects, which by their distinctiveness approach the condition of place, but by and large they are not urban places in this way.[15]

8.6
**Chek Lap Kok
airport, Hong
Kong (1998),
architect: Foster
and Partners**
Dennis Gilbert/
VIEW

To approach the condition of the airport is to accede to non-place, a reversal of the usual status of the museum. As a tourist, for example, one passes through the non-places of transit in order to attain the anthropological place of the museum, a place which one hopes is distinctively local, a place whose situatedness, as it were, makes bearable the placelessness of getting there.

If the airport exists outside of anthropological place, it also exists outside of historical time. Airports, whatever their actual age, always aspire to newness, and those, like London's Heathrow, that routinely fail in this task tend to be condemned.[16] Related to this is the assumption that airports are in some sense the most advanced and purest representation of the contemporary global economy, whatever the nature of their actual financing. The museum stood previously aloof from the world of things and money; through the Great Court, it clearly becomes part of it.

Finally, the condition of the airport sublimates the question of surveillance. It is a space of passing through, but also, as these liminal spaces tend to be, a space of authority. It needs to be said, that the notions of public-ness and circulation that are put in operation here have little to do with notions of political freedom. The ostensibly humanistic rhetoric of public access accompanies – perhaps occludes – a complex and detailed set of controls on public behaviour. Although ostensibly part of a pedestrian route through London, the Great Court remains an interior space of the museum, which grants right of passage subject to certain limitations. The route remains closed almost as much as it is open; four days a week, at the time of writing, it opens from 9am until 6pm, with an extension until 11pm at the weekends.[17] It is surveilled by guards and closed-circuit television, and large packages may not be brought through it. The visitor is subject to quite detailed controls about the consumption of food: all food consumed in the space must be bought at one of the self-service cafés, and eaten at the long benches. Museum guards prevent the consumption of sandwiches bought elsewhere, and assiduously patrol the stairways for casual picnickers. One cannot run, or play sports; one cannot make too much noise; one cannot play music; there is a complex set of rules regarding photography. Only humans may inhabit the space; there is no other kind of animal or plant life permitted. It is, it might be said, a public space in name only. In conclusion, if we think of the Great Court in terms of the airport condition, it can be seen to overturn the traditional values of the museum. Instead of a geographically situated place, it is placeless; instead of being historically situated, it exists in the present; instead of being aloof from the world, it is intensely connected with it; instead of being a place of education, it is a place of surveillance.

Waiting

I return to the idea of anxiety in the last part of this chapter. As the theme of this book, anxiety has usually been given a presence as a form of professional uncertainty about the urban. In the peculiar circumstances of the English architectural profession, the city has been the object of unusual anxiety; most of the examples I have referred to so far have been attempts to assuage that feeling by recourse to picturesque solutions, either built, or rhetorical. In both cases, the irruption of the picturesque identifies anxiety about the urban, and a desire to ameliorate it.

As will have become clear in this chapter, Foster and Partners reformulation of the Great Court of the British Museum is a different case, in that it makes an urban space out of one that previously turned its back on the urban. It made what was a curiously inward-looking, almost anti-urban institution, the British Museum, face outward to the city in which it sat, and in so doing, replaced what was by default rather than design picturesque, with what was not.[18] Here was, in other words, an urban project that although a remodelling of an existing building that had picturesque characteristics, in no way accedes to the picturesque. The Great Court is unapologetically, un-neurotically urban; it is also, as I state at the beginning of this chapter, unapologetically modern. Now these characteristics may return us to the idea of anxiety, for they disrupt traditional English notions of city life. As I suggest above, the conservative reaction by many to the substitution of French for English limestone is anxious rather than xenophobic, centred on its modernity rather than its foreign origins.

More generally, I argue that the Great Court is of itself an anxious space, because (unlike the traditional form of the museum) it is liminal. It is by definition not a place in which people settle, but pass through. In this it relates not only to the airport, an architectural form of the late twentieth century in which Foster has a great deal of expertise, but also to a set of earlier modern spaces which were closely identified with anxiety, particularly the hotel lobby.

The Frankfurt School critical theorist Siegfried Kracauer explored the hotel lobby in an essay for the *Frankfurter Zeitung* from the 1920s. He compares this quintessentially modern space unfavourably with another gathering place, the 'house of God' (Kracauer in Leach 1997: 53–8). In respect of Foster's work at the Great Court, one of the curious but useful aspects of Kracauer's essay is his use of the church as a means to read the lobby, ironically inverting a sacred space to make his critique. In the case of the Great Court, this inversion is, one could say, given material form: the museum is traditionally viewed as a secular church, yet here it is made into something like Kracauer's lobby. And if we follow his critique, then it is turned from a place of purposeful gathering to the reverse, a space of alienation and estrangement. In both, people are drawn together in public, but in the former they never achieve the sense of purpose or community seen in the latter. The inhabitants of the lobby merely wait, hoping soon to be somewhere else. Douglas Tallack's account of Kracauer's essay and its place in a wider understanding of modern urbanity is instructive here (Tallack in Leach 2002: 139–51). He describes the lobby space as, in itself, essentially purposeless. Linked with modern forms of travel, its inhabitants do not belong there. If it is like anything, it most closely resembles a stage set, a place which is only made, as it were by the social action that takes place on or in it: it is of itself essentially characterless. Worse, the lobby is not a place in which one can somehow withdraw, for unlike the street, with its size, heterogeneity and movement in which (as countless writers have described) one can lose oneself, the lobby is an interior of a certain size and disposition such that its inhabitants are on display, or worse, under surveillance. Hence its appearance so often, he argues, following Kracauer, as the classic scene of action in detective fiction. Anthony Vidler's bleak assessment of Kracauer finds in the hotel lobby modern life reduced to fragmentation and alienation; individual residents are no more than atoms in a void, 'confronted with nothing; stranded in their armchairs' (Vidler 2000: 73). He concludes that these writings of the early twentieth century foretell the destruction of what the nineteenth century understood by city life: the street dissolves into a set of bizarrely alienating spaces and the city increasingly becomes a space of atomisation. 'Kracauer's nightmare' writes Vidler, is the world made into a 'gigantic hotel atrium' (Vidler 2000: 79).[19]

The plaudits given by most critics to the Great Court on its opening suggest otherwise, that it is simply a pleasurable space that, as the humanistic rhetoric of its authors would have us believe, opens up a once private space for public enjoyment. It should also be said, as Vidler has argued, that we should be careful when appropriating the architectonic conceits of theorists working in other times and places. Kracauer's hotel lobby, he writes, whatever its claims to represent a universal modern space, is in fact a product of 'artifice and careful articulation' that distinguishes it 'from any that we might ourselves have known' (Vidler 2000: 67). We should not too easily seize upon this essay of the early twentieth century to explain a profoundly late twentieth-century structure.

Yet there are aspects of the Great Court that suggest that not only is it reasonable to invoke Kracauer here, but that a sense of anxiety is in some ways cultivated in Foster's architecture (Figure 8.7). As Frampton argues, the purpose of architecture is not simply to enclose space, but to reveal a moral condition (Frampton 1992: 343). If the modern world can be described best in terms of the space of flows, then architecture should represent it, however uncomfortable. In terms of the Great Court, this would mean something like Foster's bringing the uncanniness of the hotel lobby into the rarefied space of the museum. A way of making a critique of the modern world. I have already

8.7
Chek Lap Kok airport, Hong Kong (1998), architect: Foster and Partners
Dennis Gilbert/ VIEW

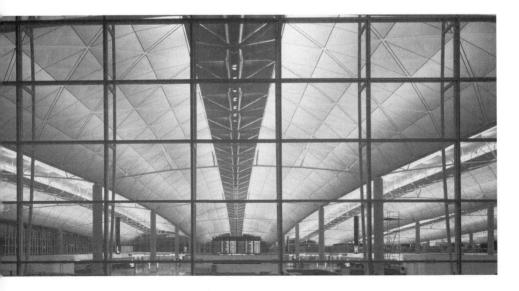

indicated how the Great Court might be a good illustration of Castells' theory. What I have not done so far is show how this illustration might be seen as a critical project in this way, in other words one which does not simply affirm the brief.

This assertion cannot be proved, and there is nothing in the critical discourse around the work that detracts from the humanistic rhetoric of its authors. But although skilled in meeting the brief of clients, and drawing in public consultation, there are aspects of Foster's work that indicate a more critical, even subversive, sensibility.[20] To illustrate what I mean, let me present the case of a film commissioned by Foster to celebrate the opening of the new Chek Lap Kok airport in Hong Kong in 1998. This is not unconnected with the Great Court, as it was the centrepiece of the exhibition of Foster's œuvre at the Court's opening, and received some critical attention as a result. My interest in it derives not only from this fact, but that it articulates a certain attitude to public space by the practice that may be seen in details of spaces themselves, but tends not otherwise to be stated. The attitude is generally an artistic one; it supposes an aloofness and detachment from the subject; it supposes the modern world actually *not* to be rational and explicable, but highly ambiguous; it supposes, finally, that the only honest approach to the world is to try to represent it as it appears. The film was made independently, by BMJ, a production company, with the help of Magz Hall and Tom Wallace, sound artists, to realise the extraordinary soundtrack. The film was, say the opening credits, commissioned by the practice explicitly to 'convey the experience' of moving through the airport. This was done by the use of cameras mounted 'as close as possible to the human viewing plane', 'including peripheral vision'. They continue: 'Ambisonic microphones were used to capture a unidirectional sound recording of the environment.'

About fifteen minutes' duration, the film provides an extremely detailed account of the building from the point of view of the traveller. Moving from the taxi rank to the departure hall, where a 360° panorama is given, to the check-in desks, to security and passport control, to the departure gates, to the baggage claim, to the departure hall again, the viewer finally mounts the express metro train that whisks the visitor away from the airport to the city. In image, the airport recedes as the train speeds away. Interspersed with these highly descriptive images of the building's function are vignettes of the life of the airport: a child clad in bright yellow ascending an escalator; a group of five Chinese stewardesses (in the only moment approaching comedy) who briefly fail to arrange themselves correctly at the check-in; muffled voices and blurred images of security checks behind a translucent screen; a man, face-on entering the rapid transit train. Huge Boeings from mainland China, Singapore and Thailand constantly take off and land, taxi and dock. The soundtrack is

extraordinarily detailed and rich, in which only rarely does one element domi-
nate any other. The overall impression is of a multiplicity and simultaneity of
events.

This impression is also true of the visual presentation of the airport,
which – through constant slow panning, and shifting from one scene to
another – gives the impression of a dynamic system or network. It is well-
populated, yet interaction between any figures in the film is seemingly
suppressed, beyond one or two incidents. Everyone, whether airport or airline
worker, or traveller, is constantly in motion; they are always seen at a distance
too, so are only rarely identifiable as individuals. Everyone appears self-
absorbed, mechanically involved in their tasks, in a scene which threatens,
but resists, absurdity.

A cinematic comparison would be Jacques Tati's *Playtime* (1968),
in which over two hours, a series of characters become progressively alienated by their self-consciously modern environment, its spectacle of efficiency
turning out to be both authoritarian and unsustainable. The sense of spectacle
is underlined by the film's extraordinary scale (a vast set, 'Tativille' was built
on the outskirts of Paris) and intricacy, every scene comprising multiple and
simultaneous gags and plotlines, many of which are only legible on repeated
viewings.[21] Only at the end is there any kind of dénouement: the film's
comedy has to do with the threat of the irrational, which constantly bubbles
under the authoritarian surfaces. So it is with the Foster-commissioned film of
Chek Lap Kok. The filmmakers present a spectacle of efficiency so complete
that it approaches the absurd. Now this reading cannot, clearly, be proved but
neither is it suppressed, and we can only conclude that the airport is to be
seen primarily as a work of art, with all the consequence that categorisation
entails.

Shown in close proximity to the Great Court, as it was in a 2001
exhibition, the film is revealing because both it and the building represent
the mass as a set of atomised individuals, alienated and estranged from
their environment, but awesomely so. The Great Court has no film equivalent,
but what it does have are a series of viewpoints from which the life of the
space is imaged in these ways. From the square opening above the south
portico, or from the stairways which encircle the drum of the Reading Room,
one now can have an image of the Court in which the public becomes a spectacle of disconnected, self-absorbed individuals, each going mechanically
about their business. It is quite a sight, but it contradicts the humanistic
rhetoric on which the Great Court was built. At the Great Court, in conclusion, a new kind of city is powerfully imagined, but it is a somewhat cruel
place in which an elevated spectator observes with amused detachment the
circulation of his inferiors.

Chapter 9

The spectacle of pleasure

Introduction

In the imagination of urban England, Manchester occupies a special place. From its emergence as the world's first industrial city in the 1820s, to its more recent existence as a post-industrial playground it has always been, as the editors of a recent anthology point out, in a hurry to be somewhere else, regardless of the consequences. It has, they write, 'been in an almost perpetual state of restructuring [. . .] talk of revolution, like the drizzle, is nearly always in the air' (Peck and Ward 2002: 1). This condition might well be described as anxious, for it shows a preoccupation with the future, with what might be, rather than the present and what is; its activity, its work, and its being is directed toward this future, heedless of what chaos it might actually bring.

This imaginative tension between the present and the future has long been the subject of commentators on the city. For Friedrich Engels, writing in *The Condition of the Working Class in England*, industrial progress had brought about the most dreadful concentrations of poverty (Engels 1993: 57–9). Alexis de Toqueville noted the same in his *Journeys to England and Ireland* (de Tocqueville 1958: 103–8). In both cases, Manchester's dreadfulness has to do with its essentially anxious nature; in its position in the vanguard of industrial progress, it renders itself unliveable. In more recent times, Manchester's dreadfulness has been the result of its abandonment by industry, a process in which it could also claim to be in the vanguard (Peck and Ward 2002: 1). Manchester as post-industrial ruin has awed and appalled visitors for a generation, the subject of much indigenously produced popular culture, especially its music, and of the novels of foreign visitors like W. G. Sebald for whom the city in the 1960s was eerily barren and empty, seemingly hollow to the core (Sebald 1996: 151).[1]

Manchester might be said to remain an anxious city, but its anxiety now springs neither from the turbulence of industrialisation, or de-industriali-sation, but something new. The city's recent history has brought about greater changes in the built fabric than at any time since the nineteenth century. What has happened in Manchester in the 1990s is new and curious; while it may not place the city in the vanguard of global change as it was in the nineteenth century, it does in many respects lead the way in England (Peck and Ward 2002: 9). It has been transformed from an industrial metropolis to one concerned with more ephemeral things: education, entertainment, computer games, the news media. This new economy is often to be found juxtaposed with the ruins of the old, or, quite often, occupying them. In Castlefield, one of the principal centres of the first industrial revolution, former warehouses have become the inevitable museums and bars. But this transformation has a very long way to go before the past becomes illegible. Something about the space of Manchester, its scale, its monumentality, yet very modern lack of density, mean that one is always made aware of the fact of transformation. The city is neither completely one thing nor the other; secure in certain aspects of its identity, it is very insecure in others. The recent past, rather like that of Liverpool discussed in Chapter 5, reveals a city whose entire existence is threatened by depopulation and suburbanisation, the centre reduced to a retail mall. As recently as 1984, the city council accepted this scenario as a probability, and planned for continued decline (Manchester City Council 1984).

The current anxiety about the city concerns its transformation into a different kind of place. This chapter deals with this problem through archi-tecture, specifically in the way certain architects have sought to remake the city in new terms. Crudely put, they imagine the city now as a place of spec-tacular consumption – of luxury goods, food and sex. The official anxiety about the location of a department store by the upmarket Harvey Nichols chain was palpable in the local news media during 1998–9, as if the presence of this store alone would heal the city's wounds. In a handful of new city buildings, particularly those by the locally based architect Ian Simpson, the idea of the city of consumption has been spectacularly realised. But it exists uneasily with other versions of the city, which may lie in ruins – literally or metaphorically – but are nevertheless present. Simpson, through his provision of calculatedly modern bars, offices and apartments has provided more successfully than anyone else an image of the new city. But the vision his work articulates, of a spectacular city of consumption, is at odds with the moral city that exists, still, in the city's reformist traditions, whose ruins can now be seen in the parlous state of its social housing and education. In this chapter, I first discuss this moral city, its history and the recent challenges to it. I then describe how one of the most spectacular of Simpson's buildings makes this challenge material.

Moral Manchester

We need to say something about Manchester's history as a moral city. By this, I do not mean to describe Manchester as an especially moral place, for it is not, but rather, I mean that it has been the site of peculiarly intense moral anxieties. Its unprecedented growth in the nineteenth century produced what seemed to be unprecedented moral conditions. The reaction of the French political philosopher Alexis de Tocqueville is indicative:

> a dense smoke covers the city. The sun appears like a disc without rays. It is in the midst of this incomplete day that 300,000 human creatures toil without ceasing [. . .] it is here that the human spirit becomes perfect and at the same time brutalised, that civilisation produces its marvels and the civilised man returns to the savage.
>
> (de Tocqueville 1958)

In this passage, the appalled philosopher presents the city in dystopian terms. Its peculiar horror is not so much a function of its squalor and degradation, for these things may be found in cities elsewhere, but rather the fact that they result from its modernity. Progress has made this state of affairs; the modern world therefore evinces a deteriorating standard of civilisation. Engels continued this idea in *The Condition of the Working Class in England* (1845) written between 1842 and 1844, while managing his father's textile mill (Engels 1993).[2] The city fascinated him precisely because of its modernity (it seemed to him to represent a city at a peculiarly advanced stage of capitalist production) – but also because this modernity had, as a by-product, unique concentrations of poverty and deprivation. As he argued by means of statistical tables, while the city was registering quite extraordinary rates of population growth as the result of migration from outlying areas, the quality of life, rates of pay and life expectancy of workers were significantly lower in the city than in the places from which they came. Engels' detailed observations covered the crowded, squalid and unsanitary conditions throughout the city. Little Ireland, next to the present day Oxford Road station, was 'the most horrible spot' (Engels 1993: 72). Hulme was 'generally sunk in filth' (Engels 1993: 73). The horror of the Old Town rendered him wordless. However dreadful his account of it seems to be, Engels writes, it cannot really convey its true depths:

> on rereading my description I am forced to admit that instead of being exaggerated, it is far from black enough to convey a true impression of filth, ruin and unihabitableness, the defiance of all considerations of cleanliness, ventilation and health which characterise the construction of this single district.
>
> (Engels 1993: 65).

'The Old Town is no less than "a Hell upon Earth"'; 'how extraordinary and shameful', he continued, 'that such a district should not only exist in the centre of the greatest manufacturing city on earth, but should somehow define it' (Engels 1993: 65). Not only were the material conditions of Manchester's central area dreadful in this way, but there was a moral vacuum at its heart too. The lack of attention to organised religion was one matter, but worse still was the design of the city itself, which seemed calculated to obscure the view of poverty from the sight of the city's wealthy inhabitants. In a much-cited description of the form of the city, Engels related how the central business district, an eerily vacant zone out of work hours, connected to the middle class suburbs by means of wide streets lined with respectable shops. Behind them the working class districts which comprised most of the city, but which one can easily avoid if the sight offends. This design seems to be the result of conscious agreement, not accident: 'I cannot help feeling that the liberal manufacturers are not so innocent after all, in the matter of this sensitive method of construction' (Engels 1993: 59).[3]

Engels and de Tocqueville represent one kind of approach to the moral aspects of Manchester. For both of them, as James Donald has argued, the nature of Manchester is a consequence of the industrial system that produced it, and that in order to effect moral improvement, one needed to change the system: this view, it barely needs to be said, informs Engels' most famous work, the *Communist Manifesto*, co-written with Marx. A different approach, but one no less concerned with the city as a moral case, is exhibited by James Kay-Shuttleworth, a Manchester doctor who became the city's chief public health officer. Writing in the 1830s, he produced an important pamphlet, *The Moral and Physical Condition of the Working Classes Employed in the Cotton Manufacture in Manchester* that observed the city in new ways. Kay-Shuttleworth's gaze on the city is a form of policing, which invokes a new model of government. Government, Donald writes of Kay-Shuttleworth's world-view, had become 'a question of welfare as well as of surveillance and discipline. It attempted to manipulate the urban environment so as to remove the sources of corruption' (Donald 1999: 31).

Kay-Shuttleworth was an early member of what might be described as Manchester's Victorian political élite – theologically nonconformist (usually Unitarian) with industrial connections, and a belief in social justice within the confines of the existing economic system.[4] His pamphlet, a prototype for many others, concluded with a policy prescription. It was from this context that *The Guardian* newspaper was formed, along with a vast series of public works, radically improving the health, circulation, and education of the city's inhabitants. Such improvements were enabled – as the Kay-Shuttleworth case shows – by observation and regulation, processes that brought the whole city under surveillance.

The historian Patrick Joyce has written in Foucauldian terms about the transformation of Manchester into a 'moral city'.[5] The process involved, generally speaking, the purification of aspects of city life that referred to the *body*, so bodily functions, blood, disease and waste were increasingly removed from public view. In the Manchester municipal code of 1893, the street was sublimated as a space of circulation in which 'standing', 'loitering' and 'remaining' were prohibited, as were 'activities which involve those who, like street sellers, 'jolt', 'jostle' or 'annoy'. The new code demanded above all that as a citizen, one

> had to be in control of oneself. The enforcement of direct moral self-control is everywhere evident in the Code [. . .] the Manchester Code governed 'riotous' and 'indecent' behaviour and language, particularly 'indecent exposure', also 'obscene, indecent and profane' books, language, songs and pictures, and bathing so as to expose the person.
>
> (Joyce 2003: 88)

All 'manifestations of corruption and decay' were, in principle, swept from the face of the city (Joyce 2003: 76). Meanwhile, the 'public' was exalted as a form of performance in which 'tact and reticence' were the desired behaviours (Joyce 2003: 124).

Much compressed, Joyce's argument is this: early nineteenth-century Manchester is an amoral chaos, whose design denied the poor; by the end of the century, it had evolved systems of regulation and surveillance that at least pretended an organisation of moral life. In it, the 'civilisation' of the bourgeois became the public ideal, through which the body was suppressed, and public behaviour tightly circumscribed. Whether or not this ideal corresponds to a lived reality is less important here than the enthusiasm with which it was pursued at an official level. It had architectural representation too, in the adoption of Venetian gothic as the default mode for public buildings: in Ruskinian terms, gothic had the appropriate connotations.[6] Alfred Waterhouse's Town Hall (1868–77) is the grandest example in Manchester (Dixon and Muthesius 1978: 165–8).

Now, this production of Manchester as a moral city has many other dimensions that could be explored. Charles Dickens and Mrs Gaskell represented the moral city in the novel, the latter being involved in the broad project of social reform though her husband, the Unitarian minister of Cross St. chapel.[7] The city's moral existence is not only part of its historical character, but persists through the twentieth century, albeit in a different, and much more conservative form. In the 1980s, in particular, through the activities of James Anderton, a controversial chief constable of Greater Manchester, the city was re-established as a site of particular moral concern. Anderton, born in Wigan, the westernmost district of Greater Manchester, had been a military policeman before his joining the civilian police in the 1950s. He rose to the top position in Britain's second largest police force in the mid-1970s, and became well known for his outspokenness on moral questions, underpinned by his fundamentalist Christianity.[8] He claimed publicly that God spoke to him, and helped him make moral decisions. His views on homosexuality were strikingly intolerant: he regarded the epidemic of AIDS as divine punishment for immoral behaviour. In London in 1987, he stated in an interview for *City Life*, a listings magazine, that 'everywhere I go, I see increasing evidence of people swirling about in a human cesspit of their own making' (*City Limits* 1987). He instituted periodic clean-up campaigns against prostitution, and exerted pressure on local magistrates to restrict the number of licensed bars in the city centre, as well as the number of off-licenses selling alcohol. His retirement in 1991 saw the beginning of a marked liberalisation of official attitudes to the night-time economy, including official support for the development of the so-called Gay Village.

Anderton's period in office coincided with the building of the monumental Arndale Centre, which may, in a number of curious, but important respects, be said to be the built representation of the modern moral city. A true megastructure, it incorporated not only 200 shops but department stores, restaurants and fast food outlets, parking for 1,800 cars, a 25-storey office tower, a bus station, flats and an embryonic subterranean rail station on Corporation St. for an underground line that was never built.[9] The project cost £100 million. It was designed by Hugh Wilson and Lewis Womersley, who had already built a smaller, but equally complex, megastructure for the University on Oxford Road, as well as much deck-access housing in Hulme just to the south of the city centre. Its architecture was controversial from the start.

By far the single largest building in the city centre, it necessitated the destruction of a number of familiar streets, and its cladding in relentless khaki and chocolate ceramic tiles drew unfavourable comparisons with public lavatories (Atkins 1976: 71).

To say that the Arndale represents the modern moral city may seem rather odd, given its status as a godless retail mall. But its condensation of the city centre into a single building which can be surveilled by day, and locked up by night, oddly confirms Anderton's authoritarian agenda. Its abolition of the street is not simply a design convenience, but an ideological position informed by a horror of it; in the Anglo-Saxon imagination, the city street is, after all, the locus of vice. The Arndale simplified the city into a number of discrete functions (retail, office work, car parking), which could be contained and controlled within a single structure. With the functions of the entire city centre consolidated into as single building, the Arndale's lack of a relationship to its surroundings was therefore of no consequence. As a visitor to the centre, one would enter it directly by car, bus or (in theory) suburban rail, without the mediation of the surrounding city, its comprehensiveness satisfying all the functions one required of the urban. Once satisfied one would leave again, having barely glimpsed what was left of the old city, let alone the exterior of the building.[10] Not only did the centre make no reference to its surroundings, but in its monolithic nature it assumed that no reference to the outside was needed. There was no scope here for morally dubious activity; everything could be observed and therefore regulated. Now in this scenario, like the Victorian one described above, Manchester is a sinful place that requires correction, and it is in this sense I describe it as a moral city, for it is place on which moral discourses are inscribed. It exhibits both moral problems and moral solutions; it has, it could be said, a crucial place in the *economy* of morality.

The city of consumption

I say that the retirement of James Anderton had an important effect on the development of an alternative model of city life. In fact, this had already been in process at an official level for some time: the city council, for example, ostensibly socialist, increasingly found itself advocating the use of market forces in the development of the city, an idea which in large part elevated consumer consumption. The political shift described here has been labelled the 'entrepreneurial turn' and it closely parallels, but predates, the changing attitudes of the Labour party nationally. The phrase 'entrepreneurial turn' used by the geographers Kevin Ward and Jamie Peck in *City of Revolution* refers to a shift in the political culture of the ruling Labour party in the middle of the 1980s. They mean principally a shift from a culture of resistance to the market, represented in an experiment from 1984–7 with municipal socialism, emulating already well-advanced political processes in Sheffield, Liverpool (see Chapter 5) and inner London. The experiment was led by Graham Stringer, who went on to become the leader of the council in 1984. As one of thirteen rebel left-wing councillors exiled by the local party from 1980, he had made contacts with a range of marginalised or disaffected social groups outside the usual working-class support base of the party. These community activists, feminists, gay rights campaigners and anti-racist groups formed the new constituency. As Steve Quilley has written, this had two distinct effects on the general direction of party policy after 1984, namely the elevation of 'equal opportunities' and a commitment to 'democratisation and de-centralisation' (Quilley in Peck and Ward 2002: 80). Resistance to the government of Margaret Thatcher was policy, as was the idea of solidarity with other politically similar councils. To imagine cities in any kind of competi- tion with each other was seen as capitulation to the market, and was therefore to be resisted (Quilley in Peck and Ward 2002: 82). Municipal socialism achieved little in Manchester, certainly compared with the policies on transport and housing seen in Sheffield, or – dramatically – the political resistance to conservatism seen in Liverpool where the council, under the influence of the deputy leader Derek Hatton, set an illegal budget, directly challenging central government's authority (Chapter 5). The changes to the built environment were limited too. One area in which change might have been visible was the policy of de-centralisation, which involved the creation of a network of local council offices, but this was abandoned almost before it was begun, given the huge capital expenditure it would have required.

Manchester's political élite was only weakly committed to the market. The framework documents produced by the planning department in the early 1980s, for example, conceptualise Manchester as the material product of historical processes about which one could do very little. In a 1984 document, Ted Kitchen, then head of planning, wrote fatalistically that office employment was likely to continue to decline, the number of vacant retail properties in the traditional commercial core was likely to rise, and that there was little the city council or anyone else could do about it. Planning emphasis was therefore placed on ameliorating a poor situation, rather than trying to effect structural change. Transport was a key issue – 'particular emphasis will be given to improving accessibility by car and public transport . . . all of which accords with the general plan to make the city centre easier to get to and more a pleasant place to move about in once there' (Manchester City Council 1984). Such statements were underpinned by the belief that the city centre was not an inhabited place, but a service centre for a population that resided elsewhere. Swift entrance and exit were the priorities.

According to Peck and Ward, the 'entrepreneurial turn' occurred shortly after the June 1987 election in which the Conservative party won an unprecedented third term in government. At this point it became clear to the local Labour party that municipal socialism had little electoral support, and their survival demanded 'critical co-operation' and eventually active participation with the private capital. The main principles were 'acceptance of a property-led strategy of urban regeneration', co-operation with the Central Manchester Development Corporation (CMDC) and the Training and Enterprise Council (TEC) and 'participation in competitive urban redevelopment schemes' such as City Pride and City Challenge (Quilley in Peck and Ward 2002: 84).[11] Driven by an élite, the council focused on a small number of prestige projects in the built environment which could show materially impressive results in a short space of time. These included the Bridgewater concert hall, replacing the Free Trade Hall as the home of the Hallé orchestra, the Millennium stadium intended for the Olympic Games (for which bids were made in 1996 and 2000), and a new terminal and runway at the airport (completed in 2000). The local party now emphasised material products rather than political process.

Regeneration occurred in broader cultural terms with the council's tolerance: I am thinking of the burgeoning economy around the nightclubs and bars, a process that began in the 1980s. This of itself I think may be included in the definition of the entrepreneurial turn, because its components – nightclubs, the music scene, the drug scene – invoke an entrepreneurial culture of the most brutal kind, with sudden flowerings of the most extraordinary phenomena followed by their equally sudden demise. This culture, I suggest, could extend to a sexual economy too. One the most remarkable, unforeseen phenomena of the night-time economy that developed in the 1990s was the development of the Gay Village around Canal St., a narrow lane alongside the Rochdale canal in the warehouse district of the city centre. For many years the site of prostitution, it also had a vestigial homosexual clientele in the form of the New Union pub at the southern end, and the Rembrandt half way along. The street was well known as a place where public sex was possible, especially at the northern end of the towpath in the undercroft of 111 Piccadilly, a Modernist office tower whose foundations straddled the canal (Haslam 1999: 200).[12] In the evening on Canal St., as was described by Dave Haslam, a DJ who published an eloquent account of Manchester's popular culture:

> prostitutes and cruisers mixed business and pleasure, the scene
> like something from a painting by George Grosz, rent boys running

in an out of pub doorways, transvestites tripping over the curb-
stones, the damp air filled with the cacophony of music, shouting,
screaming and half-heard whisperings.

(Haslam 1999: 201)

Now this sexual economy developed an extraordinary life of its own
throughout the 1990s, with the opening of numerous bars in which gay life
was openly on display. Much evolved from its furtive origins it was celebrated, even sublimated.[13] The first of the modern bars was Manto, 'designed
as if it had nothing to hide, a world away from the darkened dives around it'
(Haslam 1999: 201). Its glass frontage, and interior balcony overlooking the
dancefloor-like main space put the activity of cruising for partners on display,
both to the public walking along the street, and to the clients of the bar.
This pattern was elaborated by the majority of the new establishments. Not
only did these bars stage a vibrant sexual economy in which partners were
publicly transacted, but they also made money, to the extent that commercial
property along the street became among the most expensive in the city.
The Gay Village attracted the interest of both major developers and official
institutions: along with the conventional material regeneration in which the
city had long been expert, the city council and the local media both began
to advocate the success of the Gay Village. These distinct aspects of the
city's regeneration were linked by the emphasis on consumption, indeed
the spectacularisation of consumption. Almost all were concerned with the
consumption of food, drink, material goods and sex, and sometimes all
of these things at once. And by the middle of the 1990s, it all had official
sanction.

Representing the city of consumption

This chapter discusses a crucial point in Manchester's recent development, at
which for the first time in over a century, the city became an *aesthetic* project,
both in terms of the architectural interventions by private and public developers, and of the reimaging of the city undertaken by a political and business
élites. What was at stake in each case was the city's *look*. This was not only
a product of the IRA bomb that exploded on 15 June 1996 on Corporation St.
in the city's commercial heart, the largest peacetime explosion in Britain.
Rather, it was the result of a longer political process in which a left-wing city
council moved from an experiment with municipal socialism to a culture of
entrepreneurship. This 'entrepreneurial turn' in some ways anticipated the
changes in the Labour party that in 1997 finally led to its re-election as a party

of government. Manchester was not the only British city to make this change in direction. The experiences of Glasgow, Birmingham, Leeds and more recently Liverpool have many parallels, but it rethought itself more thoroughly than anywhere else, and within its own limited terms, it has been outstandingly successful. Such changes have had a profound impact on the built environment. Again, Manchester's experience has not been unique, but it has been profound. It has produced a more complete built version of the entrepreneurial city than anywhere else. It has also been in Manchester and other northern English cities that such transformations have been possible, politically and commercially: London has talked much, but done relatively little, hampered by high land prices, political weakness and restrictive planning (Hall 2002). If the entrepreneurial city exists, then, in these places, what does it look like? How is it represented architecturally? I discuss first the general architectural tropes that Manchester deploys, the newly revived hierarchy of streets and squares, vistas and landmarks. I then discuss in detail a signature building type of the new city, the luxury apartment block, in this case the architecturally remarkable, and ideologically revealing No. 1 Deansgate by Ian Simpson (Figure 9.1).

The city of consumption has a form that is distinct from the developer-led, low-tax, minimal planning environment found in London's Docklands, Cardiff Bay or for that matter Salford Quays, Manchester's own dock hinterland, all of which were developed in the 1980s. In these environments, a development framework was provided that spoke of commercial needs, but the visual appearance of the site was not considered as a whole. The result in each case was – the water element apart – an inward-looking urbanism, in which other than in a few set pieces, buildings were poorly related to each other and to their street contexts, styles were mixed, and the development as a whole only loosely related to the city context. It is an urbanism, but only intermittently urban in character.

The city of consumption, by contrast, *is* urban. It reasserts the core over the periphery, and in so doing it seeks to make urban realm reassuringly legible. This correction of the unfamiliar and anxious Modernist city had a big impact on Manchester. To have visited central Manchester at any time from the end of the Second World War until the mid-1980s would have been to visit a ruin. It had at the end of this period a tiny population: the area bounded by the main railway lines and the Mancunian Way counted just 150 people, almost all janitors and their families, this in an area which once had a thousand times as many. There were acres of derelict buildings: the old warehouse district around Whitworth and Sackville streets was almost deserted, the former Central Station a ruin, the canal basin at Castlefield filled with shopping trolleys and dead dogs. Anderton's policing policies, pursued during the 1980s

9.1

No. 1 Deansgate, Manchester, architect: Ian Simpson

further killed the life of the centre. Meanwhile, the Arndale shopping mall discussed above, the only large-scale commercial success of the centre and hence the only place with any life during the 1970s, closed its doors at 6 pm. There are many poetic accounts of this ruination: W. G. Sebald, arriving for the first time in 1966, found a place that seemed to 'ha[ve] been long since been deserted, and was now left as a necropolis or a museum'. Once 'one of the nineteenth century's miracle cities (it was) now almost hollow to the core' (Sebald 1996: 151). Statistically, the place was alive, softening the collapse of the textile trade with the growth of retail and higher education, but the life and the economic growth was in the suburbs. The 1984 city council document I refer to above seems to accept this picture of decline, seeking only to consolidate the regional centre (it tellingly avoids the use of 'city') to a manageable, contained indoor mall, locked up at the end of the working day. Its emphasis on heavy transport infrastructure – heavy rail, car parking, buses – likewise assumes a centre that may be briefly visited but not inhabited (Manchester City Council 1984).

The picture at the time of writing is rather different. The core has been reasserted in several ways, most obviously in terms of population. In 2003, the central area population approached 20,000, the size of the whole city in the late eighteenth century, at the beginning of its period of industrial growth. The repopulation of the core became council policy in the late 1980s, supported by the CMDC at the same time. As the geographer Brian Robson, has described, the policy made connections between demographic change, the reimaging of the city as a site of spectacular consumption. The council's support for city centre repopulation was aimed, he wrote,

> at stemming the population loss and hence high rate base of the city, creating a mix of housing tenures to dilute the high proportion of council-owned property within the city boundaries; bringing in a high-spending population that could support the growth of consumer-based land uses of the centre.
>
> (Robson in Peck and Ward 2002: 37)

Material support for this came principally in the form of grants to assist the purchase of land, or in the conversion of disused buildings for residential use, but the result was the rapid creation of a self-sustaining market for such development. Growth has been so rapid in this sector that land values for residential now outstrip that for any other kind of development in the city centre, a record being recently set by the volume builder Wimpey, who paid £8 million for a quarter-acre gap site, putting it on a par with New York, Tokyo and central London (*Manchester Evening News* 2002).

The core has also reasserted itself as a business location.[14] The creation through public and private means of a central housing market, and the continued relative buoyancy of the central office market, helped produce and sustain a range of new centrally located retail and leisure facilities. Shopping boomed, encouraged by the redesign of the centre after the 1996 bomb. The restaurant trade did likewise, aided by a council-promoted annual festival of food and drink. New bars opened every week through the 1990s. Most museums extended their premises and added retail and leisure compo-nents.[15] The Hallé got a new concert hall, with vast areas of circulation space in which one could shop, eat and drink, activities which the orchestra's previous home had rather discouraged. In general the city centre began, by the mid-1990s, to look as if it operated within a market economy: money was circulating, construction boomed, derelict factories became luxury flats, the centre itself got bigger especially to the immediate south, reurbanising the industrial hinterlands of Knott Mill, Castlefield and St George's. And this look of market success increasingly represented itself in the visual arts and mass media, especially television, where a generation of drama programmes (*Queer as Folk*, *Cold Feet*, *Cutting It*) provided richly textured images of a glamorous city-centre life of conspicuous consumption. Canal St., the epi-centre of the city centre's booming gay culture, replaced Coronation St. it could be said: the loft apartment replaced the working-class terrace as a metonym for the city as a whole.

These centralising processes had become, by the early 2000s, market driven, but they were earlier defined by an urban élite that included politicians, architects and property developers. The sources for this definition are a series of urban design framework documents produced by the city council and CMDC and other agencies from the late 1980s: they include *City Pride: A Focus for the Future* (1994) and *City Pride 2: Partnerships for a Successful Future*, *City Development Guide* (1995) and perhaps most import-antly the guidance provided for the international urban design competition after the 1996 bomb.

What were the design solutions that these documents offered? Let us take the 1995 *City Development Guide* as an example, for it both sum-marised a local theory of urbanism that was in operation, and it provided the design basis for subsequent documents. Broadly, what the *Guide* contained could be described in terms of the so-called new urbanism, a reassertion of traditional urban form after the traumatic irruption of Modernism in the city. Concretely, this meant the remaking of streets and squares with a legible urban hierarchy, the clear policing of the boundaries between private and public space, the use of landmarks to identify and signify the urban hierarchy, and in architecture the reassertion of more or less traditional forms of building

in which type, use and circulation are all clearly legible (a building's entrance would always be clearly marked, for example. Likewise its edges and corners) (Figure 9.2). In Europe, the new urbanism is closely associated with Léon Krier and Aldo Rossi, the former building the Poundbury extension of Dorchester for HRH Prince Charles (see Chapter 2). In the US, the new urbanism has been responsible for the town of Celebration, built for the Disney corporation near Orlando, Florida, and Seaside in the same state on the north western Mexico Gulf coast. Generally associated with a socially conservative agenda, the new urbanism rejects Modernist social engineering in favour of an acceptance, or even enhancement of the status quo. In the US in particular, new urbanist development has tended to be aimed at relatively high-income, professional families on the basis that not only can they afford to buy, but that they will most readily reproduce the social behaviour modelled by the architecture. Whatever aspects of the new urbanism are successful can then be applied to housing for lower income groups.[16]

Manchester's 1995 interpretation of the new urbanism imagined the city under the following criteria: first, a hierarchy of streets. Here the street is imagined not simply as a traffic artery, but as a social place. A major road is differentiated from a high street, a secondary street from a minor street, and a minor street from private areas within development blocks. Second was density and a mix of uses, a direct challenge to Modernist

9.2
**Housing for
The Guinness
Trust, Hulme,
Manchester
(*c.*1997), architect:
OMI Architects**

planning practice which since the Athens Charter of 1933 had sought to decongest and simplify the city, separating out ('zoning') different functions spatially. Third, the *Guide* stressed permeability: 'all streets should lead somewhere', it stated, 'streets should encourage movement . . . there should be a variety of routes through an area . . . the grain of streets should become finer around nodes of activity'. Fourth, was transport, with the emphasis on keeping visitors in the city centre, rather than speeding them away from it.[17] Fifth, was the landmark: 'public places and areas where people congregate should be emphasised as focal points.' Sixth, was 'quality', by which was meant a sympathetic and considered architectural engagement with existing urban space. Seventh, was identity, meaning the contribution urbanism might make to the way a city was understood. Eighth, was security, which is to say the belief that busy streets are essentially self-policing.[18] Ninth, was urban sustainability, which contained the implicit critique of modern urban forms for being wasteful of resources and environmentally damaging. Consistent with the new urbanist agenda, the *Guide* opened with the relatively humble statement that urban design was important for the city, but could not resolve profound economic or social problems. These would have to await larger economic solutions. But that said, a poor urbanism might hinder economic recovery, while a good urbanism might positively encourage it.

The urbanistic achievements of the city since 1996 have followed most of these principles. After the 1996 IRA bomb, the major innovation was the making of New Cathedral Street, a new pedestrian way linking, in a straight line, the Royal Exchange with the Cathedral, and making possible for the first time an axial view from St Anne's square to the Cathedral district. At the same time, new pathways were built and old ones revived along all the waterways, routes now lined from Oxford Road to Castlefield with new bars and restaurants (Figure 9.3). Capital and information supposedly flowed along these new or revived arteries, past and through the local hub of Atlas, a bar designed by Simpson and which acted for a time as a kind of clearing house of development ideas, the meeting place of developers, architects and young urbanites on their way to the clubs. The city built larger and more portentous nodes and hubs too, in Exchange Square by Martha Schwartz, around the Cathedral, in Castlefield, along Deansgate, in the Northern Quarter, in Hulme, providing at least the *look* of a city through which capital and information freely flowed. The new city represented, it might be said, Castells' idea of the space of flows, scattering the urban fabric with the international hotels, designer clothes stores and coffee bars. A variety of (mostly) symbolic bridges were made too, which imaged the flow of capital around the city: across the Bridgewater canal in Castlefield (Wilkinson Eyre 1995); across the highway to

9.3
**Dukes 92 pub,
Castlefield,
Manchester (1998)**

the airport (Wilkinson Eyre 1997); across the river Irwell, symbolically link-ing Manchester and Salford (Santiago Calatrava 1995); across the six-lane Mancunian way between the city centre and Hulme (Arca 2002); across Corporation St. to replace the one dramatically lost in 1996 (Stephen Hodder 1998) (Figure 9.4); and several across the Manchester Ship Canal.

Building the city of consumption

What I have not discussed so far has been the moral aspect to the way the city of consumption was represented. The intellectual origins of the recon-struction were, as I have pointed out, the constellation of interests around the so-called new urbanism, a tendency, which, as I described in Chapter 2, could be both socially conservative and authoritarian. The residents of Poundbury live according to a strict set of rules that govern both the exterior form of their buildings, and by extension, certain aspects of their lives as lived in public. At Manchester, the reconstruction had less to do with the desire to return to a morally certain past than the production of an environment that provided a better stage for the city of consumption. The revival of traditional urban forms such as the street and the square was a means of making consumption spectacular again, after its banishment to the hermetic and inward-looking Arndale. But the reconstruction of Manchester was not strictly traditional, for the re-establishment of a legible urban realm in the centre was accompanied by the building of a number of visually dramatic neo-Modernist structures. One of the best known of these is Urbis, a museum of urban life, designed by Ian Simpson, who along with EDAW was responsible for the masterplan of the city centre after the bomb (Figure 9.5). Set in newly made grounds between the cathedral and Victoria Station in what had been an NCP car park, it was unlike anything else in the city when built. A seven-storey triangular wedge, its tallest aspect is a curved prow, barging onto Corporation Street; Urbis sweeps around the perimeter of a roughly four-sided site, defining rather than filling it. The exterior has more public and more private sides, as it were, faced in ground glass, making it simultaneously luminous and opaque. It is intended to be a landmark. Before its design or content were finalised, Simpson spoke of his desire to give it certain formal characteristics – height, to be visible, to provide a vantage point, to sweep down, to open up, to gather, to be a sculpture (interview with Simpson, November 2001).

9.4
**Merchants Bridge,
Castlefield,
Manchester
(1998), architect:
Wilkinson Eyre**

Its exhibits consist of a travelogue-like view of a handful of world cities, which rhetorically place Manchester in the context of the world city, positing equivalence between it and São Paolo, Mumbai, Paris, Tokyo, Los

Angeles, Singapore and St Petersburg. As Mark Crinson has argued, this is more rhetorical than real, for it leaves unquestioned Manchester's actual status as a city (Crinson 2002–3: 20–3). In Engels' time, it was the greatest manufacturing city in the world; it no longer is an industrial city of global significance. And it is no longer one of the world's largest cities, as it was only a century ago; that place has been taken by cities no less than ten times its size, of which São Paolo is one. Urbis and its exhibits spectacularise the city of consumption, representing a series of world metropoles as visual tableaux, to be touristically consumed; even their negative characteristics are presented in this way, high rates of crime and poverty in the Brazilian metropolis adding local colour. On the top floor, an exhibit puts the visitor literally in the space of the tourist, through back projection placing the visitor in real time in a tour of the cities that are the museum's subject.

Urbis is a clear representation of the city of consumption, its outward form, and display modes aping those of the department store, which it will in all probability one day become.[19] Urbis, although built by a Manchester architect, and promoting a specifically local agenda – namely the city's desire to accede once more to a pantheon of vaguely defined 'world cities' – suffers from a national problem. Its financial troubles exactly parallel those of the Millennium Dome, another spectacular structure whose exhibition

9.5
Urbis, Manchester (2002), architect: Ian Simpson

programme similarly lacked definition or purpose, and whose targets for visitor figures were similarly out of step with pubic demand. The elision of the boundary between the museum and the world of commerce is something that – as I have shown in this book – is certainly a national, and in large part international, phenomenon. There are aspects of Manchester's case that are peculiarly local, however, and I will spend the rest of this chapter discussing another of Simpson's buildings in this context.

No. 1 Deansgate

No. 1 Deansgate, was the last, and most prominent piece of the post-bomb rebuilding of the city centre planned by Ian Simpson and EDAW. A fourteen-storey triangular steel and glass slab lifted above a three-storey retail podium by means of a raking transfer structure, it dominates this part of Deansgate, effectively closing the vista down Market St. (Figure 9.6). Its form is certainly demonstrative. Perhaps not a totally original form in world terms, it is a radical departure from the Portland stone neoclassical form of the few Victorian buildings that survive in the area, and is equally a contrast to the bare concrete of the Ramada hotel opposite. A residential building, it contains 88 apartments over the 14 floors, including 8 penthouses selling for between £1.25 million and £1.75 million, then a record for central Manchester.

I alight on this building out of all the new ones put up in Manchester in recent years partly because of its type; the residential apartment block is the type most representative of change. In 1990, there was practically no market for residential buildings in the central city. A decade later, it was the strongest of all property markets, to the extent that office developers were being outbid by those proposing residential development (the so-called 'slot site' in the Great Northern scheme off Deansgate is a case in point – worth £6 million as land for an office scheme, it fetched a third more because it was bought for apartments). Tall towers have become the liveliest part of this market, with, at the time of writing, about twenty such schemes in the city centre under development, and several more on the city fringes at Salford Quays.[20] Building type is indicative of a profound shift in the use of Manchester, in its understanding of itself as a city. Further, however, I am interested in the form of the building itself, because its seems to stage the specifics of this new kind of inhabitation; through its visibility, it stages the city of consumption; visibility is present, we could say in both its calculated status as landmark (it can be seen from all over the city) but perhaps more importantly in its transparency. It is this latter point that I will elaborate.

9.6
**No. 1 Deansgate,
Manchester,
architect: Ian
Simpson**

Let me say something about transparency in architecture. Transparency and modernity are linked; to build an explicitly transparent building is a sign of modernity. Modernity has, as Anthony Vidler has written, been 'haunted [. . .] by a myth of transparency' (Vidler 1992: 217). This haunting has to do with the qualities that transparency itself represents:

> transparency of the self to nature, of the self to the other, of all selves to society, and all this is represented, if not constructed from Jeremy Bentham to Le Corbusier, by a universal transparency of building materials, spatial penetration, and the ubiquitous flow of air, light and physical movement.

'To put it another way', he continues, 'transparent architecture functions as a metaphor for a new kind of society, in which nothing is hidden, and everything is open to public view' (Vidler 1992: 218). It is a materialisation of the idea expressed by Patrick Joyce that the nineteenth-century city increasingly made itself legible, open to scrutiny, and that a new kind of self was cultivated, self-aware, self-conscious, on public display (Joyce 2003: 4). Le Corbusier's architecture of the 1920s and 1930s put intimate functions on display; the bathroom and dressing rooms were elevated to become major parts of the house, while windows were designed to bring exterior views into the interior and vice versa; everything was devoted to the free movement of light, space and air – hence his horror of curtains. Transparency in this case signified a new politics of personal space. Vidler quotes Walter Benjamin, arguing for the need for transparency in architecture from the point of view of political debate:

> To live in a glass house is a revolutionary virtue par excellence. It is also an intoxication, a moral exhibitionism, that we badly need. Discretion concerning one's own existence, once an aristocratic virtue, has become more and more an affair of petit bourgeois parvenus.
>
> (Benjamin in Vidler 1992: 218)

For a particularly good built example of the rhetoric of transparency in modern architecture, I turn to the city of Brasília, built by Lúcio Costa and Oscar Niemeyer between 1957 and 1960.[21] The monumental aspects of the city are well known, a simple cross describing a monumental government axis traversed by a great highway. Less well-known in image are the residential districts, which in the central part of the city comprise groups (*superquadras*) of six to eight slab blocks on *pilotis*, with, on one side, a lattice of brick or tile covering service corridors, and on the other side a largely glazed façade opening onto a central square[22] (Figure 9.7). The point of this transparency was political. Brasília was not only a nationalistic project, but in the view of its authors a prototype of a future Brazilian society. A notoriously unequal society, despite relative tolerance in the area of race relations, Brazil could be changed by experimenting with a standardised living type for all citizens. So at Brasília, the theory was that all strata of society would live in the same kind of housing, share the same schools and public facilities. A critical adjunct to this was the form of the housing block which explicitly put its residents on display, as (supposedly) a form of social levelling – a technique which was disturbing, and possibly offensive to a middle-class Brazilian sense of propriety. James Holston describes this design feature as follows:

> Just as the elimination of ornament from the façade denies the public display of individual status in architecture, and thus achieves a levelling of private individuals in relation to the public sphere of representations, so the transparency of glass exposes the private domain – previously concealed behind ornamented walls – to a new public scrutiny. The glass transparency turns the domestic domain inside out, so to speak, by the simple technique of dissolving the barrier that prevents one from seeing what goes on inside.
>
> (Holston 1989: 184)

'The end result', continues Holston, 'is a new kind of all-public façade in which the private plays almost no role (Holston 1989: 186–7). Unsurprisingly, the glass façade was not popular, resisted by residents anxious to maintain privacy, and who objected to their lives being the object or public scrutiny and, possibly, entertainment.[23] Now here the failure of the Brazilian apartment block per se is less important than the way it identifies transparency with morality. The dissolution of private life is conterminous with an opening up to a collective life, in which equality is a key term. There can be no true equality with the emphasis on privacy – privacy must be resisted.

Let us move on forty years to the transparent façade of No. 1 Deansgate. No. 1 Deansgate shows an unusual degree of permeability to the outside. It has what the architect calls a 'buffer zone', a glazed balcony-like space surrounding the exterior of each flat, the glazing to the outside controlled electronically according to the weather: when it rains and the resi-dent is out, the windows automatically close. The extent to which the interior is visible can be controlled by the individual resident by means of steel

9.7
**Superquadras
at SQS 308,
Brasília (1959),
architect: Marcello
Campello, Sergio
Rocha, José
Ricardo Abreu,
Luiz Acioli**

louvres, but the architect clearly tempts them to expose as much of themselves as possible. Individual elements propose exhibitionism: a bath in one
of the triplex penthouses has an unimpeded view of the city, in theory putting
the bather on display to the public. The residents of the building had, at the
time of writing, furnished the 'buffer zones' of their apartments with contemporary furniture and indoor plants. Not only that, it was well-known that Fabien
Barthez and the two Neville brothers, all players for Manchester United, had
bought apartments in the building and could, with patience and luck, be seen
from the pavement outside. The extent of the glazing, and the clarity of the
views, both from the inside out, and from the outside in, are remarkable, and
invite comparison with early Modernist structures. Ludwig Mies Van der
Rohe's proposed glass tower for Berlin is a clear point of reference.

The interior of the building also proposes a redefined relationship
between work and home lives, instead of the separation Benjamin describes in
the classic bourgeois scenario. Here, rooms are built as studies or offices, and
take their stylistic cues from the workplace rather than the home. It is nothing
new to imagine a study in a residential building, but it is rare to see it have such
a clear architectural expression – and rare until now to see the architectural
lines so blurred between work and play. This conscious blurring, between interior and exterior, between work and play, can be related to the idea in Castells
of the space of flows requiring social spaces in which business may be equally
transacted as in the office. The penthouse show apartment was set up as a

faux-architectural office with perspectives of Simpson's work lining the walls, as if – in an amusing conceit – the building had been designed there.

How do we interpret this? What does transparency signify here? Does it involve the moral programme of architectural Modernism in which the boundary between public and private is rhetorically dissolved in order to make a new kind of society? Is the transparency of Simpson's building equivalent to the transparency of the façades of the apartments in the Brazilian capital? Do its residents, like the Brasilienses, seem to resent the intrusion of the outside into their private lives and seek to prevent it?[24]

The fact that they do not, thus far, suggests that a different conception of transparency operates here. Far from representing a moral programme, the transparent façade has much more in common with a department store window, where luxury goods are rendered spectacular to encourage their consumption. Indeed, the building in fact has shops at ground-floor level, and is adjacent to a new retail development containing both a Harvey Nichols, and in a nearby building, a Selfridges. The retail development is integral to the apartment complex; it provides the local stores, the local eating places, the rationale for the place being a reasonable one in which to set up home. The 'buffer zone' that is an integral part of the Simpson building has not (as at Brasília) been a cause of conflict, but much as its author intended, seemingly celebrated.[25] It is an informal dining area; most residents seem to have put dining furniture out there, which puts them on display as they eat (Figure 9.8). And residents are frequently visible from the street. The effect, the spectacularisation of consumption, exactly parallels the processes visible in department stores, or perhaps even more closely, the contemporary restaurant, in which plate-glass windows put the diners on display. The overall effect is not to bring the private and the public closer together, but, if anything, the reverse – by making consumption spectacular in this way, society becomes more, not less, fragmented, as it makes that much more visible the difference in lifestyle made possible by differences of wealth. This play of openness does something else too: in a market-orientated economy, it brings social life into the realm of the market. Dining at home, previously a private experience, an intimate and informal one that could be carried out more or less in secret, is now made the subject of public display in which the furniture, the food and manners all become matters of public attention; dining at hosme therefore takes on many of the characteristics of restaurant dining. The transparency here does not have a socially moral effect, but is about display.

The advertising copy makes clear the fact that the building's transparency does anything but make a more egalitarian society, quite the reverse: it is about establishing distance between the resident and the rest of the city

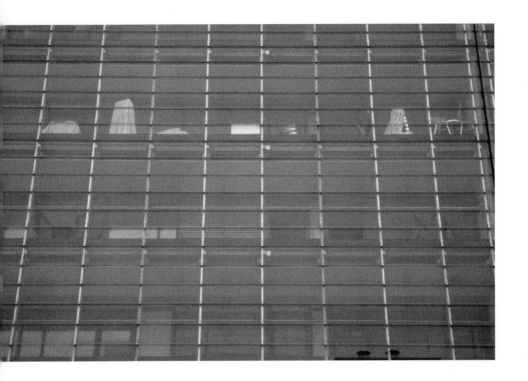

9.8
**No. 1 Deansgate,
Manchester,
architect: Ian
Simpson**

while remaining at its heart. Not only does its transparency reveal the consumer power of it residents, but the views also put the residents in a position of visual power: 'Pour a drink, step out onto the sun terrace', the copy reads,

> Put your feet up. Far off are empty hills, above you the sky. But beneath is the bustling, ant-like activity of Manchester's prime corporate, commercial and leisure district. You are all-seeing but totally uninvolved. And the feeling this brings – of deep relaxation, of unwinding – is almost palpable.
>
> (Crosby Homes 2002: 5)

Simpson, notes that at the top of the building, 'you get a fantastic aspect across the city. It's very tranquil and relaxing' (Blanchard 2002b) (Figures 9.9 and 9.10). Both Simpson and the selling agents locate the idea, albeit untheoretically, in terms of the relationship between the view and power. Both state clearly that the view over the city is a powerful one, and that those who have it gain a sense of pleasure – specifically relaxation – from this. One's relationship with the centre is already powerful – the activity is described as 'ant-like' – and elsewhere in the selling brochure, the potential

buyer is imagined as someone with actual power in that world. 'So much of your time is spent in control', it states. Being temporarily removed from the centre generates a (powerful) sense of release (Crosby Homes 2002: 5).[26]

Here in summary is a building that materialises superbly the city of consumption. Its transparency has nothing whatever to do with the moral transparency of Modernism, except for being a formal reference point; instead, it is the transparency of the department store, the glass frontage serving as a shop front for the privileged residents to display their ability to consume. And from their high apartments, their views encompass the spectrum of wealth that comprises the city, confirming them in their privileged status.

9.9
No. 1 Deansgate, Manchester; views out, architect: Ian Simpson

seen in a new light

Views of a living city are always intriguing, especially at night.
Manchester at night is breathtaking from No.1 Deansgate.

9.10
**No. 1 Deansgate,
Manchester,
architect: Ian
Simpson**

Chapter 10

Staging the city

Introduction

The starting point of this book was the English anxiety about the urban. It has been principally about ideas expressed in architectural discourse, ideas which have, as has been shown, a variable relationship with observable reality. Anxiety about the urban is expressed in various places: in the observable facts of de-industrialisation and de-urbanisation in the great cities of the north of England; in the less observable, but still widely felt, degradation of the existing public realm; in a vague feeling, a source of much journalistic angst, that the streets and squares and parks of England are becoming ever more decayed, ever more threatened, ever more compromised by traffic and violence. As we have seen, anxiety is clearly represented in architectural and other writings; in, above all, the pronouncements of Richard Rogers, who regrets the loss of 'civility' in present day London, the quality that brought his parents to the city half a century previously (Rogers 1997: 105); his later report for the British government's Urban Task Force describes traumatic urban conditions, in which English cities appear primitive and uncivilised by comparison with their European counterparts. Anxiety is strongly present in the writings of Jane Jacobs, still influential forty years after their publication (Jacobs 1962). It is present too in the work of Jacobs' contemporaries Kevin Lynch, Marshal Berman, Richard Sennett; in the statements of Norman Foster about his plans for Trafalgar Square; in the architectural polemics of Peter Rowe, Ken Worpole, Joseph Rykwert, Roger Scruton and even HRH Prince Charles. These are a few of the sources that have been frequently referred to here.

This anxiety in the English discourse about the urban has been productive of a variety of architectural responses. The urban places I have discussed in detail in the book – the Millennium Dome, Poundbury, the Albert

Dock, Trafalgar Square, the British Museum, Canary Wharf, post-bomb Manchester – exemplify different responses to the anxiety about the English city, responses that vary from the appropriation of distinctly foreign urbanisms, to the retreat into picturesque aesthetics, to the appropriation of a self-consciously modern and placeless aesthetic. What I argue in this concluding chapter is that in each of these cases, the response is essentially theatrical. In other words, each response represents a new idea of city life, but that in each case the new city is not so much materialised, as staged. The city becomes, as it were, a form of theatre. This is not, by any means, a new idea. But it bears restating in relation to contemporary urbanism, especially the English kind.

Urban theatre has been tremendously important, I argue, in establishing new corporate images for cities, and the closely related process of attracting economic investment to those places, as well as tourism – but so far it has had little impact on more widely held views of city life, and on population movements towards a more mobile, ex-urban, de-centred way of living. For at the same time as the dramatic urban initiatives described here in the central city, the government's advice on future development included recommendations to develop a vast ex-urban region to the north and east of London, stretching from Milton Keynes to Cambridge. Not only this, but there were proposals for several new airports (Bicho 2003; Hall 2003; Hetherington 2003). Underpinning this was a belief, intellectually legitimised by the planner Peter Hall, in the urban region, as opposed to the traditional form of the city (Hall 1969; Hall 1989). Theatre is therefore a superficial form, unquestionably important in broad cultural terms, but less so as a phenomenon of urbanism per se. In the following, I say more about what I mean by theatre, before moving on to describe the ways in which my examples have been essentially theatrical. I conclude with a discussion of some of the problems of the theatrical mode of urbanism.

On theatre

What am I claiming when I say that recently English urbanism tends to *stage* the city rather than build it? Starting in the broadest possible way, by theatre I mean a cultural spectacle that presupposes a performer and an audience, a spectacle with both temporal and spatial dimensions. I imagine dance, and performed music in this category, but not film, which can exist, at least in theory, without an audience. Theatre's spatial dimensions include a stage, and I would contend that the architecture of the recent past in England has been preoccupied with making stages, on which the user or inhabitant becomes a performer, whose actions can be viewed as theatre. Now the idea that the theatre and the city might be closely related has a long history, which unsurprisingly received much attention in the eighteenth century. As the architect Dennis Sharp has written 'the idea of the city as theatre is an essentially eighteenth century one' (Sharp 1989: 59).

The historian John Brewer has described how in England at that time, the theatre was a focus of profound anxieties about public life. It was the subject of considerable hostility in what he terms the 'Protestant consciousness'. The stage was thought of 'as a place of trickery and deceit, full of illusions and magic, similar to those which the Roman Catholic Church had used to bamboozle ignorant observers' (Brewer 1997: 332). Tourists to England, he continues 'came to see the English stage as a microcosm of English society, a place which accorded much liberty to the ordinary man' though which was also famous for appalling rudeness and licentiousness (Brewer 1997: 352). As Brewer goes on to describe, an argument also elaborated by Stallybrass and White (1986), the theatre becomes a focus of attempts to order urban English society. It was not the 'only site of this process' but perhaps the most important one given the very close identification between it and urban life. The aim, the 'great labour of bourgeois culture', Stallybrass and White continue, was 'the creation of a sublimated public body without smells, without coarse laughter, without organs, separate from the Court and the Church on the one hand, and the market square, alehouse, street and fairground on the other' (Stallybrass and White 1986: 93–4).

Richard Sennett, in *Fall of Public Man*, theorised these eighteenth-century phenomena to help explain the historically close relationship between the city and the theatre. Why should we regard them as so closely linked? Sennett writes that the affinity between the two is 'logical' given what he terms the 'expressive experience' in both realms (Sennett 1977: 37). He continues in more detail:

> First the theatre shares a problem, not with society in general, but with a peculiar kind of society – the great city. The problem is one of audience – specifically how to arouse belief in one's appearance among a milieu of strangers. Second, there can arise in a great city rules for making believable appearances before strangers that have a continuity of content with the rules governing response to the stage at the time. The audience can thus play a common role in both realms. Third, to the extent a common problem of audience is solved through a common code of believability, a public geography is produced, according to two criteria of publicness: the

world external to immediate surroundings and personal loyalties becomes consciously defined, and movement through diverse social circumstances and groups of strangers with the aid of this common code becomes comfortable. Fourth, to the extent that a public geography exists, social expression will be conceived of as presentation to other people of feelings which signify in and of themselves, rather than as representation to other people of feeling present and real to each self.

(Sennett 1977: 38–9)

What Sennett describes here are certain problems of audience and reception common to both the city and the stage. In both realms, to properly exist one must be, as he puts it, believable. One must, in other words act in a way that is convincing to others, and which makes sense. This condition of believability is attained through codes and conventions, which if adhered to properly, lose their distinction as codes per se, so that what is perceived signifies directly. To put it another way, social expression under normal conditions comes to seem natural and unmediated, as does acting: its condition as representation becomes, as it were, obscure. Sennett is not thinking here specifically of architecture, although what he says clearly has architectural implications. Specifically, if what he says is right, then architecture becomes a frame for theatrical action, which is to say a stage set.

Now this idea of architecture as theatre is very strongly stated in many of the sources I have cited in this book, and it is worth elaborating in some detail who says what exactly in this regard, and when. Beginning chronologically, I will mention first Jacobs' very influential *Death and Life of Great American Cities*, cited with approval by the very different figures of Rogers and Scruton (Jacobs 1962; cited in Rogers 1997, Scruton 1994). Its account of the traditional city form based on the author's experience of living in Greenwich Village, deploys, in one famous passage, the metaphor of the dance to describe the character of the street-life in the neighbourhood. It is

an intricate ballet in which the individual dancers and ensembles all have distinctive parts which miraculously reinforce each other and compose a harmonious whole. The ballet of the city sidewalk never repeats itself from place to place, and in any one place is always replete with new improvisations.

(Jacobs 1962: 60–1)

She continues in some detail:

I know the deep night ballet and its seasons best from waking long
after midnight to tend a baby and, sitting in the dark, seeing the
shadows and hearing the sounds of the sidewalk. Mostly it is a
sound like infinitely pattering snatches of party conversation and,
about three in the morning, singing, very good singing. Sometimes
there is sharpness and anger or sad, sad weeping, or a flurry of
search for beads broken. One night a young man came roaring
along, bellowing terrible language at two girls whom he had apparently picked up and who were disappointing him. Doors opened, a
wary semi-circle formed around him, not too close until the police
came. Out came the heads too, along Hudson Street, offering
opinion, 'Drunk, Crazy, a wild kid from the suburbs'.

(Jacobs 1962: 63)

In this account, Jacobs uses the metaphor of the dance to explain what she
regards as the underlying order beneath the apparent chaos of the traditional
city. It is a rhetorical means of explaining the value of traditional city form to
a reading public whom, she imagines, to be sceptical of it. It is a carefully
chosen metaphor, and its elaboration over several pages in the book demands
that it be taken seriously. It also elaborates an important subject position
on the part of the observer. Jacobs may be a part of her neighbourhood, but
the use of the theatrical metaphor puts her in the position of a privileged
observer – in effect a theatregoer – for whom the city is an entertaining
spectacle. The traumatic events she alludes to in the second passage – the
anger and sadness, and the violence of the young man – do not actually
threaten the observer at all, but provide an experience of threat that (as Freud
described) is a means of letting off steam, of having the necessary experience
of danger without any threat to one's own person.[1]

Continuing from Jacobs chronologically, we find much use of the
theatrical metaphor in the work of the *Architectural Review* and its circle
in the immediate post-war period. The articles on the picturesque and on
Townscape by de Cronin, Hastings and Gordon Cullen are premised on the
idea of the theatre. In the special issue on Italian Townscape (discussed in
Chapter 4), the entire point of the exercise is described as 'good or bad
theatre'; architecture per se scarcely matters. Hastings introduces the issue
by describing an impressionistic photograph of a fountain in the following way:

Thus the scene above. Is it St Peter's? Who can tell? Who cares?
What matters is the bowler hat raised in silhouette against heaven
and man, the makebeliever, pushed back where he belongs – on
the set – behind a glittering screen of H_2O.

(*Architectural Review* 1962: 382)

In a later discussion of the townscape of Sabbioneta, Hastings writes:

> there can be no more doubt about it, we have walked straight onto
> the stage. What's more the curtain's up and the scene set for
> Montagues and Capulets, or rather mummers and mystery players
> – they performed in the street in the middle ages with conse-
> quences almost certainly fruitful for townscape.
>
> (*Architectural Review* 1962: 439)

These are commentaries on images, and the images by Hastings' wife
confirm the theatrical metaphor, emphasising the city as stage set. The issue
is replete with empty piazzas, with occasional figures who are represented for
their theatrical potential; ambiguous and often mysterious, like the sinister
figure in sunglasses on page 428 of the article, they imply a narrative structure
that is never exactly revealed. This view of the city as theatre is confirmed
in Hastings' sometime collaborator, Gordon Cullen, whose concept of
Townscape posited the city as a stage set inhabited by colourful performers.
I discussed examples of this in Chapter 2. There is, for example a highly
ambiguous photograph of a man in a doorway, and a textual analogy
comparing Townscape to a formal dinner party, in which the setting stages
theatrical relations between individual players ('It is found that Miss X's sharp
but good-natured wit is just the right foil to Major Y's somewhat simple
exuberance. And so on. It begins to be fun. Conformity gives way to the
agreement to differ within a recognised tolerance of behaviour' (Cullen 1961:
11)). Another example of the theatrical metaphor in use in the circle of the
Architectural Review includes the book that emerged from the CIAM 8 conference, titled *The Heart of the City* (Tyrwhitt, Sert and Rogers 1952). Here the
volume was introduced with a cartoon by Saul Steinberg of the Piazza San
Marco in Venice, where gesticulating waiters and strutting pigeons become
indecipherable from each other. In the text, Philip Johnson and the editor of
the *Architectural Review*, J. M. Richards, describe the attractions of the
theatre of American drugstores and Italian piazzas respectively.

These related ideas about Townscape from the immediate post-
war period are underpinned by a belief in the city as a form of theatre. In
recent years in England, as this book has made clear, they have been most
clearly taken up by Richard Rogers, whose images and text describing the
possible transformation of London's civic spaces articulate a view of the city
as theatre. 'The public domain is the theatre of an urban culture', he writes. 'It
is where citizenship is enacted, it is the glue that can bind an urban society'
(Rogers 1997: 16). On the same theme he states 'democracy finds its

physical expression in the open-minded spaces of the public realm, in the quality of its street life. Central to this is the way its buildings contain or act as backdrop to the spontaneous and chaotic enactment of everyday life' (Rogers 1997: 152). He writes of his enjoyment of cities'

> combination of ages, races, cultures and activities, the mix of community and anonymity, familiarity and surprise, even their sense of dangerous excitement [. . .] their grand spaces as much as the animation that simple pavement cafes bring to the street, the informal liveliness of the public square, the mixture of workplaces and shops and homes that make living neighbourhoods.
>
> (Rogers 1997: 15)

In these statements, which are, as I have argued, close to the views of those of the British government, the idea of the city as theatre is elaborated further to include the idea of democracy. The earlier concepts of city as theatre, in Jacobs and (especially) the *Architectural Review* tend to stop short of any political justification for their belief in the public realm. For Jacobs, the urban theatre she advocates is, besides being for her personally more attractive, a means of increasing personal safety for individual residents. For Hastings and his colleagues at the *Review*, urban theatre is rarely presented as anything more than a means of making the city into a pleasurable spectacle for consumption by the bourgeois tourist – nowhere is this truer than in the special issue on Italy. Rogers' work incorporates many of these values – indeed his city is invariably only described in terms of the pleasures of the bourgeois realm, such as drinking in pavement cafés, going to concerts, strolling in gardens – but he imbues them with the sense that they contribute to the enactment of democracy. The pleasurable act, therefore, of cappuccino drinking in a pretty square is a means of enacting the public realm, and confirming the political condition of democracy. The act is, as he puts it, 'the physical expression' of democracy. Although there are clearly problems with this idea – not least that the pavement café is as typical a feature of totalitarian regimes as it is of western-type democracies – the idea that urban theatre is somehow the physical enactment of civilisation has a distinguished history.[2] See, for example Habermas (1989) and Arendt (1958). This is not, obviously, a complete survey of the idea of the city as theatre, but I hope to have shown that it has a history, and that in terms of the English city, it is pervasive as a theory.

English urbanism as theatre

Thinking specifically about the places I have described in this book, how do they exist in terms of theatre? Let me provide a brief survey. The ideas of picturesque urbanism in Chapters 2 and 4, the village of Poundbury and the Mediterranean urban models, are straightforwardly theatrical as their authors make clear. In the case of Poundbury, the design of the centre of the town by Léon Krier is an exceptionally clear example of a stage set, the market hall in particular being a place for the acting out of traditional forms of assembly.

Milton Keynes (Chapter 3) is a different case, but arguably no less theatrical. It is in one sense the most realistic of the places I discuss, in that the plan tries to accommodate actually existing behaviours and modes of living. Hence the emphasis on motorised circulation, through the system of roads, and the refusal of neighbourhood structures. As I argued, this plan attempted to formalise contemporary living styles that had emerged, but in a piecemeal fashion in the most industrialised societies. But the form of the plan spectacularises such modes of existence, making circulation self-conscious; it sublimates it, theatricalises it, so inhabitants become performers on a stage. The city does not (unselfconsciously) take existing architectural forms and put them in a new place, but it makes something new that inevitably draws attention to itself and makes the city into an object of consumption.

The Albert Dock, Liverpool, turns a previously obscure industrial building into a theatrical spectacle for consumption by tourists, staging, most commentators have pointed out, a deracinated version of the historical past (see Buchanan 1988). Trafalgar Square, as I argued in Chapter 6, stages the idea of civility. Formalising a previously ragged and insecure place, it stages the idea of a civilised public life. The images of the remodelled square provided by architects are explicit about this purpose; a leisured public stroll amiably about a neoclassical stage, performing civility. Canary Wharf provides a very different kind of stage set, a spectacle of modernity that could, implicitly, be anywhere. Its architects and tenants operate globally, and the development closely resembles those by the same architects in the US and Asia. Canary Wharf, like the World Financial Center in New York, stages modernity and efficiency and the flow of capital – as do, in different ways, the Great Court of the British Museum (Chapter 8) and the remodelled area around New Cathedral Street in central Manchester (Chapter 9). All these places are in different ways theatrical. All stage the city, or otherwise put it on show; all make the city self-conscious; all in some way force the visitor to define him or herself as a spectator or performer, or both.

Problems with theatre

Perhaps theatricality simply is the condition of city architecture, to extend Sennett's argument that the city and the theatre are inextricably linked. But there are conceivably models of urban architecture that are unspectacular. For example, the interest in process in architecture in the late 1960s threw up models of development which were anything but spectacular – Peruvian *barriadas*, Brazilian *favelas*, and the temporary architecture of protest in the US all became objects of considerable interest (see Hughes and Sadler 2000). Or for an example in the developed world, Reyner Banham's discussion of Los Angeles (1972) revealed a city that undoubtedly had spectacular elements, but whose principal characteristic was an unselfconscious kitsch, seemingly freed from the need to signify anything. This interest in unself-conscious forms of building, more concerned with process than a finished result, and more often than not eschewing the use of architects, is opposed to the idea of the city as theatre as described here.[3] There exists therefore an alternative to theatre in models for thinking about the urban; there needs to be one too, because theatre as a model has a number of serious problems; what follows is the beginning of a critique.

What is wrong with theatre? To begin with, there is the puritan critique of it as an idea. As Brewer points out in his analysis of eighteenth-century English culture, the theatre is marked by very considerable hostility: it is a popular cultural form, but a poorly regarded one; its productions are regarded as immoral and impure, and its audiences little better (Brewer 1997: 352). But a more profound critique concerns its emphasis on the world of appearances. For the philosopher Jean-Jacques Rousseau, it was precisely the theatrical character of urbanism – its concern for the world of appearances, its dissimulation, and its essentially leisured quality that made the city a morally undesirable place to be. Hence the lack of theatres in Calvinist Geveva. In Sennett's *Fall of Public Man*, Rousseau's position is neatly summarised:

> the great city is a theater. Its scenario is principally the search for reputations. All city men become artist of a particular kind: actors. In acting out a public life they lose contact with natural virtue. The artist and the great city are in harmony and the result is a moral disaster.
>
> (Sennett 1977: 119)

This view of Rousseau's was developed and expanded in much more recent times by the American art critic Michael Fried, who, in a much cited essay 'Art and Objecthood' of 1967, argued that art and theatre were naturally opposed: 'theatre is now the enemy of art', he wrote; theatre was a corrupt, impure art form which had the power to corrupt other cultural forms, and therefore had to be resisted – though, he argued, it had infected the practice of sculpture, with disastrous results, specifically Minimalism (Fried 1967).

The moral dimension to this critique of theatre is questionable, with its roots in anti-Catholicism, and an understanding of purity that conflicts with postmodern theories of art. Indeed, it now seems only reactionary to pursue the idea of purity in the arts; bizarre to wish to forbid any of the arts on these grounds. Yet there may be something in these old anti-theatrical arguments. The postmodern approach to the arts, despite its claims to heterogeneity, can be an oddly totalising one, reducing the visual arts to a play of surfaces alone. Postmodern architecture may be a good example of the limitations of it in terms of material practices. It was a necessary stylistic move as a means of combating a debased and unpopular Modernism, and its initial appearance spoke of an embrace of heterogeneity. But it quickly became a style, which did little more than dress modern structures in historical clothes. In the same way, to describe the city only in terms of the play of surfaces, as pure spectacle, is an oddly reductive way to describe the city. The city of spectacle becomes (in the words of Christine Boyer):

> a place of escape, a wonderland that evades reality, for there is nothing more to think about in pure entertainment. There is no outside world, no place from which we feel alienated, for this formalistic city is known and comfortable; it is above all a place to enjoy oneself.
>
> (Boyer in Ellin 1996: 142)

If this is right then the appeal to city life in such writers as Jacobs and Sennett is misguided. They celebrate the traditional city and its spectacular life, but they tend to disregard the fact that the spectacle is a function of distinct historical circumstances. They wish to recreate the traditional city by means of attention to its spectacular aspects alone, without attention to the underlying facts that produced it in the first place; what they propose, in other words, may be said to confuse effect with its cause. The focus of attention on the spectacular city is a limited reading of the city, as limited as postmodern architecture's appropriation of the historical façade.

I want to turn now to the question of anxiety. In my opening remarks, I argue that the theatrical turn in the modern English city is a response to the trauma of the loss of the urban, through de-industrialisation, depopulation and related processes. Now I want to suggest that an important, further problem with theatre as a model for city building is that it is – in this case – essentially neurotic, born of the compulsion to repeat the trauma. In Freud's thinking on psychological trauma, he notes the propensity of neurotic patients to unconsciously re-enact the moment of greatest pain, typically in the form of dream, but also in the form of neurotic behaviours driven by unconscious impulses. Freud writes of the desire to repeat:

> the traumatic neuroses give a clear indication that a fixation to the moment of the traumatic accident lies at their root. These patients regularly repeat the traumatic situation in their dreams; where hysteriform attacks occur that admit of an analysis, we find that the attack corresponds to a complete transplanting of the patient into the traumatic situation.
>
> (Freud 1977: 274–5)

In psychoanalytical terms, the compulsion to repeat the city as theatre might be said to be neurotic: it is a desire to repeat the trauma of the loss of the city; its return in the form of (unreal) theatre is the equivalent of the representation in dream, or other appearance in the unconscious. Specifically in terms of (say) Trafalgar Square, it might be said that the desire to remake it in formal terms, to represent a civilised public life, re-enacts the trauma of its loss. Such a public world (as Jacobs and other make clear) is receding or actually gone, and to remake the space in which it occurred makes a neurotic memorial of it. Obviously this hypothesis cannot be proved one way or the other, and some readers may object to the use of psychoanalytical ideas so directly. Nevertheless I hope to have shown that in terms of the language used by architects and planners, we can speak of both trauma, and a desire to return to the site of that trauma in order to re-enact it; these new public spaces are surrounded by a discourse about loss. If this is right, then I suggest that merely revisiting the site of the trauma out of compulsion will do nothing to restore the loss; it merely underlines the fact that the loss has occurred. These theatrical public spaces arguably therefore only serve the neuroses of their authors; in no way do they restore the genuine urban life they are supposed to. Real life – if we can speak of such a thing – I think no longer occurs in these spectacularised old centres, but as commentators as different as Marc Augé, Reyner Banham, Rem Koolhass, Lars Lerup and Martin Pawley have argued, on the unspectacular urban fringes, in the airports, on the urban freeways, in the business parks.

The final problem of theatre is that it turns itself into a product for consumption by a necessarily privileged audience. This was explicit in Jacobs, whose account of the theatre of the night in her neighbourhood puts the reader in the position of one who can enjoy the violence and disorder of the city without being affected by its consequences. It is explicit in the much earlier writings of Le Corbusier on theatre. In a speech from the thirties, translated and reprinted in the *Architectural Review* in 1989 in a special issue of the journal about theatre and architecture, Le Corbusier describes his entrance to Brazil:

> We landed by zeppelin at Pernambouc and I was struck by the sight of Negroes hanging from the cables of this hilarious instrument [. . .] and these Negroes were starving [. . .] I said 'Minister, do not build a theatre for travelling theatre companies. What you need above all are theatrical means, the boards. So put up stages everywhere in your immense, gargantuan country, so that people can create their own theatre, for themselves, at any time.
>
> (Le Corbusier 1989: 80)

Here, dramatically, the city's inhabitants become players who perform for the benefit of an audience who in this case is literally raised above them, in that most theatrical means of transport, the airship. The poverty-stricken condition of the players is a matter of curiosity rather than urgent attention. Their picturesque nature in this state deserves, Le Corbusier thinks, enhancement rather than amelioration. They should be provided with theatres in order that they better perform their picturesque condition. I alight on this curious example to show that the treatment of the city as theatre has a long history that always invokes a superior position on the part of the viewer; to invoke the city as theatre is never value free.

In this regard, Marshall Berman raises two issues with Jacobs in his book *All that is Solid Melts into Air* (1983). First, he thinks that her invocation of the metaphor of the dance to describe the street-life of her neighbourhood is 'misleading' in terms of her desire to represent its spontaneity:

> the years of élite disciplined training required for this sort of dance, its precise structures and techniques of movement, its intricate choreography, were worlds away from the spontaneity, openness and democratic feeling of the Jacobean street.
>
> (Berman 1982: 318)

But it is also an oddly revealing metaphor, as it confirms Jacobs' essentially privileged position in the scheme she describes, in which the neighbourhood seems to exist for her pleasure. The same idea is confirmed a little later when

Berman suggests that her view of the world is essentially a picturesque one, an urban pastoral. She insists, he writes

> on a vibrant neighbourhood with a mix of shops and residences, with constant activity on the sidewalks, with easy surveillance of the streets from within houses and stores, there will be no crime. As we read this, we wonder what planet Jacobs can possibly have been thinking of.
>
> (Berman 1982: 324)

Conclusions

Berman's critique of Jacobs (a rare thing in itself) usefully points up the fantasy element in much contemporary urbanism. As I have argued, in different ways the urbanistic schemes that I have described all theatricalise the city rather than build it; they are primarily concerned with the play of surfaces, while in quite unspectacular places, mostly on the city's fringe, the nature of the city's core economic and social activity continues to change and mutate. I see no reason to change this view, in spite of the apparent re-centralisation of English cities during the 1990s. The spectacular public architecture of that period was accompanied, for the most part by flat or gently growing city economies and populations. Even the relatively rapid growth of central London towards the end of that decade did not in any way match the projected growth on the outer fringes of the conurbation, particularly the axis from Milton Keynes to Cambridge.[4] The 1990s in England produced a convincing look of (re-)urbanisation, which resembled that of other states that remade their cities in the same decade, but the underlying demographic patterns of England suggested continuing de-urbanisation (see Schoon 2001). England's cities remained for the most part sluggish performers by comparison with (say) Spanish cities, especially Barcelona or Madrid; neither did they register the astonishing, albeit mostly suburban, growth of cities in the American south and west, among them Atlanta and Los Angeles. The booming English economies were generally not urban, but concentrated in small settlements with good connections to London – for example, Oxford, Cambridge and the M4 corridor.

I suggest that it is the knowledge of this continued decline that has been productive of a panic, which in turn has led to a superficial, theatrical reassertion of the urban in terms of design solutions alone. The effect of this parallels that of the Disney theme parks, Disneyland in Los Angeles and Disney World near Orlando, Florida, which have been described in detail by

Sharon Zukin. In both cases, Zukin finds the urban very literally made into spectacle, a replacement for what no longer exists outside the park's boundaries. At Disneyland, the Main Street USA exhibit does this most explicitly, reconstructing the form of the once ubiquitous American town centre as a series of storefronts; she argues – somewhat hyperbolically, it must be said – that the exhibit represents what can no longer be seen in reality. It has become a monument to a lost urban way of life (Zukin 1991).

Now the spectacularisation of the English city has taken place for different reasons. Some of the development has been led by the profit motive, but all of the projects I have discussed have been public projects in one sense or another: At one extreme there is 'World Squares for All', which to begin with expressly forbade a commercial element; at the other there is the No. 1 Deansgate development in Manchester, a block of private apartments for sale. But even here the land was publicly owned, and the scheme had to conform to a masterplan formulated by a public agency (Peck and Ward 2002: 133–54). As I hope to have shown, there is a moral imperative at work in the schemes I have discussed; the attempt to reassert the urban realm may have been unconsciously motivated, as I suggest above, by a neurotic compulsion to return to the site of past trauma – but the superficial motivation has been stated in humanistic terms. The oath of Athenian citizens has been much quoted.

But if this is all true, the results of these schemes are oddly comparable to Disney's. What we get is a series of façades, of stage sets, in which the performers are inevitably those with time on their hands – tourists, the young, the leisured. To limit the experience of the city to these groups is a mistake. What I am arguing for, finally, is not an end to these spectacular projects – an end to them will come soon enough, as sure as they will be in favour once again in the future – but a more realistic, less neurotic way of conceptualising the city. The spectacularisation of city life has been a refreshing, and perhaps necessary response to the technocratic and functionalist approach to the city of the 1970s, but it has its limits, as this book has shown. Let us think about margins as much as centres, of work as much as play, of ways of being in the city that do not correspond to bourgeois forms of entertainment – and let us find ways of imagining the city in these terms as well.

Notes

1 The anxious city

1 The largest peacetime bomb explosion in mainland Britain occurred on Corporation St., central Manchester on 15 June 1996, devastating a large part of the city's retail space. The reconstruction and improvement of the centre took four years and cost around £1 billion. For an account of the process, see Peck and Ward 2002: 133–54.

2 By the end of the decade, there were at least six low-cost airlines operating from Britain to continental European cities, offering fares at sometimes extraordinary discounts. Their success was in marked contrast to that of the traditional airlines – the national carriers of Belgium and Switzerland collapsed in 2002, while the Irish low-cost carrier Ryanair saw its market capitalisation exceed that of British Airways.

3 At the time of writing, planning permission for a 47-storey tower designed by Ian Simpson on Manchester's Deansgate had been granted. The tower was to include a Hilton hotel, and over 200 apartments. Its height far exceeded that of any other residential tower in the UK.

4 Kuala Lumpur built the Petronas Towers, the world's tallest; Chongqing, now thought to be the world's largest city, is at the time of writing, building 1,000 km of new motorways, and 600 km of new railways.

5 I have avoided the use of the word 'regeneration' here, the usual term to describe recent urban changes. 'Regeneration' is an ideological term, used by politicians and professions of the built environment to imply that change is organic, and has continuity with the past. I believe that urban change in England has been much more disruptive, and discontinuous than 'regeneration' allows; to use it as a term would be to suggest complicity with a political programme.

6 None of these terms is of course fixed (see Marwick 1980 for an overview of the problem). But what I mean by a revolution in bourgeois taste can be illustrated by the change in patterns of residential living by young professionals living in commuting distance of major English cities. In the 1970s, they often aspired to a pseudo-rustic life on the periphery, an anti-urban existence in the clearest symbolic, if not actual terms. In the mid-1990s, property markets allowing, they sought centrally located apartments decorated in a minimalist style. This is a generalisation, but can be supported by the evidence of private housebuilders: none of the major companies had urban divisions in the 1970s, while almost all did by the end of the 1990s.

7 Joyce (2003) makes a similar argument about the nineteenth-century city.

8 The decline is yet more marked if one considers only the inner city. The Manchester of 300,000 that Engels described in the 1830s had simply vanished by the 1970s, dispersed to outlying suburbs and other towns.

9 In the case of Berlin, population decline has accelerated since 1989, in spite of the vast building works associated with the city's reunification.

10 The Netherlands was, and is, Europe's most densely populated nation.

11 Key texts here would be Dickens, *Hard Times* (1854); Gaskell, *Mary Barton* (1848) and *North and South* (1855); Lawrence, *Sons and Lovers* (1913). See discussion of the idea of the industrial city in Williams 1973: 215–32.

12 English cities do not, typically, contain large bourgeois populations close to their centres, and consequently lack the spaces of socialisation and consumption that such populations require. The English bourgeois has been for much of the twentieth century suburban rather than urban, its spaces of socialisation the golf club, the country pub and the sub- or ex-urban shopping mall. Manchester, Birmingham, Leeds and Liverpool are nearly all inner city, wealth residing on the urban fringe rather than in the centre. Continental European cities tend to concentrate wealth at the centre, by contrast. In the US, despite the hollowing of urban cores, many cities, even quite small ones, have maintained a bourgeois centre albeit not on the European scale: see Washington DC, Boston, Philadelphia, even Atlanta.

13 Hutton does not cite Wiener, and I can find no other direct connection between these texts – but their argument about the city is strikingly similar.

14 See Schoon 2001 for a detailed elaboration of this thesis. Each chapter of *The Chosen City* takes a different aspect of contemporary urban life, arguing that its corroded state derives from the failure of the wealthy to participate.

15 Burgeoning because of the rapidly rising property values in the centres of English cities since the mid-1990s. Increases of 100 per cent over five years were commonplace, not only in London.

16   There is perhaps no psychic phenomenon which is so unconditionally reserved to the city as the blasé outlook [. . .] just as an immoderately sensuous life makes one blasé because it stimulates the nerves to their utmost reactivity until they finally can no longer produce any reaction at all, so, less harmful stimuli, through the rapidity and contradictoriness of their shifts, force the nerves to make such violent responses, tear them apart so brutally that they exhaust their last reserves of strength and, remaining in the same milieu, do not have time for new reserves to form. This incapacity to react to new stimulations with the required amount of energy constitutes in fact the blasé attitude which every child of a large city evinces when compared with the products of the more peaceful and more stable milieu.

(Simmel in Leach 1997:73)

17   Given the absolute symmetry of the four towers, it is quite impossible to get your bearings in this lobby [. . .] I will take as the most dramatic practical result of this spatial mutation the notorious dilemma of the shopkeepers on the various balconies. It has been obvious since the opening of the hotel in 1977 that nobody could ever find any of these stores, and even if you once located the appropriate boutique, you would be most unlikely to be as fortunate a second time.

(Jameson in Leach 1997: 245)

18 I emphasise that this is not an architecturally determinist argument. England's city spaces may, I believe, be anxiety producing, but because of the way its citizens have learned to inhabit city space rather than anything inherent in the architecture.

19 All Manchester's new public spaces are anchored by at least one retail development. Public spaces punctuate a more or less continual experience of shopping.

20 Ecological catastrophe is the particular anxiety of Rogers' *Cities for a Small Planet* (1997). The statistics on the energy consumption of large cities are indeed impressive, although it is nowhere made clear that cities in their current state consume *more* energy than their equivalent populations living in smaller concentrations.

Notes

21 See for example Radio 4 (2003) *Costing the Earth*, 31 July in which over a 30-minute documentary, the contemporary redevelopment of Birmingham was contrasted unfavourably with that of Rotterdam and Frankfurt.

22 Their messages read, respectively: 'Christians and those of many other faiths in the United Kingdom and from around the world were united in celebration at this New Year marking the beginning of the third millennium since the birth of Jesus Christ [. . .]' (Millennium Experience 2000: 5); 'a baby is born – and your whole world changes. The birth of Jesus even changed how much of the world measured time. These millennium events recall that birth – like a two thousandth birthday party!' (Millennium Experience 2000: 6).

23 Like the Millennium Dome, this was the largest in the world when built. It measured 365 feet in diameter, and was 100 feet high. It also contained a variety of ill-defined, humanistic exhibits. Formally, it differed somewhat from the later design: it was based around a central box ring girder, defining the circumference of the Dome, supported by 24 steel-lattice struts. It was surfaced in an aluminium alloy. The struts are superficially similar to those in the Rogers building, although their deployment was not. The Dome of Discovery was demolished in March 1952 after only 11 months.

24 Power was devolved to the Scottish Parliament and Welsh Assembly during the first New Labour government, and referenda were planned for devolution of some English regions in the second term.

25 The Dome was meant as a national, which is to say, British, project. The anxieties it raises seem to me however peculiarly English ones, and its authors little concerned with the non-English aspects of Britishness. And by this time, it should be noted that Wales, and particularly Scotland, were seeking their own distinct symbols of architectural identity.

26 Davey writes here of 'Britain', although his position is uncritically Anglocentric.

27 There was unquestionably a media campaign against the Dome during the year of its operation. However unfair this may have been, what is important here is the fact that the campaign was conducted in terms of anxiety, both in the metaphorical sense of what the building represented (or failed to represent), and in terms of the visitor experience.

28 There was a series of high-profile sackings during its operation. Jennie Page, the chief executive of the New Millennium Experience Company, was replaced in February by the flamboyant P. Y. Gerbeau. Three chairmen of the company came and went within four months.

29 Much of the Greenwich peninsula has now been redeveloped. Certainly, industrial decay must now be consciously sought out, and one is more likely to be struck by the modernity of the public infrastructure, and the number of new apartments.

30 This is a generalisation, obviously, but the evidence of the professional journals in the mid part of the century is of a profession little concerned with the exterior appearance of buildings than of their function.

31 I imply that New York is not an American city. In its density, its heterogeneity, and its relationship with the car, it is much more like a European one.

32 Indeed it could be argued that some of the new public spaces in English cities have exacerbated the anti-social tendencies in English urban life. The new spaces of Millennium Square (Leeds), Concert Square (Liverpool) and Deansgate Locks (Manchester) for example, have the appearance of places meant for polite behaviour, but their concentrations of bars orientated to the very serious consumption of alcohol, makes them unusable after dark for the very young, the very old and families.

33 The relationship between architecture and social order is complex and ambiguous, and a constant theme here. Patrick Joyce's work on the nineteenth-century city, which describes social liberalism as a form of discipline, is an important source. See Joyce (2003).

34 It also needs to be said that the relationship between Manchester City Council and the archi-tectural profession has been unusually close: the RIBA has been effusive in its praise for MCC as a client, twice awarding it prizes for its support for architectural design. No other English city yet approaches Manchester's obsession with urban design, although others may show more impressive results in the less-specific field of regeneration. Design is my focus here, however.

35 Liverpool was awarded the title. The other competitors were Oxford, Birmingham, Belfast and Bradford. Liverpool's bid was led by the theatre impresario Sir Bob Scott, who helped secure Manchester's 2002 Commonwealth Games.

2 The picturesque city

1   For a summary of such tendencies see especially Ellin 1996 and Frampton 1992: 290–300.

2   The Tesco and Sainsbury chains build their out-of-town stores to resemble giant oast-houses and barns.

3   This is itself underwritten by a deterministic view of architecture. Krier agues 'function follows form' (Frampton 1992: 297).

4   This is certainly true of the *Architectural Review*, the *Architect's Journal*, the *RIBA Journal*, and to a lesser extent, *Building*. The great exception is *Architectural Design*, which made a point of supporting the historicist revivals of the 1980s.

5   *The Englishness of English Art* is based on the Reith lectures broadcast by the BBC in 1955.

6   No doubt an exaggeration, but the picturesque was, and is, very widely understood as an aesthetic mode in England.

7   For a discussion of the Grand Tour, and its relations to aesthetics, see Chapter 3.

8   This idea is developed at greater length by the historian John Barrell in *The Dark Side of the Landscape* (1980).

9   Reynolds' remarks might be compared with John Ruskin's later critique of Gower Street, London, for its regularity. My thanks to Mark Crinson for drawing my attention to this.

10 Reynolds thought architecture should be perceived only as 'scenery', the 'background of a picture' (Hussey 1927: 187).

11 For Foster on Cullen, see Jenkins (2000) 616–8. Schoon approvingly cites the imaginary new town 'Civilia', designed on Townscapist principles in Schoon 2001: x, as does Glancey in several reviews.

12 These were its premises from 1925 until 1986.

13 By all accounts, Hastings cut a terrifying figure. Built 'like Edward VII in his later years' he was 'an autocrat cast in the eighteenth century mould', 'an ayatollah', 'a cruel poseur' (Carter 1987). See also editor J. M. Richards' description of his deteriorating relationship with Hastings. The chief sacked Richards on a whim in 1972 after three decades of service (Richards 1980: 248–9).

14 Interestingly, Hastings' own relationship to the city was tenuous. He lived on a Sussex farm and until the early 1970s made only infrequent visits to London.

15 Rogers expressed the same view in interview with me (London, 8 May 2001).

16 The authoritarian other with which Townscape contrasts is invariably France, and French-influenced Modernism. The new Brazilian capital of Brasília, inaugurated in 1960, was frequently described in the pages of the *Review* in these terms for its long formal axes, and huge scale.

17 Here Hastings seems to be contrasting an (old-fashioned) object-centred analysis, with (new) one focused on space. In this respect at least, Townscape is an alternative to mainstream architectural criticism.

18 In retrospect this seems very like Kenneth Frampton's call for a 'Critical Regionalism'. See Frampton 1996: 314–27, discussed further in Chapter 4. The reference to the International

Notes

Style makes clear that this is not meant to facilitate a straight revival of a historical architecture.

19 The choice of the country house location over an urban one is significant. It was apparently felt that London would be too distracting if the conference were to be held there, although there was an excursion. See account in Mumford (2000).

20 This is Jacobs of the influential *Death and Life of Great American Cities*. Her link to Cullen here instantiates the transatlantic importance of both her work and Cullen's work.

21 The comparison with surrealism could be taken further: this opening image of 'Townscape' closely resembles the introductory double spread of Brassai's *Paris de Nuit*, likewise a depiction of rain-soaked cobbles.

22 The photographs Cullen used were not his own, but came from a variety of sources. Many were taken by Eric de Maré, with whom Cullen collaborated on various projects.

23 See Brassai, *Paris de Nuit* as well.

24 My view of Townscape might be read alongside Patrick Joyce's critique of liberalism in the nineteenth-century city. In both cases, a performance of freedom is dependent on agreed forms of restraint. In the above passage, Cullen seems happy to accept this paradox. See Joyce (2003).

25 Duany had been involved in the design of two of the best-known new urbanist settlements, both coincidentally in Florida: Seaside, on the northern Gulf coast, and Celebration, a suburb of the inland city of Orlando.

26 In this respect Poundbury could not be more different from Milton Keynes.

27 This is not a characteristic of Krier's per se, but of the fact that in this case he was working in England. His schemes for Luxembourg and Washington DC are by contrast highly formal in the French tradition, a response to the existing character of the site.

28 Krier also built a house for himself at Seaside.

29 Laubin trained with Colin Rowe at Cornell, and was impressed by his theory of the Collage City. He suggested the paintings are an attempt to image Rowe's urban philosophy. See the Laubin website for more: www.carllaubin.com (accessed 24 February 2003).

30 Laubin wrote that what he depicted was based on his living situation in Hertfordshire: 'what I painted was what I see every day' (Laubin 2003).

31 Writing about Covent Garden, the subject of an earlier image, Laubin describes the heterogeneity of its projected population in spectacular terms: 'people in evening dress next to people in fancy dress, diners, entertainers, pickpockets, police, dustmen, office workers, almost every form of humanity one can think of passes through Covent Garden. . .' (Laubin 2003).

32 Confirmed by Laubin in a letter to the author, February 2003.

33 She felt untrained for job of pigeon-keeping, on top of which she had concerns about public health.

34 For an architectural discussion of the building codes developed in American new urbanism, see Dutton (2000).

35 Extensively investigated in the accounts of Celebration, Florida in Frantz and Collins (1999) and Ross (2000). The opposing, mainly architectural, view is that building codes have been in operation for centuries, 'often to exemplary results' in the US according to John Dutton. See Dutton 2000: 70

36 Lebbeus Woods: 'What worries me, Léon, is that your feelings for a kind of unity seem to comply with that control picture. It seems I can take David Fleming and Susan Denyer's views, and your idea of a total planning architecture and put them together into something fairly totalitarian.'

3   The free city

1   However, this is changing, and there is now an incipient café culture, albeit based around national chains, in the cultural quarter around the art gallery.

2   The main axis of Midsummer Boulevard now has a number of monumental buildings besides the shopping mall: a church, an art gallery and a theatre. But these are recent additions, modifications to the original plan.

3   The government's urban policy at the time of writing was to encourage development on areas where economic growth was strongest. Milton Keynes was one pole of development, Cambridge and the so-called Thames Gateway the others. Declining areas of the industrial north would be provided with grants to clear up redundant sites. Peter Hall (1969) advised on the policy. Useful summary and critique in the *Observer* (2003).

4   It ought to be noted, however, that most of these established cities exist inside much larger metropolitan regions. Manchester's hinterland is 2.6 million, Liverpool's 1.5 million and so on.

5   Milton Keynes was never solely a state product, unlike earlier new towns: from the beginning, half of its houses were for sale. It has never been anything other than prosperous.

6   It was never thought of a dormitory town for London.

7   The *grand projet* mode of urbanism is admittedly a phenomenon of the 1980s. It was not available as a mode in the 1960s.

8   For surveys of Jacoby's work, see Jacoby (1977).

9   His images of Milton Keynes represent many more human figures than his images of other places. See Jacoby (1977).

10   The key post-war new towns include Harlow, Skelmersdale, Warrington-Runcorn, and in Scotland, Cumbernauld. For accounts of them, see Brett (1980), Ward (1993) and Hall, P. (1996). Glendinning and Muthesius (1994) discuss the new towns in terms of public housing. Although new towns fell from favour in the early 1970s, the Town and Country Planning Association (TCPA), Peter Hall and Colin Ward, continued to argue in their favour, from a variety of standpoints. Current government policy suggests a revival of the idea.

11   Richard Llewelyn-Davies (1912–81) is the key figure here. Studying at Cambridge in the 1930s, he was impressed by the social commitment of many scientists there, and helped bring about a rebellion against the department of architecture's long–standing commitment to Beaux-Arts forms. He worked for William Holford during the Second World War, building housing and munitions factories. He later worked for Leslie Martin on railway buildings, and became professor of planning at the Bartlett, where he helped to develop an interdisciplinary approach to architecture. His practice was responsible for Washington New Town as well as Milton Keynes.

12   For a critique of 'negative' planning, see 'Non Plan: An Experiment in Freedom', Banham, *et al.* (1969). They complain: 'Somehow, everything must be watched; nothing must be allowed simply to "happen"' (435).

13   The grid is clearly recognisable when approaching Luton airport from the north. The indoor leisure complex, 'Xscape' is, tellingly perhaps, the city's most visible landmark.

14   This proposal was initially supported by Fred Pooley, leader of Buckinghamshire council.

15   Its population density of 25 to 30 dwellings per hectare would be a quarter of that of industrial Manchester at its peak. See Llewelyn-Davies *et al.* 1970: 31.

16   This is the one aspect of Milton Keynes that is definitely picturesque, as Banham (1976) noted. But the city mostly resists the picturesque, as I argue later.

17   'The main road system provides a number of alternative routes between any two points of the city and thus affords a choice of experience even on a routine trip' (Llewelyn-Davies *et al.* 1970: 16).

Notes

18 McKean's review of it for *The Times* shows some anxiety in his response, a good indicator of its difference: it is 'expensive' and 'dishonest', but nevertheless at the same time 'highly exciting' and 'American'.

19 Jacoby, born in Halle in 1926, was a trained architect who branched into the subsidiary practice of architectural rendering, that is, making detailed perspective drawings from architectural plans. The practice has been largely replaced by computer-generated images (see Chapter 6 for examples by Foster and Partners).

20 The shopping centre closely resembles Mies' IIT buildings, Chicago (1952–6).

21 The mound resembles both contemporary land art, and neolithic structures such as Maes Howe in Orkney. Contemporary with Jacoby's drawing, artists such as Michael Heizer, Robert Morris, Dennis Oppenheim and Robert Smithson were making work that made explicit reference to such prehistoric buildings. What Jacoby represents is a mild version of this artistic tendency.

22 The stadium plan was always linked with attempts to attract a major football club to the city. This has been realised in a vestigial form with the arrival of Wimbledon FC in the 2003–4 season. The transfer, deeply unpopular with supporters of the south London club, was the subject of a deal made between the city and the club's management in 2002, after the rejection of Dublin as a possible home. Their home is for the time being the 20,000-capacity former National Hockey Stadium, which bears little relation to the spectacular City Club venue.

23 Jacoby's use of the helicopter to symbolise a modernity located *just* in the future compares well with Le Corbusier's biplane motif in his cityscapes of the 1920s. Both indicate a moment of personal freedom that is on the point of being realised. By contrast, Léon Krier's biplanes, which frequently appear in his urbanistic perspectives, speak of a nostalgia for a now vanished past.

24 'Xscape', an indoor ski-slope and entertainment complex which opened in 2001 is the nearest equivalent to the City Club. Situated adjacent to the arts quarter, its glass and aluminium half dome rises to 47 metres, and contains themed restaurants and bars, clothes stores, a nightclub, a climbing wall and a 16-screen cinema as well as the slope. But the skiing is the main attraction: it clearly defines the exterior form, forcing the other attractions to the periphery. And unlike the City Club, there is no pretence that this is a public space.

25 The kind of attention Jacoby illustrates seems to return the spectator to pre-industrial conditions in which the performing arts were never the object of single-minded attention, but an accompaniment to more general forms of socialisation. The development of audience discipline is the subject of Sennet 1977: 206–9.

26 See, for example, the underground metro stations in Liverpool and Glasgow, the bus station of the Arndale shopping centre in central Manchester, and the rail terminals at Altrincham and Bury.

27 This is precisely the ideal of Cedric Price's architecture, discussed later.

28 An earlier, smaller, image has the glass in a safe position back from the balcony. A decision has therefore been made in the larger image to shift the bottle to the dangerous position, and inject a note of uncertainty.

29 My thinking about these pictures derives from T. J. Clark's account of them in *The Painting of Modern Life* (1984): 201–2 and 263–7. Clark argues that the mechanical nature of the representation is a means of describing the essential strangeness of the scene. The activity Seurat describes is quite new: the modes of dress, the place, and the (unprecedented) class mixing were all new, and still unsettling phenomena at the time they are painted.

30 This and other remarks on the relationship between Webber and Llewelyn-Davies come from a conversation with David Dunster, September 2003.

31 The class dimensions of this image have, as far as I am aware, gone unremarked. Clearly in retrospect Webber extrapolates a general pattern of living from the privileged circumstances of his own university position. He and his peers may consume the city in this radically de-centred way, but those lower down the class scale are likely to exist in much closer contact with specific urban places. At the heart of Milton Keynes are therefore assumptions about city life based on middle-class, professional modes of consuming it. The relationship between class and mobility has perhaps been eroded through the availability of mobile phones – but this precise technology could not have been anticipated by Webber.

32 There were autobiographical elements to Webber's theory. Not only was he from LA, but his work involved much communication with colleagues at Penn State, on the other side of the US. Webber's working relationships were therefore transcontinental. From personal correspondence with David Dunster, September 2003.

33 Webber's influence is curious in respect of the political differences between the two men. Llewelyn-Davies was a communist for most of his adult life, and his architecture is under-pinned by a belief in social improvement directed by the state. His commissions included, appropriately, hospitals. Webber's work supposes a capitulation to the market, albeit a highly rational and pragmatic one.

34 Jencks wrote acerbically of Webber that his theory 'was all an attempt to explain why [he] felt his much maligned Los Angeles was, after all, a most urbane place in spite of its sprawl' (Jencks 1985: 330).

35 It ought to be noted however that since the early 1990s, LA has developed a substantial downtown core, which includes new public spaces such as Pershing Square, and public buildings including Frank Gehry's Disney concert hall, and Rafael Moneo's cathedral. At the same time, the density of settlements such as Santa Monica would seem to be increasing. The thesis that LA is a vapid, insubstantial, centreless place of a new kind no longer really applies – it is a much better description of Atlanta, or Phoenix.

36 Constable, after the painter, Lawrence after the novelist D. H. Lawrence, and Montagu after the aristocratic family who are the biggest landowners in this part of Hampshire. 'Constable country' was perhaps misnamed, as it described an area centred on what is now Stansted airport. Banham, interestingly, shied away from the picturesque Suffolk countryside where the painter lived and worked, favouring the development of an area that was already partially ruined.

37 It needs to be stressed that the plans for culture and entertainment at Milton Keynes were vastly more ambitious than anything achieved at previous new towns. The plans for Harlow and Stevenage, for example, assumed a largely working-class population with little time for culture of any kind. High culture especially was assumed to reside in London. Small theatres and dance halls were part of the plans, but did not in any sense define the centre. Milton Keynes, by contrast, makes the consumption of all forms of culture a central image of the city.

38 The essay is 'The Beaubourg Effect: Implosion and Deterrence'. Baudrillard writes:

> Beaubourg is really a compression sculpture by César: the image of a culture flattened by its own weight, the mobile automobile suddenly frozen into a geometric block [. . .] culture at Beaubourg is crushed, twisted, cut out and stamped into its tiniest basic elements – a bunch of transmissions and defunct metabolism, frozen like a science-fiction mechanoid

> (Baudrillard in Leach 1997: 210)

39 Littlewood (1914–2002) was a radical theatre director, with a commitment to working-class subjects and performers.

40 The 'cybernetic revolution' is an anachronistic term meaning computerisation.

Notes

41 For more on this, see Williams 2000: 58–90; Caute 1988: 25, 29–30.

42 This is, obviously, not an argument that can be proven. However, Jacoby's drawings seem to me to be qualitatively different in tone from the classic city perspectives of the Modernist period. See for comparison, Le Corbusier's drawings of 'a City of Three Million Inhabitants' (1922) in which the architect's taste forms the city; he personally identifies himself with it.

43 Hastings, writing from his Sussex farmhouse, reiterates Stanley Baldwin's view that 'England is the country'. For more on this, see Chapter 1, and Wiener (1980).

44 In this respect, Civilia is really a revival of the sentiments expressed in the *Architectural Review's* 1962 special on Italy.

45 I think Woodhead conflates the *Architectural Review* with the *Architect's Journal*. No matter: both were published by the same firm, and in this case shared a hostility to Milton Keynes.

46 This reiterates the earlier (interwar) fears of ribbon development, expressed as the image of London as an 'octopus' (Clough Williams-Ellis was the author of this term, the architect responsible for the highly picturesque fantasy of Portmeirion). See Hall, P. (1996): 80–2.

47 Banham wrote:

> 'the ideals behind MK's loose, unfocused grid plan were not really alien to the Picturesque method proposed by the *Review*. It was never a rectangular grid, American style. It looked more like a piece of coarse netting dropped askew on the map, the major roads serpenting to avoid accidents of topography, to avoid areas of natural beauty and historic sites – consulting the genius of place in all, as Alexander Pope had instructed the founders of the picturesque two centuries or more ago'.
>
> (Banham 1976: 359)

4 The Mediterranean city

1 The idea of a competition is sometimes expressed in business terms, the quality of the public realm being held out as reason for business to locate to one city or another. English cities are sometimes described as losing out in this kind of competition, although in the European Union, the UK has consistently attracted more foreign investment than any other member nation. For an account of the idea of inter-urban competition within Europe, see Peck and Ward (2002): 76–94.

2 This is precisely the role Kenneth Frampton sees remaining for modern architecture – a form of romantic resistance against the inevitable onslaught of modernity. See Frampton (1996: 314–27) and my discussion of it later in this chapter.

3 Another indication of this sentiment was the RIBA's 2003 annual conference, which was held in Rotterdam to showcase (successful) urban development abroad.

4 The political influence of this idea can be traced through the British government's Urban Task Force, chaired by Lord Rogers, which reported in 1999.

5 For further reading on the Grand Tour, I refer the reader to Hibbert (1987) or Wilton and Bignamini (1997).

6 See account of Oxford in Hibbert 1987.

7 Smith had given up a professorship at Glasgow University to accompany the Duke.

8 On entering a strange town the tourist (would) at once ascend the highest steeple to gain a good view of it and take note of any interesting buildings worthy of further inspection. He must then make drawings, take measurements, study the details of architecture and decoration, list valuable contents, sketch the layout of their courtyards and gardens, constantly bearing in mind his future as the inheritor of family possessions and as patron of artists who would one day enhance them.

(Hibbert 1987: 37)

9 On Rome, 'first experiences of the city were commonly disappointing, and often exasper-
   ating' (Hibbert 1987: 155). For a full account of the difficulties of Italian travel see the same
   source, 155–81.

10 This is not entirely true, of course, with Pevsner and Betjeman's interest in Victoriana forming
   an alternative ideological strand in the journal. But the attraction of the Georgian for
   Modernists was very strong. See J. M. Richards' work on industrial architecture
   for example, a highly selective view of the nineteenth century (Richards 1958).

11 It opens with a bizarre excursus on the (English) cooked breakfast:

   > When a hundred thousand breakfast tables are loaded every day at 8 a.m., winter and
   > summer, rain or fine, with bacon, planning may be said to be a fairly developed science.
   > When they, the breakfast tables, are concentrated at twelve-foot centres more or less,
   > and the bacon is still brought home, *town*-planning, the art of getting bacon to breakfast
   > tables when they are densely packed, is operating too. The question then arises, is a
   > congestion of breakfast tables a nice or nasty thing to have?

   (Hastings 1962: 383)

12 The CIAM Athens Charter (1938) proposed that the city could be understood in terms of the
   functions of work, leisure, residence and circulation. See Mumford (2000).

13 Catalunya in Catalan, Cataluña in Castillian Spanish. I use the anglicised version of the name
   here.

14 Foreign interest in Spain's architecture accompanies a series of rapid political changes in the
   country, marked by huge public spending on infrastructure and culture. The key dates are:

1975	death of the dictator General Franco
1976	restoration of democracy
1981	the resistance of a military coup
1982	the election of the centre-left PSOE
1986	membership of the EEC
1992	Barcelona Olympics and Madrid, European Capital of Culture.

   Throughout this period, Spain's regional politics have become ever more centrifugal.
   Catalonia, which regards itself as a 'pais' or country, has the right to raise its own taxes. For
   a useful general account of post-Franco Spain see Hooper (1986).

15 There were several magazines dealing with property ownership in Spain published regularly
   in 2003. Catalan cuisine was represented by a proliferation of cookery books on the subject,
   while Manchester holds an annual 'Festa Catalana' in mid-summer.

16 In 2003, it was probably easier and cheaper, for Londoners to visit Barcelona for the weekend
   than, say, Liverpool.

17 It is significantly smaller than these cities: 4 million in the metropolitan area, as opposed to
   6 million (Paris) and 7.5 million (London).

18 See Washington Irving's account of Spain, for example.

19 Seen by the author when resident in Spain from 1990–3.

20 Further sources for this idea: George Orwell, *Homage to Catalonia* – an account of the city
   during the civil war. And a novel which describes the capacity of Barcelona for self-reflexive
   exoticisation – Eduardo Mendoza's *Sin Notícias de Gurb* (1991) in which an extraterrestrial
   arrives in Barcelona during the 1992 Olympics, and reports his bizarre experiences.

21 These are the Casa Lléo Morera (Domènech i Montaner), the Casa Amatller (Puig i Cadafalch)
   and the Casa Batlló (Gaudí). The block itself lies on the Passeig de Grácia, 200 m north of the
   Plaça de Catalunya.

22 The airport, which combines the aesthetic of the Mies van de Rohe pavilion with some
   restrained neo-classical details, has also been the subject of exoticisation in the accounts of

Notes

Hughes (1992) and Castells (1996), the latter discussed in Chapter 8. It is in these accounts, like the other major projects, essentially ruinous and non-functional, a surreal monument to architectural hubris.

23 On the evidence of a visit made in 2003, these problems seem to have been resolved. The original tiling has been replaced, and the safety nets have gone.

24 The images in Bofill (1985), an officially sanctioned publication, show Walden 7 in rather poor repair. The nets Hughes describes have yet to be installed, but the exterior tiling is evidently patchy.

25 The Parc de L'Espanya Industrial, and the Parc de Joan Miró are the best examples of public spaces that capitalise on the surreal.

26 The idea of competing versions of Catalan architecture is alluded to by Bohigas in 1990. Modernism is alive and well, he reports, whereas Ricardo Bofill's variant of postmodernism has not been widely adopted despite that architect's success abroad. In Catalonia, he 'is a rather isolated figure. There is hostility to him [. . .] and he does not exert a great influence' (Davies 1990: 25).

27 New Brutalism was the tendency of the mid-1950s associated with the architects Peter and Alison Smithson, the sculptor Eduardo Paolozzi, and the critic Reyner Banham. For Banham's quasi-manifesto, see Banham (1955), reprinted in Banham (1996): 7–15.

28 It has quickly become established as a major economic pole in a globalised economic system. Spain is relatively unusual amongst European countries in having two such cities. See Castells (1996).

29 Of course, no building is simply a product of market forces, as much as architects would like to believe that this could be the case. Buildings always exist in a framework of regulation, or lack of regulation, and as Will Hutton has argued, markets themselves are social phenomena with variable effects according to their location.

30 The British profession was in some ways literally excluded from Docklands. In the original scheme, the masterplan was drawn up by SOM, while they and a handful of US practices contributed the designs for the main buildings, as the developers felt that British firms lacked the requisite experience. Troughton McAslan was the only British practice involved, and they contributed one of the most superficially American buildings. For more, see Chapter 7.

31 Bohigas refers to Baroness Thatcher here.

32 Curiously, one of these figures, Castells, is Catalan, although he was working in California at the time. It ought to be said too that his argument in *The Rise of the Network Society* describes processes of urban re-centralisation in the major metropolitan centres as a result of information technologies, but a de-centralisation elsewhere. Neither centralisation nor de-centralisation carry the unequivocal values for Castells that they do for Bohigas. See Chapter 8 for more on this.

33 Bohigas discounted Krier's urbanism in 1990 as overly dependent on archaic architectural forms (Davies 1990: 35). But in later remarks he did describe his own views on urban form as 'very conservative' (Melhuish 2000: 8). The difference between Krier and Bohigas is not, it seems to me, all that great; see the similarly unlikely parallels in Britain between HRH Prince Charles and Richard Rogers.

34 Barcelona's grid is notable both for its great extension, and (with a few much-visited exceptions) the uniformity of its buildings. There is very little variation in height, and relatively little in the treatment of façades. It is a very different kind of grid to that found in American cities, where the geometry imposes order on what would otherwise often be extremely heterogeneous. For example, downtown Houston, Dallas or LA have quite radically varying building heights (and types) in the same rectilinear block.

35 The airport terminal, designed by Bofill, makes use of classical motifs, albeit very restrained ones. Apart from the Walden 7 housing scheme, Bofill has built relatively little in Barcelona.

5 The city in ruins

1 Keith Hackett, Liverpool City Council: 'there is a voyeuristic element in the way people come to look at cities in decline' (Middleton 1991: 80).

2 The dispute involved 500 dock workers who refused to accept new terms and conditions. Locked out of their former place of employment, they demonstrated at the dock gates between from 1995 to 1996.

3 Objective 1 status identifies regions whose GDP falls below 75 per cent of the EU average. Originally it mostly benefited southern Europe and Ireland. It now covers large areas of post-reunification Germany.

4 Islington is the most commonly cited example.

5 Kinnock, November 1985: 'Militant Tendency is a maggot in the body of the Labour Party' (Parkinson 1985: 15).

6 Hatton wrote of Sheffield and Islington councils that they styled themselves as rebels on the Liverpool model, but 'when it came to the crunch, they just didn't have our bottle' (Hatton 1988: 90).

7 The area originally covered by the Merseyside Task Force was small: a few hundred acres on the waterfront south of the city centre, Bootle to the north, and part of Birkenhead opposite Liverpool on the other side of the Mersey.

8 The site was abandoned after the festival, and has never been redeveloped, although there has been a business park built nearby, and some low-density suburban housing. It remains an isolated site, not easily accessible from the city centre.

9 There was resistance from curators in some these cities to the creation of a Tate of the North, an institution that could be seen as a rival to their own. Interview with Alan Bowness, October 2003.

10 Conformed in interview with Bowness, October 2003. Bowness thought the Dock on first sight was 'fantastic', and his view was shared by the majority of the trustees, as well as James Stirling. Their response was, it seems, *aesthetic* more than anything else.

11 The important parts of the report's discussion of Liverpool read as follows:

> Apart from the Scottish National Gallery of Modern Art in Edinburgh, there is no comprehensive collection of modern art outside London. The public cannot therefore experience what has been one of the most fertile fields of creativity and perceptual renewal in our time; and young and potential artists cannot meet face to face the highest achievements of the tradition in which they are to work. It is not sufficient for the millions in the north of England that London is within a three or four hour journey. The full experience of art can be achieved only by regular exposure, and must have a place within the community [. . .] Some six years ago the Director and the Trustees began to explore possibilities in the great cities of the north of England. When they saw the Albert Dock in Liverpool, they knew they had found the right place. Built by Jesse Hartley in 1841–48 it is one of the finest and grandest industrial buildings in England [. . .] there is a political will to enrich a city which is undergoing a traumatic transformation; money could be found. [. . .] The buildings are magnificent in scale, built in brick over a great cast iron Doric arcade that runs around the whole dock and detailed in monumental simplicity. [. . .] [T]he new gallery will, we hope, serve sensitively and flexibly the needs of the northern community within reach of Merseyside. It will seek all means of integrating itself into the artistic and cultural life of that community.
>
> (Tate 1986: 21–4)

12 The scale of investment in cultural facilities at the Albert Dock was unprecedented until the Lottery-led museum boom of the mid-1990s.

Notes

13 For a longer discussion of the loft gallery phenomenon in New York, see Williams (2000): 100–17.

14 'Downtown' signifies the area around Houston St. now universally know as SoHo.

15 Much of lower Manhattan was zoned for industry, not residence.

16 Kaprow was responsible for the phenomenon of 'Happenings', vaguely structured performances involving the participation or implication of an audience. They invariably occurred in downtown lofts. See the account on Kaprow (1993: 15–26); commentary in Williams (2000: 93–4). The minimalists I refer to here included Carl Andre, Eva Hesse, Robert Morris, Richard Serra and Robert Smithson, all of who lived and worked in downtown loft spaces.

17 The name 'SoHo' is itself an indicator of the area's gentrification – it was invented in the 1960s by property developers.

18 There was a notorious headline on 30 October 1975 in the *New York Daily News* at the height of the fiscal crisis, referring to the president's attitude to the problem: 'Ford to City: Drop Dead'.

19 There was at the time of writing a campaign originating in the city council to have the whole waterfront, including these buildings, declared a world heritage site – were this to transpire, it would give the whole site the character of a historical ruin.

20 The Three Graces is a name, as far as I can tell, that dates from 2002 when a public competition was held to design a fourth public building to fit alongside the existing buildings to the south, in an area of very low-density development adjoining the maritime museum. The competition was won by Will Alsop; it was unclear at the time of writing whether his pod-like proposal would actually be built, owing to a lack of clarity about its use. The North West Development Agency (NWDA), the embryonic regional parliament, was known not to favour the idea.

21 There is something very curious in these arguments, in that they all invoke the ruin as *authentic*, against the perceived inauthenticity of the American approach to old buildings. The ruin is in fact accompanied by all manner of artifice, in their representation, and their reconstruction. The demand for ruins, as is well know, led to the creation of ersatz ruins at Stourhead and other English gardens.

22 Fountains Abbey, the largest of all Cistercian monasteries in England, was founded in the early twelfth century and was completed in the thirteenth century. It lies in North Yorkshire, 32 km to the northeast of York on the River Skell, and is arguably the most spectacular of English medieval ruins. Managed by the National Trust, it is a world heritage site.

23 In retrospect, Piper's view seems to presage the fascination of 1960s artists with the concept of entropy. See especially the work of the American Robert Smithson, discussed throughout Williams (2000).

24 Although Alan Bowness' initial response to the Dock – it was a 'fantastic place' – admits this type of reading. It is not difficult to imagine that the quality he alludes to has to do with the Dock's terrible condition as much as its usefulness as a building. Interview with Bowness, October 2003.

25 This idea derives from a discussion in August 2003 with Fiona Bradley, a former curator at the gallery.

26 The institutions that were nationalised included the Walker Art Gallery, the Liverpool Museum, and the Lady Lever Art Gallery in Port Sunlight.

27 This continues at Liverpool. It is a common source of employment for local art students.

28 As Jemima Pyne recalls, the relationship between the director of the Liverpool operation, Richard Francis, and Alan Bowness was a somewhat oedipal one. The tensions there were represented in a series of unusual policies at Liverpool: not only education, but also the creation of a corporate graphic identity long before London.

29 This is Jemima Pyne's phrase. Interview with Pyne, 28 August 2003.

6 The architecture of civility

1 In this context, Rodney Mace notes the symbolic nature of the square for foreign powers as much as England. During the Second World War, Hitler apparently wanted Nelson's column re-erected in front of the Reichstag in Berlin after a successful military conquest of Britain. See Mace 1976: 17.

2 Charles Saumarez Smith, the director of the National Gallery, referred to the square as particularly 'disgusting' before renovation, a sentiment that recalls many earlier views of the square's incivility cited by Mace. Interview with Saumarez Smith, 27 September 2001.

3 My argument here is informed partly by a panel discussion at 'Square Politics', National Gallery, May 2003, involving Richard Sennett, Alan Hudson and myself. The conference was organised by the National Gallery in conjunction with the University of Westminster.

4 The works were *Ecce Homo* by Mark Wallinger, *Regardless of History* by Bill Woodrow and *Monument* by Rachel Whiteread. The plinth was originally intended for a sculpture of William IV, which was never realised. The project was run by the RSA, and ran from 2000 to 2002.

5 This was Sennett's view at 'Square Politics'.

6 Deborah Cherry, papers at Association of Art Historians' conference, London, April 2003, and 'Square Politics'.

7 This is Manuel Castells' argument in *The Rise of the Network Society* (1996). The poor, he argues, historically place themselves at the centre, so that their plight is visible – to hide on the margins is to capitulate to poverty. Hence the extremes of wealth and poverty in such global cities as London, New York and Los Angeles. Trafalgar Square is a local instance of this phenomenon.

8 Political demonstrations have been very frequent since the square's reformation in the nineteenth century: see table in Mace (1976): 299–322. Key moments of dissent in recent years include the anti-apartheid campaign outside South Africa House; the demonstration against the so-called 'poll tax' in 1990, which directly led to the resignation of the Prime Minister, Margaret Thatcher; the Stop the City protests throughout the 1990s; and in the early years of the twenty-first century, the protests on 1 May against global capitalism.

9 For a general discussion of this idea in nineteenth-century England, see Joyce (2003): 109. He writes, 'the connections between technologies of light and forms of surveillance, especially policing, are striking'.

10 Elsewhere, the twin fountains at the centre of the square are described in as a means of preventing meaningful assembly: dividing any crowd in two, they also prevent the square from maintaining a single point of focus for a charismatic speaker.

11 All events must now conform to a cultural programme, which is to say that Trafalgar Square is now envisaged, at an official level, as a species of open-air theatre. A GLA official is responsible for programming the square.

12 In the Roman idea of *civitas*, citizenship, originally of the city of Rome, and later the territories under its jurisdiction, was a privilege conferred by birth or in exceptional circumstances by imperial decree. It could also be lost. In exceptional circumstances, foreigners could be Roman citizens, such as when, for example, it was politically expedient that this was the case. It provided rights, namely the right to vote for the magistracy and to stand oneself as a magistrate, to appeal to the public against magisterial rulings, to marry legally and to hold property, in return for responsibilities including the paying of taxes, military service and more minor civic duties such as road maintenance. See Sherwin-White (1939) for a full account.

13 For Karl Marx – who with Hegel is the first to make use of the term – 'civil society embraces the whole material intercourse of individuals within a definite stage of the development of productive forces' (Marx 1972: 267). Civil society is categorically not the state, but the commercial and industrial life of the state, and the mass of relationships that it must involve.

14 To be fair to Rogers, his use of the term is fleeting, and does not itself carry a great deal of weight. It may not even be his particular word, but that of Philip Gumuchdijan, his co-author on *Cities for a Small Planet*.

15 The coffee house, and the social and commercial life that it embodied, is the origin of the financial trade of the City of London.

16 For Mandeville, literary critic and author of the 'wicked' *Fable of the Bees*, public morality was impossible – all that was conceivable was self interest, but that this was of itself a force for progress (Solkin 1993: 13–14).

17 Likewise, in Britain, the academic interest in eighteenth-century discourses of politeness in (for example) the work of Solkin and John Brewer seems to me a response to the brutal nature of free-market thinking, and its application by the governments of Margaret Thatcher and Ronald Reagan. The eighteenth century represented some alternative possibilities, albeit rather aristocratic ones.

18 Scruton's hostility to Modernism, and to Modernist architects is hyperbolic – Le Corbusier's rhetoric is equal to that of 'Lenin and Hitler' while Denis Lasdun's Institute of Education building in Bloomsbury, London is 'almost as repulsive the activities that are contained within it' (Scruton 1994: 18).

19 This list nicely reveals Scruton's traditional moral principles.

20 I resist determinism throughout this book, although I argue at several points that there may be a connection between architecture and social behaviour that is culturally specific, which is to say learned. In the broadest sense my argument about anxiety makes this point. The English anxiety about city life – which I think is real – is a conditioned response.

21 Robert Putnam has been particularly influential on Tony Blair. Putnam, in return, regards New Labour's approach to poverty and deprivation in the UK as the most 'innovative and sustained' of any western government (J. Hall 2003).

22 Sennett's inclusion needs to be qualified here by saying that civility is not a term he uses. But he is concerned with the same issues as DeMott, Carter, Putnam *et al*.

23   Only religion possesses the power, the majesty and the sacred language to teach all of us, the religious and the secular, the genuine appreciation of each other on which a successful civility must rest. Critics who insist that religion is a danger to civility are misreading both America and religion – and generally have no better ideas.

(Carter 1998: 18)

24 To see this argument developed at length with reference to the nineteenth-century English city, see Joyce (2003).

25 Carter is African-American and his work makes something out of his racial origins.

26 Two of the public spaces discussed in this book, Liverpool's Albert Dock (Chapter 5) and Canary Wharf (Chapter 7) were built during Conservative rule. And as discussed here, the reformation of Trafalgar Square was also initiated during this period.

27 In the view of Lord Rogers, the chair of the Urban Task Force, the government has, in the end, done very little to address his concerns about the built environment, and certainly in comparison with countries such as Spain, architecture and design have a low priority. But for a British government to take interest in these matters at all is a significant change.

28 I am paraphrasing Saumarez Smith, 2001.

29 Saumarez Smith again: he related the story of the railings outside the National Portrait Gallery on Irving Place, a small section of greenery just north of the square proper, and an area which the Foster plan envisaged formalising as part of the main plan. The railings appeared only in the 1960s after pressure on Westminster City Council from Roy Strong who then worked at the gallery. Directly outside Strong's office, on the street there was regularly to be found

an escapologist, whose activities Strong and others found distracting. The railing afforded them a degree of protection.

30 Foster and Stirling, by contrast, exhibited existing schemes, the Hong Kong and Shanghai Bank, and the Stuttgart gallery respectively.

31 For a discussion of the complete scheme, see Davey 1987. Davey's reservations centre on the lack of clarity about the way public life is described; it is a scheme predicated on the provision of a lot of new public space, but it is unclear what kind of life will actually occur in them, especially along the newly pedestrianised Embankment. 'What will people do on the shallow steps in the still noisome waters of the Thames?' (Davey 1987: 70).

32 After the show, the drawings appeared in the *Architectural Review* (Davey 1987), *A New London,* written with Mark Fisher (Rogers and Fisher 1992), and *Cities for a Small Planet* (Rogers 1997).

33 Rogers' belief in the interconnectedness of public space and civil society was confirmed in discussion with the author in London on 8 August 2001.

34 A large part of the book's thesis concerns environmentally 'sustainable' architecture.

35 This account is based on a conversation with Spencer de Grey, London, 21 August 2001.

36 De Grey clearly emphasised this difference in approach. Without naming Rogers, he said he was personally 'suspicious' of an approach to urban design that began from an ideal image. De Grey 21 August 2001.

37 A decision which was later reversed. A café now sits at the foot of the steps leading to the gallery terrace.

38 Confirmed in an interview with Jeremy Dixon and Edward Jones, London, November 2001.

39 It must be said however that the images produced by the two practices use quite different representational techniques. Foster's computer-generated images contrast with the pen-and-wash of the Rogers images, the latter clearly invoking the picturesque tradition. Foster's treatment of individual figures is quite different too, with rather more differentiation and detail – individuals in the Rogers images are mere silhouettes. But the kinds of activities they are engaged in are remarkably similar in each case.

40 Confirmed by Livingstone at 'Square Politics', National Gallery, 30 May 2003.

41 For further remarks on this subject, see Williams (2003).

7 'America, E14'

1 The process is usefully summarised by Merrifield: 'Speculation in the built environment simultaneously ameliorates and internalises capitalism's inner contradictions and contains within this dialectical nexus the source of its own restabilisation and destabilisation' (Merrifield 1993: 1250).

2 Zukin's book is excellent on its own terms, but it is concerned with identifying and describing broad global phenomena, whereas my concern here is the local.

3 Hall provides a useful critical commentary on his own work at Docklands in Hall (1996: 342–60).

4 Hall thought it was 'a modest and unradical scheme', which showed the British talent for neutralising radical ideas by institutionalising them (Hall 1996: 357).

5 A high wing turboprop with four engines, it was capable of very short take-offs and landings, but it was small, slow and its range limited it to journeys of only a few hundred miles. Production ceased almost at the same time as the airport was opened.

6 These were consequently the only buildings taken seriously by the architectural press.

7 For a (critical) discussion of the informal quality of the redevelopment until Canary Wharf, see Davies (1987).

8 As Zukin (1992) points out, the schemes involved the same keynote architect (Pelli), and the same masterplanner (SOM). The locations differed, however. Although both made use of

reclaimed land, the New York development adjoined the financial district of Wall St., while Canary Wharf was several miles from central London.

9   For changes in the design of the tower, see *Building Design* (1991). It was shorter and fatter than Pelli originally wanted.

10 LA City Hall was built in 1928 by Austin, Parkinson, Martin and Whittlesey. Like Pelli's building, the central feature is a tall tower on a square plan, set on a podium, and capped by a pyramid. It is about thirty storeys tall, and was until 1957 the tallest building in LA. There is an observation deck on the twenty-seventh floor.

11 Brooks Brothers is a chain of department stores specialising in smart-casual menswear; perhaps he means the building has the store's sense of restraint, and attention to surface detail.

12 The Docklands Light Railway opened in 1989, as a line with two branches running from Tower Hill through the Isle of Dogs to North Greenwich. It was a cheap and cheerful system, with fully automated three-car trains running on elevated tracks. It initially ran only during the working week. An extension of the Jubilee Line of the Underground, which opened in 2000, provided a more substantial transport solution.

13 I have borrowed her phrase for the title of this chapter.

14 This is an early instance of planning giving way to 'masterplanning' – the former being a function of the state, the latter generally a function of commercial architecture departments.

15 See Colin Davies' remarks: 'The London Docklands phenomenon has probably dealt the death blow to town planning as we know it in Britain. [. . .] And this is seen not as a public scandal, but as a triumphant success (. . .).' (Davies 1987: 31).

16 'It is an invasion, and one more of Vandals rather than Goths', he continued. See Kenneth Powell, 'The American Revenge', www.theworldandi.com/ accessed 10 September 2003. The remarks were made in a speech to the RIBA, and Maxwell Hutchinson, then president, spoke in support. Lord St John, as Norman St John Stevas was a minister in Mrs Thatcher's first cabinet, but regarded as 'wet' (or dissident).

17 Quoted in Frampton 1992: 42. See Morris (1902).

18 The developers continue to be sensitive about the way Canary Wharf is perceived. During the writing of this book, Canary Wharf plc repeatedly refused permission to reproduce the perspective drawings discussed in this chapter, despite the fact that they were already in the public domain, and widely published. Their objection was that they were early images that did not accurately represent the development now; they offered some 'more accurate' contemporary pictures instead. The images can be found in *Archictectural Review* (1987: 35).

19 This is reminiscent of nineteenth-century Parisian critiques of the remodelling of their city by Baron Haussman, the Prefect of the Seine. For example, the journalist Edmond Goncourt, wrote:

> I am a stranger to what is coming, to what is, as I am to these new boulevards without turnings, without chance perspectives, implacable in their straight lines, which no longer smack of the world of Balzac, which make one think of some American Babylon of the future.

> (Goncourt in Clark 1985: 35).

20 Curiously, this highly stratified state of affairs has come about though increased security controls due to terrorism. It is impossible to enter Canary Wharf by private car unless one has the appropriate permit. Barriers seal the entrance and exits to the main boulevard. Traffic is, as a result, eerily light.

21 The *capriccio* was a fashionable mode of architectural presentation at the time. See Carl Laubin's work for Dixon:Jones, for example.

22 However, the move from the City was never entirely happy. According to Kenneth Powell, journalists of the right-wing, socially conservative *Daily Telegraph* wished that 'the Jubilee line would never get there and the place would become cut off so the paper could then conveniently move back somewhere more sensible' (Powell 1993: 28).

23 I think she refers to *Stalker*, a 1979 film by the Russian director, in which the arrival on earth of an alien object leads to the creation of a forbidden zone around it. The zone, it is said, allows those to enter it to realise their fantasies. Evidently this sense of Tarkovsky's work has no parallel at Canary Wharf.

24 For the *Guardian* cartoonist Steve Bell, the puniness of the DLR line was a perfect illustration of the problem.

25 It might be noted that the views toward the City now increasingly connect with Canary Wharf, as Norman Foster has built towers in both places. The Swiss Re tower (or 'erotic gherkin') is clearly visible from Docklands.

26 EPCOT is one of the main attractions of Disneyworld Florida.

8 The museum, the city and the space of flows

1 This was not, in fact, realised, although the bookshop in the Great Court much more resembles a general bookshop than the old one.

2 Colin St John Wilson, The New British Library, 1977–1998. St John Wilson had earlier been involved in plans to extend the existing library at the British Museum. The St Pancras site was chosen after opposition to earlier plans (1974) to erect a large new building in the historic area of Bloomsbury.

3 See Jenkins 2000.

4 Foster did try to argue that the stones were, geologically speaking, the same, as they belonged to the same rock layer, with one end of it in France, and one in England.

5 Castells has long been associated with studies of the built environment, having collaborated with the planner Peter Hall, for example on *Technopoles of the World* (1994).

6 There are obvious parallels with Melvin Webber's concept of the 'nonplace urban realm', discussed in Chapter 3.

7 Ironically or not, Castells clearly sees a theological dimension to the space of flows. To inhabit the space of flows is to participate in a quasi-religious rite. This particular dimension of the idea makes it particularly useful to account for the contemporary museum space, which has been long regarded in theological terms, a replacement for the church or cathedral.

8 For more on Bofill, see Chapter 4.

9 Compare the British Museum with the Pergamon Museum in Berlin, or the Louvre in Paris: the narrative structure is very similar.

10 The flattening of hierarchies is not by any means total – but the new arrangement is a significant move in that direction.

11 From a conversation with Richard Rogers, 2001. See Chapter 1 for more on the English confusion of private with public.

12 The novelist Howard Jacobson wrote: 'It used to be one of the unsurpassable joys of life for people working in the library to look up from their labours and show their profiles to parties of spectators allowed so far into the reading room and no further. Gaze upon us ye unlettered masses and marvel!' (Jacobson 2000).

13 The hub-and-spoke metaphor was literalised in airport designs of the 1970s, with the circular satellite terminal a common design. Paris Charles de Gaulle and London Gatwick are good examples of this approach.

14 For more discussion of Augé, see Chapter 7.

15 Eero Saarinen's highly expressive work at New York JFK (1956–62) and Washington Dulles (1958–63) are unusual examples of terminal buildings meant as distinctive places.

16 Martin Pawley regards Heathrow as a city, rather than an airport, having in effect displaced the historic centre of London as the principal site of commerce and information exchange in that city. Its failure to be 'non-place' in Augé's terms is of little consequence.

17 For a comparison, consider the Arndale shopping centre in Manchester, a discursively 'private' space criticised for sealing off large parts of the public realm out of hours. The opening hours of the Arndale and the supposedly 'public' Great Court are very similar.

18 The British Museum's relationship to the city context is a particularly good example of picturesque urbanism. One comes upon the great Greek façade on Museum Street almost by surprise; there are no long axial views that lead up to it, little sense of formality. It faces a set of rather domestically scaled residential buildings, lined at street level with little shops and restaurants. This is no imperial set piece: the contrast with Berlin, Paris or Washington is striking.

19 Fredric Jameson's nightmare too: see his account of the Westin Bonaventure Hotel in 'The Cultural Logic of Late Capitalism' (Jameson in Leach 1997: 238–246) (discussed in Chapter 1).

20 See Chapter 6 on Trafalgar Square. The great difference between the Rogers and Foster projects for the square, in spite of their superficial similarity, was the design process. Rogers seems to have begun with an image of a Mediterranean-type civilisation; Foster with a public consultation exercise, in which the outcome was supposedly not prefigured.

21 The critic Noël Burch wrote: 'it not only begs for multiple viewings, but demands to be seen from several different seats in the auditorium'. See www.frenchculture.org/cinema/festival/tati/playtime.html/. Accessed 13 September 2003. For an academic account of the film, see Iain Borden in Leach 2002: 217–35.

9 The spectacle of pleasure

1 By popular music, I am thinking of the lyrics of such groups as The Fall, The Smiths, Joy Division and New Order. For an account of popular culture and Manchester, see Haslam 2000.

2 Engels does not cite de Tocquecville, although he was well read in other existing accounts of Manchester.

3 See discussion of Engels in comparison with Mike Davies' account of contemporary Los Angeles in Le Gates and Stout (1996): 158–9.

4 One much-visited memorial to this liberal élite is the Quarry Bank Mill complex at Styal, on the fringes of Manchester, now a tourist attraction run by the National Trust. The Greg family who owned it were Unitarians; they ran the complex on liberal lines, providing a local form of welfare state for their employees, who lived on the site. By the standards of the early nineteenth century, it was a model society, and if there is a Unitarian cathedral, then it is the mill building here. But the Gregs' society left unquestioned the capital basis of their activities, and the essentially exploitative character of their relation to the labouring poor.

5 Joyce uses this term.

6 See Ruskin's argument about gothic and northern European identity in *The Stones of Venice* (Ruskin 1851–3).

7 The site also saw the founding of the great liberal newspaper, the *Manchester Guardian*, in 1821.

8 It ought to be made clear that Anderton's faith differs radically from that of the nineteenth-century liberals; his certainty is in stark contrast to the Unitarian sublimation of doubt.

9 It was said that the station, like a submarine ruin at low tide, became visible again after the 1996 IRA bomb. The author could not get close enough to the site at the time to see if this was true.

10 Skylights were finally introduced in 1994, the first time daylight penetrated the building.

11 CMDC corresponds to the Merseyside Development Corporation, and the London Docklands Development Corporation discussed in Chapters 5 and 7 respectively. A government agency, it was responsible for bringing disused land into circulation. Its powers over land and planning by definition brought it into conflict with local government.

12 Noted unexpectedly by the author in 1994. At the same time the towpath was recommended as a walk in a family oriented tourist handbook, the *Good Britain Guide*, edited by Alastair Aird.

13 The older gay venues, such as the New Union, were furtive and seedy places, coy about the sexual orientation of their customers. Likewise the older gay clubs tended to be hidden away in liminal zones of the city, and indeed seemed to cultivate a furtive aesthetic. Dave Haslam describes the hardcore gay Archway club as

> rudely furnished, the tarted up damp bricks and steel beams from the railway arch fused with a few cold metal rails, a small balcony and a DJ box suspended on the back wall. Nothing was fake about the Archway, just stripped down and very dark, a bit claustrophobic.
>
> (Haslam 1999: 200)

14 The importance of the centre as a business location for the professions is illustrated anecdotally by Rosemary Mellor, quoting a Manchester actuary:

> If you walk the streets at lunchtime and you go into various watering holes you can bump into people which you don't outside the city centre . . . being near each other and bumping into people, it's more of a social than a real business need . . . but there's an argument for seeing people, you bump into them, you lunch with them and so on.
>
> (Mellor in Peck and Ward 2002: 228)

15 The three largest museums, the Manchester Museum, the Museum of Science and Industry and the City Art Gallery (now the Manchester Art Gallery) were extended under a joint scheme, partly funded by the Heritage Lottery Fund.

16 For a longer discussion of the new urbanism, see Nan Ellin's important *Postmodern Urbanism* 1996.

17 This is a major shift in thinking. The 1984 city centre plan imagines the centre as a retail mall visited by an entirely suburban population, whose transport needs concern rapid entrance and exit. Circulation within the city is of no consequence.

18 The *Design Guide* did not refer to Jane Jacobs, but this idea is a major part of her *Death and Life of Great American Cities* (1962).

19 It is ideally placed for retail, between Selfridges and the old Corn Exchange shopping mall. By contrast with the success of all of Manchester's other museums, Urbis' visitor figures have fallen to below half of what was required for it to break even. At the time of writing, it seemed likely that the £5 admission charge would be abolished for visits to the permanent exhibition.

20 At the time of writing, a 47-storey tower, also designed by Ian Simpson, is under construction at the southern end of Deansgate. The tower, the tallest residential building in the UK, was to have 200 apartments, built on top of a Hilton hotel. The developers reported that almost all the apartments had been sold off-plan.

21 The dates refer to the design process, and the realisation of the monumental parts of the plan. It was clear on the city's inauguration in April 1960 that it was barely finished.

22 This was the pattern in the blocks built in the first phase of the south wing on the city. Later phases, especially on the north wing, have been much more varied in their treatment.

23 When first built, the blocks were known as the *televisão de candango*, the 'candango's television', the candango being the poor itinerant worker from the northeast who was largely responsible for the capital's construction.

24 My account of Brasília and transparency is possibly incomplete. The official view of the trans-
    parency of the apartment buildings was that it was essentially moral in purpose. But
    Niemeyer's architecture has played with questions of voyeurism; in fact, he positions himself
    as a kind of voyeur, his studio on Copacabana providing an excellent view of the sunbathing
    girls on the beach (whom he like to draw) while above his desk can be seen a photograph of
    two naked girls from the head down, objectified as sexual bodies. Niemeyer was not in fact
    responsible for the design of the apartment blocks. But I wonder if at some level the presen-
    tation and reception of transparency was not more complex than either Lúcio Costa or James
    Holston would like to admit (interview with Niemeyer, Rio de Janeiro, September 2001).
25 Although it must be said that as its louvred windows open and close automatically according
    to the weather, it may be a technically difficult area to modify. There is no place to hang
    curtains or blinds without disrupting the louvre mechanism.
26 Of course, this brings to mind the passage by Michel de Certeau from the essay 'Walking in
    the City' in which he discusses the power of city views:

> To be lifted to the summit of the World Trade Center is to be lifted out of the city's grasp
> [. . .] when one goes up there he leaves behind the mass that carries of and mixes up
> any identity of authors and spectators. His elevation transforms him into a voyeur. It puts
> him at a distance. It transforms the bewitching world by which one was possessed into
> a text that lies before one's eye. It allows one to be read, to be a solar eye, to be looking
> down like a god.
>
> (de Certeau 1984: 92)

10 Staging the city

1   Being present as an interested spectator at a spectacle or play does for adults what play
    does for children, whose hesitant hopes of being able to do what grown up people do
    are in that way gratified. [. . .] accordingly his enjoyment is based on an illusion; that is to
    say, his suffering is mitigated by the certainty that firstly, it is someone other than
    himself who is acting and suffering on stage, and, secondly, that after all it is only a
    game, which can threaten no damage to his personal security.

    (Freud 1985b: 121–2)

2   In Europe, the countries that are the greatest exponents of the pavement café – Italy, Spain,
    Portugal, Greece – all had notably authoritarian political régimes for some, or most or the
    twentieth century. Of course, I would not argue that the pavement café is somehow a cause
    of authoritarianism – but what is clear from these examples, is that it is certainly no protec-
    tion against it, whatever Richard Rogers might argue.
3   Although it parallels the critiques of theatre made from within that cultural form at the time.
    See, for example, Augusto Boal (1991) *Teatro do Oprimido*. The essays were originally
    published between 1962 and 1973.
4   For a downbeat assessment of the spectacularisation of the English city, see Peck and Ward
    2002; also Crinson 2003 on Manchester's Urbis centre.

Bibliography

Aird, A. (2003) *The Good Britain Guide*, London: Ebury Press.

Alberge, D. (2000) 'Call for action on Museums Blight', *The Times*, 15 December.

Allinson, K. and Thornton, V. (1993) *A Guide to London's Contemporary Architecture*, Oxford: Butterworth.

Allison, L. (1981) *Condition of England: Essays and Impressions*, London: Junction Books.

Apollo (1988) 'Tate Gallery Liverpool', 127, 314, April: 264–6.

Appleyard, B. (1986) *Richard Rogers: A Biography*, London: Faber & Faber.

Architects' Journal (1980a) 'Shopping Centre, Milton Keynes', 172, 42, 15 October: 747–58.

Architects' Journal (1980b) 'Shopping Centre, Milton Keynes', 172, 43, 22 October: 797–807.

Architect's Journal (1986) 'Model Exhibition', 184, 41, 8 October: 22–3.

Architect's Journal (1990) 'Barcelona', special issue, 192, 2, 11 July: 22–54.

Architect's Journal, (1997) 'Wilford under Fire over Stirling Tate Alterations', 205, 6, 13 February: 9.

Architect's Journal (1998) 'Docklands Defined', 207, 6, 12 February: 27–41.

Architectural Association Quarterly (1974–5), 6, 3–4: 1–7.

Architectural Design (1993a) 'Architecture in Arcadia', special issue, 63, 5–6, May–June.

Architectural Design (1993b) 'New Practice in Urban Design', special issue, 63, 9–10, September–October.

Architectural Record (2001) 'A Brilliant Shell Game at the British Museum', 189, 3, March: 149–54.

Architectural Review (1951) 'The South Bank Exhibition', CX, 656, August: 72–138.

Architectural Review (1962) 'Italian Townscape', special issue, 131, 783, June: 382–444.

Architectural Review (1987) 'Docklands Challenge', special issue, 181, 1080, February: 30–85.

Architectural Review (1988) 'Monster Emerges from London Docks', CLXXXIII, 1095, May: 4, 9.

Architectural Review (1991) 'Airports', CLXXXIX, 1131, May: 4–90.

Architectural Review (1999) 'Gold for Barcelona', CCV, 1126, April: 17–19.

Architectural Review (2000) 'Magic Bubble', CCVII, 1238, April: 52–7.

Architecture and Urbanism (1985) 'César Pelli', special issue, July.

Arendt, H. (1958) *The Human Condition*, Chicago: Chicago University Press.

Astragal (1991) 193, 26 *Architect's Journal*, 26 June: 6.

Atkins, P. (1976) *Guide Across Manchester*, Manchester: Civic Trust for the North West.

Augé, M. (1995) *Non-Places: Introduction to an Anthropology of Supermodernity*, trans. John Howe, London and New York: Verso.

Bailey, M. (2000a) 'Mandela Supports British Museum's Global Role', *The Art Newspaper*, XI, 109, December: 1.

Bailey, M. (2000b) 'Master of the Speaking Objects', *The Art Newspaper*, XI, 109, December: 30.

Baillieu, A. (2002) 'Championship Contender', *RIBA Journal*, 109, 6, June: 7.

Baird, G. (1995) *The Space of Appearance*, Cambridge, Mass.: MIT Press.

Banham, R. (1955) 'The New Brutalism', *Architectural Review*, 118, December: 354–61.

Bibliography

Banham, R. (1972) *Los Angeles: The Architecture of Four Ecologies*, London: Penguin.

Banham, R. (1976a) 'The Open City and its Enemies', *The Listener*, 23 September: 359–60.

Banham, R. (1976b) *Megastructure: Urban Futures of the Recent Past*, New York: Harper & Row.

Banham, R. (1986) 'The Quality of Modernism', *Architectural Review*, CLXXX, 1076: 54–6.

Banham, R. (1996) *A Critic Writes: Essays by Reyner Banham*, Berkeley and Los Angeles, Calif.: University of California Press.

Banham, R., Barker, P., Hall, P. and Price, C. (1969) 'Non-Plan: An Experiment in Freedom', *New Society*, 20 March: 435–43.

Barker, P. (1995) 'Architecture: In Conversation with Richard Rogers', *Modern Painters*, 8, 2, Summer: 78–83.

Barrell, J. (1980) *The Dark Side of the Landscape: The Rural Poor in English Painting 1730–1840*, New York: Cambridge University Press.

Bendixson, T. (1969) 'Milton Keynes: The Newest New Town', *Architectural Review*, CXLIV, 870, August: 102–8.

Bendixson, T. and Platt, J. (1992) *Milton Keynes: Image and Reality*, Cambridge: Granta Editions.

Benjamin, W. (1973) *Illuminations*, ed. Hannah Arendt trans. Harry Zohn, London: Fontana.

Benjamin, W. (1979) *One-Way Street and Other Writings*, trans. Edmund Jephcott and Kingsley Shorter, London: New Left Books.

Benjamin, W. (2000) *The Arcades Project*, trans. Howard Eiland and Kevin McLaughlin, Cambridge, Mass.: Harvard University Press.

Berman, M. (1983) *All that is Solid Melts into Air*, London: Verso.

Bicho, R. (2003) 'Plans to Increase UK Airport Capacity', *The Guardian*, 14 January.

Binney, M. (2000) 'Review of British Museum Great Court', *The Times*, 2, 7 November: 18.

Blair, A. (2001) 'Improving Your Local Environment', speech, Croydon, 24 April.

Blanchard, T. (2002a) 'Manchester, United', *Observer Magazine*, 19 May: 22–9.

Blanchard, T. (2002b) 'Homing Instincts', *Observer Magazine*, 20 October.

Boal, A. (1991) *Teatro do Oprimido*, Rio de Janeiro: Civilização Brasileira.

Bofill, R. (1985) *Ricardo Bofill: Taller de Arquitectura* with an introduction by Christian Norberg-Schulz, New York: Rizzoli.

Bohigas, O. (1983) *Resena y catálogo de la arquitectura a*, Barcelona: Liman.

Bohigas, O. (1999) '10 Points for an Urban Methodology', *Architectural Review*, CCVI, 1231, September: 88–91.

Bohigas, O., Buchanan, P. and Lampugniani, V. M. (1991) *Barcelona: City and Architecture*, Barcelona: Gili.

Breton, A. (1991) *Nadja*, Paris: Folio.

Brett, L. (1980) *A Broken Wave: The Rebuilding of England, 1940–1980*, London: Allen Lane.

Brewer, J. (1997) *The Pleasures of the Imagination: English Culture in the Eighteenth Century*, London: Harper Collins.

Brownill, S. (1990) *Developing London's Docklands: Another Great Planning Disaster?*, London: Paul Chapman.

Bryson, B. (1996) *Notes from a Small Island*, London: Black Swan.

Buchanan, P. (1980) 'Milton Keynes and the Architecture of Innocence', *Architectural Review*, CLXVIII, 1003, September: 155–6.

Buchanan, P. (1984) 'Regenerating Barcelona with Parks and Plazas', *Architectural Review*, CLXXXV, 1048, June: 32–46.

Buchanan, P (1986) 'Barcelona: Rebuilding the Public Realm', *Architectural Review*, CLXXXIX, 1071, May: 58–63.

Buchanan, P. (1988) 'Tate on the Mersey', *Architectural Review*, CLXXXIV, 1097, July: 18–27.

Buchanan, P. (1989) 'Quays to Design', *Architectural Review*, CLXXXV, 1106: 38–44.

Buchanan, P. (1990) 'Making Places in Spain', *Architectural Review*, CLXXXVIII, 1121, June: 29–31.

Building (1988) 'New Tate of the Art', 253, 7549, May: 31–3.

Building (1991) 'Canary Wharf: A Landmark in Construction, 256, 7717 (42), supplement, October: 4–114.

Building (1999) 'Barcelona First Place to Win RIBA Medal', 19 March: 9.

Building (2000) 'We Hate to Say it But Charles Was Right', 265, 8130, 31 March: 36–41.

Building Design (1979) 'Midsummer at Milton Keynes, The Shopping Centre', 456, 27 July: 13–15.

Building Design (1988) 'Regional Criticalism', 889, June: 26–9.

Building Design (1991) 'Pelli Says Canary Tower "Started Out Slimmer" ', 1048, September 13: 6.

Building Design (2002) 'Rogers Tells Prescott "Show Me the Money" ', 1554, 1 November: 1.

Burke, E. (1958) *A Philosophical Enquiry into the Origin of our Ideas of the Sublime and Beautiful*, London: Routledge & Kegan Paul.

Caldwell, M. (1999) *A Short History of Rudeness*, New York: Picador.

Campbell, P. (1992) 'The Wearer as Much as the Frock', *London Review of Books*, 9 April: 19–20.

Carter, H. (2003) 'Glory of Greece, Grandeur of Rome . . . and Docks of Liverpool', *The Guardian*, 7 March.

Carter, J. (1987) 'The Ayatollah of QAG', *Architect's Journal*, 28 January: 27.

Carter, S. L. (1998) *Civility: Manners, Morals and the Etiquette of Democracy*, New York: Basic Books.

Casabella (1983) 'Lost Opportunities', 47, 494, September: 42–3.

Casabella (1987) 'I Grande Progetti di Barcellona', 51, 533, March: 36–9.

Castells, M. (1996) *The Rise of the Network Society*. Oxford: Blackwell.

Castells, M. and Hall P. (1994) *Technopoles of the World: The Making of Twenty-First Century Industrial Complexes*, London: Routledge.

Caute, D. (1988) *Sixty-Eight: The Year of the Barricades*, London: Hamilton.

Certeau, M. de (1984) *The Practice of Everyday Life*, trans. Stephen Rendall, Berkeley and Los Angeles, Calif.: University of California Press.

Chaney, E. (1998) *The Evolution of the Grand Tour: Anglo-Italian Cultural Relations since the Renaissance*, London: Cass.

Chilvers, I. (1990) *The Concise Oxford Dictionary of Art and Artists*, Oxford: Oxford University Press.

City Limits, 18 December 1987.

City Pride Strategic Planning Group (1994) *City Pride: A Focus for the Future. Manchester, Salford, Trafford and Tameside from the Present into the Twenty-First Century*, Manchester: City Pride Strategic Planning Group.

City Pride Strategic Planning Group (1998) *City Pride 2: Partnerships for a Successful Future. Manchester, Salford, Trafford and Tameside from the Present into the Twenty-First Century*, Manchester: City Pride Strategic Planning Group.

Clark, T. J. (1984) *The Painting of Modern Life: Paris in the Art of Manet and his Followers*, London: Thames & Hudson.

Collins, P. (1965) *Changing Ideas in Modern Architecture 1750–1950*, Montreal: McGill-Queens University Press.

Commission for Architecture and the Built Environment (2001a) Annual Report and Accounts.

Commission for Architecture and the Built Environment (2001b) Mission Statement.

Connaissance des Arts (1988) 'Quand L'Art Moderne Rejeunit Les Monuments: Liverpool – Dock Pour La Tate', 127, 314, April: 264–6.

Cook, P. (1986) 'London Collection', *Architectural Review*, CLXXX, 1076, October: 49–53.

Costa, L. (1957) 'O Relatório do Plano Piloto de Brasília', *Modulo*, 8.

Country Life (1991) 'Pushing Poundbury', 185, 42, 17 October: 62–3.

Coward, R. (2001) 'Wonderful, Foolish Dome', *The Guardian*, 13 March.

Cox, H. (1965) *The Secular City*, New York: Macmillan.

Bibliography

Crinson, M. (1996) *Empire Building: Orientalism and Victorian Architecture*, London: Routledge.

Crinson, M. (2002–3) 'Urbisville', *Mute*, 25, Winter–Spring: 20–3.

Crinson, M. (2003) *Modern Architecture and the End of Empire*, Aldershot: Ashgate.

Crosby Homes North West Ltd. (2002) *No. 1 Deansgate*, promotional brochure.

Cruickshank, D. (1986a) 'Visions of a Modern City', *Architect's Journal*, October, 28–31.

Cruickshank, D. (1986b) 'Buying the Big Three', *The Times Literary Supplement*, 24 October.

Cruickshank, D. (1987) 'Vision of Mersey', *Architectural Review*, CLXXXI, 1080, 55–64.

Cruickshank, D. (1991a) 'The Bride: Spirit of an Age', *Architect's Journal*, 2–9 January: 22–7.

Cruickshank, D. (1991b) 'Capital Ideas', *Architect's Journal*, 194, 24–5, 11–18 December: 22–67.

Cullen, G. (1949) 'Townscape Casebook', *Architectural Review*, 106, 636, December: 363–74.

Cullen, G. (1961) *The Concise Townscape*, London: Architectural Press.

Daniels, P. W. and Bobe, J. M. (1993) 'Extending the Boundary of the City of London? The Development of Canary Wharf', *Environment and Planning A*, 25: 539–52.

Davey, P. (1987) 'North Bank Show', *Architectural Review*, CLXXXI, 1084, June: 68–74.

Davey, P. (1989) 'Three on the Waterfront', *Architectural Review* CLXXXV, 1106, April: 46–54.

Davey, P. (1996) 'Delight: The Bride of Denmark', *Architectural Review*, CXCIX, 1191, May: 106.

Davey, P. (1998) 'Outrage', *Architectural Review*, CCIII, 1215, May: 37.

Davey, P. (1999a) 'Public Realm', *Architectural Review*, CCVI, 1229, July: 27–8.

Davey, P. (1999b) 'Urban Rescue', *Architectural Review*, CCVI, 1230, August: 26–7.

Davey, P. (2000a) 'Postmodern Urbanity', *Architectural Review*, CCVII, 1236, February: 34–5.

Davey, P. (2000b) 'Meeting the Millennium', *Architectural Review*, CCVII, 1238, April: 47.

Davey, P. (2000c) 'The Station Not the Airport', *Architectural Review* CCVII, 1240, June: 44–5.

Davey, P. (2000d) 'Quay Performance', *Architectural Review*, CCVII, 1241, July-August: 56–60

Davey, P. (2000e) 'Common Decency', *Architectural Review*, CCVIII, 1245, November: 44–5.

Davies, C. (1987) 'Ad Hoc in the Docks', *Architectural Review*, CLXXXI, 1080, February: 31–7.

Davies, C. (1990) 'Modernism is Alive and Well', *Architect's Journal*, 192, 2, 11 July: 24–5.

Davies, C. (1991) 'Eastern Promise', *Architect's Journal*, 193, 46, 11–18 December: 56–63.

Davis, M. (1990) *City of Quartz*, London: Verso.

Davis, M. (1999) *The Ecology of Fear: Los Angeles and the Imagination of Disaster*, London: Macmillan.

De Grey, S. (2001) interview with the author, London, 21 August.

DeMott, B. (1996) 'Seduced by Civility', *The Nation*, 9 December: 11–19.

De Tocqueville, A. (1958) *Journeys to England and Ireland* trans. George Lawrence and J. P. Meyer, London: Faber and Faber.

Dickens, C. (1858) *Hard Times for These Times*, London: Chapman and Hall.

Dixon, R. and Muthesius, S. (1978) *Victorian Architecture*, London: Thames and Hudson.

Domus (1974) 'Milton Keynes Development Corporation, Central Milton Keynes', 541, December.

Domus (2001) 'Il Monumento nel Museo', 834, February: 36–53.

Donald, J. (1999) *Imagining the Modern City*, Minneapolis: University of Minnesota Press.

Doron, G. M. (2002) 'Untitled: A Reply to Richard Rogers', *Archis*, 2: 41–3.

Duncan, C. (1995) *Civilizing Rituals: Inside Public Art Museums*, London: Routledge.

Dutton, J. A. (2000) *New American Urbanism: Re-forming the Suburban Metropolis*, Milan: Skira.

Edwards, B. (1992) *London Docklands: Urban Design in an Age of Deregulation*, Oxford: Butterworth Architecture.

Ellin, N. (1999) *Postmodern Urbanism*, Oxford: Blackwell.

Elsner, J. and Rubiés, J. P. (eds) (1999) *Voyages and Visions: Towards a Cultural History of Travel*, London: Reaktion.

Engels, F. (1993) *The Condition of the Working Class in England*, David McLellan (ed.), Oxford: Oxford University Press.

Financial Times (1984) 14 January: 4.

Forty, A. (2000) *Words and Buildings: A Vocabulary of Modern Architecture*, London: Thames and Hudson.

Foster and Partners (2001) *Foster Catalogue 2001*, Munich: Prestel.

Foucault, M. (1977) *Discipline and Punish: The Birth of the Prison*, trans. Alan Sheridan, London: Penguin.

Frampton, K. (1992) *Modern Architecture: A Critical History*, London: Thames and Hudson.

Frampton, K. (1995) *Studies in Tectonic Culture: The Poetics of Construction in Nineteenth and Twentieth Century Architecture*, Cambridge, Mass.: MIT Press.

Frampton, K. (1996) *Modern Architecture: A Critical Introduction*, London: Thames & Hudson.

Frampton, K. (1999) 'Seven Points for the Millennium: An Untimely Manifesto', *Architectural Review*, CCVI, 1233, November: 76–80.

Frantz, D. and Collins, C. (1999) *Celebration USA: Living in Disney's Brave New Town*, New York: Henry Holt & Co.

Freud, S. (1965) *New Introductory Lectures on Psychoanalysis*, New York: Norton & Co.

Freud, S. (1966) *Introductory Lectures on Psychoanalysis*, New York: Norton & Co.

Freud, S. (1977) *Introductory Lectures on Psychoanalysis,* trans. and ed. James Strachey, New York: Norton.

Freud, S. (1985a) *The Penguin Freud Library, Vol. 12: Civilization. Society and Religion*, London: Penguin.

Freud, S. (1985b) *The Penguin Freud Library, Vol. 14: Art and Literature*, London: Penguin.

Fried, M. (1967) 'Art and Objecthood', *Artforum*, June, 5, 10: 12–23.

GA Document Extra 12 (1999) *Norman Foster*.

Gaskell, E. (1849) *Mary Barton: A Tale of Manchester Life*, Leipzig: Bernard Tauchnitz.

Gaskell, E. (1998 [1855]) *North and South*, ed. Angus Easson, Oxford: Oxford University Press.

Garreau, J. (1991) *Edge City: Life on the New Urban Frontier*, New York: Doubleday.

Gifford, J., McWilliam, C. and Walker, D. (1984) *The Buildings of Scotland: Edinburgh*, London: Penguin.

Gilloch, G. (2002) *Walter Benjamin: Critical Constellations*, London: Polity.

Glancey, J. (1989) *New British Architecture*, London: Thames & Hudson.

Glancey, J. (2000) 'A Feast for the Eyes', *The Guardian*, 27 November.

Glancey, J. (2001) *London: Bread and Circuses*, London: Verso.

Glancey, J. (2002) 'Visions of Utopia', *The Guardian,* 30 October.

Glendinning, M., and Muthesius, S. (1994) *Tower Block: Modern Public Housing in England, Scotland, Wales and Northern Ireland*, New Haven and London: Yale University Press.

Gómez, J. J. (2001) 'El Modelo de "Ciudad Dispersa" Se Impone en el Urbanismo Europeo', *El Pais*, 28 July.

González, A. and Lacuesta, R. (2002) *Barcelona: Architectural Guide 1929–2002*, Barcelona: Editorial Gustavo Gili.

Gosling, D. (1996) *Gordon Cullen: Visions of Urban Design*, London: Academy Editions.

Graham, B. (1989) *Bruce Graham of SOM,* New York: Rizzoli.

Greater London Authority (2002a) *Making Space for Londoners*, July.

Greater London Authority (2002b) *Squares Annual Report 2002: Trafalgar Square and Parliament Square Garden*, November.

Guardian, The (2000) 'Last Days of the Dome – No One Ever Quite Knew What it was For', 29 December.

Guardian, The (2001) 'There for What Purpose?', 7 September.

Habermas, J. (1989) *Structural Transformation of the Public Sphere: an Inquiry into a Category of Bourgeois Society,* trans. Thomas Burger and Frederick Lawrence, Cambridge: Polity Press.

Bibliography

Habermas, J. (1991) *The Structural Transformation of the Public Sphere: An Inquiry into the Category of Bourgeois Society*, Cambridge, Mass.: MIT Press.

Hall, C. (2002) *Civilising Subjects: Metropole and Colony in the English Imagination, 1830–1867*, Cambridge: Polity.

Hall, J. (2003) 'A Very Civic Servant', *The Guardian*, 1 October.

Hall, J. A. (ed.) (1995) *Civil Society: Theory, History, Comparison*, London: Polity Press.

Hall, P. (1969) *London 2000*, London: Faber & Faber.

Hall, P. (1989) *London 2001*, London: Unwin Hyman.

Hall, P. (1996) *Cities of Tomorrow*, Oxford: Blackwell.

Hall, P. (1999) *Cities in Civilization*, London: Phoenix.

Hall, P. (2003) 'Getting the Message', *The Guardian*, 19 February.

Harbison, R. (1977) *Eccentric Spaces*, London: Deutsch.

Hardingham, S. (2001) *London: A Guide to Recent Architecture*, London: Ellipsis.

Hartwell, C. (2001) *Pevsner Architectural Guides: Manchester*, London: Penguin.

Harvey, D. (2000) *Spaces of Hope*, Edinburgh: Edinburgh University Press.

Harwood, E. and Powers, A. (eds) (2001) 'The Festival of Britain', special issue, *Twentieth Century Studies*, 5.

Haslam, D. (1999) *Manchester, England: The Story of the Pop Cult City*, London: Fourth Estate.

Hatton, B. (1990) 'The Development of London's Docklands', *Lotus International*, 67: 55–89.

Hatton, D. (1988) *Inside Left: The Story So Far*, London: Bloomsbury.

Haug, C. J. (1982) *Leisure and Urbanism in Nineteenth Century Nice*, Lawrence: The Regents Press of Kansas.

Hendry, F. (1988) 'Tate and Bile: Liverpool's Bitter Artistic Pill', *The Guardian* (letters), 26 May: 20.

Hetherington, P. (2002) 'Rogers Laments Failing Vision', *The Guardian*, 26 January.

Hetherington, P. (2003) 'The New Town that Could Be a New City', *The Guardian*, 19 February.

Heynen, H. (1999) *Architecture and Modernity: A Critique*, Cambridge, Mass.: MIT Press.

Hibbert, C. (1987) *The Grand Tour*, London: Thames Methuen.

Hillier, B. (1996) *Space is the Machine*, Cambridge: Cambridge University Press.

Hillier, B., Peponis, J. and Simpson, J. (1982) 'National Gallery Schemes Analysed', *Architect's Journal*, 27 October.

HM Government, Department for Culture, Media and Sport (2000) *Better Public Buildings*, London: HMSO.

HM Government, Department of Environment, Transport and the Regions (1999) *Towards an Urban Renaissance*, London: HMSO.

Holston, J. (1989) *The Modernist City: An Anthropological Critique of Brasília*, Chicago: University of Chicago Press.

Hooper, J. (1986) *The Spaniards: A Portrait of the New Spain*, London: Penguin.

Hughes, J. and Sadler, S. (eds) (2000) *Non-Plan: Essays in Freedom, Participation and Change in Modern Architecture and Urbanism*, Oxford: Architectural Press.

Hughes, Q. (1964) *Seaport : Architecture and Townscape in Liverpool*, London: Lund Humphries.

Hughes, R. (1992) *Barcelona*, London: Harvill.

Hussey, C. (1927) *The Picturesque: Studies in a Point of View*, London: Putnam.

Hutchinson, M. (1989) *The Prince of Wales: Right or Wrong? An Architect Replies*, London: Faber and Faber.

Hutton, W. (1996) *The State We're In*, London: Vintage.

Irving, W. (1853) *The Alhambra*, London: H. G. Bohn.

Jacobs, J. (1962) *Death and Life of Great American Cities*, London: Jonathan Cape.

Jacobs, J. (2000) *The Death and Life of Great American Cities*, London: Pimlico.

Jacobson, H. (2000) 'Curiouser and Curiouser', *The Independent*, 30 November.

Jacoby, H. (1977) *Architectural Drawings, 1968–1976*, London: Thames & Hudson.

Janusczczak, W. (1988) 'Stirling Statement', *Architect's Journal* 27, 187, 6 July: 27–43.

Jencks, C. (1977a) *The Language of Post-Modern Architecture*, London: Academy Editions.

Jencks, C. (1977b) 'MBM and the Barcelona School', *Architectural Review* CLXI, 961, March.

Jencks, C. (1983) *Modern Movements in Architecture*, London: Penguin.

Jencks, C. (1985) *Modern Movements in Architecture*, London: Penguin.

Jencks, C. (ed.) (1991) 'Post-Modern Triumphs in London', *Architectural Design*, profile 91.

Jencks, C. (1993) *Heteropolis: Los Angeles, the Riots and the Strange Beauty of Hetro-Architecture*, London: Academy Editions.

Jenkins, D. (1992) *Clore Gallery, Tate Gallery Liverpool: James Stirling, Michael Wilford and Associates*, London: Phaidon.

Jenkins, D. (2000) *On Foster . . . Foster On*, Munich: Prestel.

Jenkins, S. (1986) 'Master Builders with Feet of Clay' *Sunday Times*, 21 December: 28.

Jewell, N. (2002) 'The Fall and Rise of the British Mall', *Journal of Architecture*, 6, Winter: 317–78.

Jones, E. and Woodward. C. (1992) *A Guide to the Architecture of London*, London: Weidenfeld & Nicholson.

Joyce, P. (2003) *The Rule of Freedom: Liberalism and the Modern City*, London: Verso.

Kalliney, P. (2002) 'Globalization, Postcoloniality, and the Problem of Literary Studies in *The Satanic Verses*', *Modern Fiction Studies* 48, 1, Spring: 50–82.

Kaprow, A. (1993) *Essays on the Blurring of Art and Life,* ed. Jeff Kelley, Berkeley and Los Angeles: University of California Press.

Kay-Shuttleworth, J. (1970 [1832]) *The Moral and Physical Condition of the Working Classes Employed in Cotton Manufacture in Manchester*, London: Cassell

Kennedy, M. (2000a) 'Museum Fined in Portico Fiasco', *The Guardian*, 17 November: 6.

Kennedy, M. (2000b) 'Two Years and £100m Later, the Court Opens', *The Guardian*, 6 December.

Kenny, M. and Kertzer, D. I. (eds) (1983) *Urban Life in Mediterranean Europe: Anthropological Perspectives*, Urbana, Ill.: University of Illinois Press.

Krauss, R. (1993) *The Optical Unconscious*, Cambridge, Mass. and London: MIT Press.

Krier, L. (1992) *Architecture and Urban Design 1967–1992*, London: Academy Editions.

Langmuir, E. (1989) *The Pan Art Dictionary Vol. 1 – 1300–1800*, London: Pan Books.

Laubin, C. (2003) Letter to the author, 3 March.

Lawrence, D. H. (1956 [1913]) *Sons and Lovers*, London: Heinemann.

Leach, N. (ed.) (1997) *Rethinking Architecture: A Reader in Cultural Theory*, London: Routledge.

Leach, N. (ed.) (1999) *Architecture and Revolution*, London: Routledge.

Leach, N. (ed.) (2002) *The Hieroglyphics of Space: Reading and Experiencing the Modern Metropolis*, London: Routledge.

Le Corbusier (1929) *The City of To-Morrow and its Planning*, London: J. Rodker.

Le Corbusier (1989) 'Corb on Spontaneous Theatre', *Architectural Review*, CLXXXV, 1108, June: 80–3.

Lefebvre, H. (1991) *The Production of Space*, Oxford: Blackwell.

Le Gates, R. T. and Stout, F. (eds.) (1996) *The City Reader*, London: Routledge.

Lerup, L. (2000) *After the City*, Cambridge, Mass.: MIT Press.

Lister, D. (2000) 'The Great Court Opens with its Back to the Wall', *The Independent*, 6 December.

Llewelyn-Davies, R. (1951) 'Endless Architecture', *Architectural Association Journal*, July: 106–12.

Llewelyn-Davies Weeks Forestier-Walker and Bor (1970) *The Plan for Milton Keynes*, Wavendon: Milton Keynes Development Corporation.

London Docklands Development Corporation (LDDC) (1990) *London Docklands Architectural Review*, Huntingdon: LPL.

Lynch, K. (1961) *The Image of the City*, Cambridge, Mass.: MIT Press.

Bibliography

McConnell, T. (2002) 'Manc's Man', *Property Week*, 13 September.

Mace, R. (1976) *Trafalgar Square, Emblem of Empire*, London: Lawrence & Wishart.

McGuire, P. (2000) 'The Great Court', *Architectural Review*, CCVIII, 1236, February: 74–9.

McKean, C. (1980) 'A Masterpiece of Order out of Chaos', *The Times*, 1 April.

Malone, P. (ed., 1996) *City, Capital and Water*, London: Routledge.

Manchester City Council (1984) *Manchester City Centre Local Plan*, Manchester: Manchester City Council.

Manchester City Council (1995) *City Development Guide*.

Manchester Evening News (2002) 8 October.

Marcuse, H. (1956) *Eros and Civilization: A Philosophical Inquiry into Freud*, London: Routledge & Kegan Paul.

Marcuse, H. (1964) *One-Dimensional Man*, London: Routledge & Kegan Paul.

Maré, E. de (1996) 'Gordon Cullen: My Friend and Colleague', *Architectural Review*, CC, 1196, October: 81–5.

Martin. A. (2003) 'There is Such a Thing as Smoke Without Fire', *The Wharf*, 23 January: 4.

Marwick, A. (1980) *Class: Image and Reality*, Collins, London.

Marx, K. (1972) *Economy, Class and Social Revolution*, ed. Z. A. Jordan, London: Nelson.

Mateo, J. L. (1985) 'Deu Anys D'Arquitectura Catalana 1975–85', *Quaderns*: 164

Mateo, J. L. and Cervelló, M. (1993) 'Entrevista con Pasqual Maragall', *Quaderns*: 7–17.

Maxwell, R. (1974–5) 'The Beautiful City', *Architectural Association Quarterly*, 6, 3–4, unpaginated reprint for MKDC.

Mead, W. E. (1914) *The Grand Tour in the Eighteenth Century*, Boston and New York: Houghton Mifflin.

Melhuish, C. (2000) 'Bohigas on the Public and the Market in Barcelona', *Architect's Journal*, 7 December: 8.

Mendoza, E. (1991) *Sin Notícias de Gurb*, Barcelona: Seix Barral.

Merrifield, A. (1993) 'The Canary Wharf Debacle', *Environment and Planning A*, 25: 1247–65.

Middleton, M. (1991) *Cities in Transition: the Regeneration of Britain's Inner Cities*, London: Michael Joseph.

Miles, M., Hall, T. and Borden, I. (eds) (2000) *The City Cultures Reader*, London: Routledge.

Millennium Experience (2000) *Millennium Dome Official Handbook*, London: New Millennium Experience Company.

Mitchell, W. (1995) *City of Bits: Space, Place and the Infobahn*, Cambridge, Mass. and London: MIT Press.

MKDC (*c.*1974) *Leisure in Milton Keynes* (pamphlet), Milton Keynes: MKDC

Mkweb.co.uk/shopping/displayarticle.asp?id=215. Accessed online 10 July 2004.

Moore, C. (2001) *You Have to Pay for the Public Life*, Cambridge, Mass. and London: MIT Press.

Morris, S. (2000) 'British Museum's £97m Makeover that Became a Pale Imitation', *The Guardian*, 25 August: 3.

Morris, W. (1902) *Architecture, Industry and Wealth: Collected Papers,* London, Bombay and New York: Longmans, Green.

Morris, W. (1984) *News from Nowhere and Selected Writings and Designs*, London: Penguin.

Muir, H. 'Mandela Statue Judged Wrong for Square', *The Guardian*, 7 May: 9.

Mumford, E. (2000) *The CIAM Discourse on Urbanism 1928–1960*, Cambridge, Mass. and London: MIT Press.

Observer (2003) 'Housing Crisis', supplement, 6 April: 1–6.

Olympia and York (1990) *Canary Wharf Prospectus*.

Orwell, G. (1967 [1938]) *Homage to Catalonia*, London: Secker and Warburg.

Prince of Wales, HRH the (1984) The 150th Anniversary of the Royal Institute of British Architects, A speech by HRH the Prince of Wales, Royal Gala Evening at Hampton Court Palace, 30 May. Online. Available www.princeofwales.gov.uk/ (accessed 25 February 2003).

Prince of Wales, HRH the (1987) The Corporation of London Planning and Communication Committee's Annual Dinner, A Speech by HRH the Prince of Wales, Mansion House, London, 1 December. Online. Available www.princeofwales.gov.uk (accessed 25 February 2003).

Prince of Wales, HRH the (1989) *A Vision of Britain*, London: Doubleday.

Packer, W. (1988) 'Learning to Live in the Albert Dock', *Financial Times*, 31 May: 19.

Parkinson, M. (1985) *Liverpool on the Brink*, Hermitage: Policy Journals.

Pawley, M. (1998) *Terminal Architecture*, London: Reaktion.

Pawley, M. (1999) *Norman Foster: A Global Architecture*, London: Thames & Hudson.

Pearman, H. (2000) 'Empire in the Sun', *Sunday Times Magazine*, 26 November.

Pearman, H. (2002) 'Lofty Ideals, Low Impact', *The Sunday Times*, 17 March.

Peck, J. and Ward, K. (eds) (2002) *City of Revolution: Restructuring Manchester*, Manchester: Manchester University Press.

Pelli, C. (1990) *Cesar Pelli: Buildings and Projects, 1965–1990*, New York: Rizzoli.

Pelli, C. (1993) *Cesar Pelli: Selected and Current Works*, Mulgrave, Victoria: Images.

Pevsner, N. (1964) *The Englishness of English Art : An Expanded and Annotated Version of the Reith Lectures Broadcast in October and November 1955*, London: Penguin.

Pevsner, N. (1969) *The Buildings of England*, vol. 36, *Lancashire*, vol. 1, *The Industrial and Commercial South*, London: Penguin.

Piper, J. (1947) 'Pleasing Decay', *Architectural Review*, CII, September: 93.

Planner (1993) 'Deconstructing the City: The Experience of London Docklands, 79, 2, February: 16–18.

Pople, N. (2001) 'Caught in the Web', *RIBA Journal*, 108, 2, February: 36–44.

Popper, K. (1966) *The Open Society and its Enemies*, London: Routledge & Kegan Paul.

Porter, R. (1995) *London: A Social History*, Cambridge, Mass.: Harvard University Press, 1995.

Powell, K. (1992) *Norman Foster and the Architecture of Flight*, London: Blueprint.

Powell, K. (ed.) (1993) *World Cities: London*, London: Academy Editions.

Powell, K. (1994) *Richard Rogers*, Zürich: Artemis.

Powell, K. (2000) 'Holding Court', *Architect's Journal*, 7 December: 24–31.

Press, I. (1979) *City as Context: Urbanism and Behavioural Constraints in Seville*, Urbana, Ill.: University of Illinois Press.

Progressive Architecture (1988a) 'Tate Gallery Liverpool', 69, 10: 35–6.

Progressive Architecture (1988b) 'Americans in London Docklands; Architects: César Pelli, Kohn Pedersen Fox Associates, and Skidmore Owings & Merrill', 69, 6, June: 27–29.

Putnam, R. D. (2000) *Bowling Alone: The Collapse and Revival of American Community*, New York: Touchstone.

Rasmussen, S. E. (1937) *London: The Unique City*, London: Jonathan Cape.

Rasmussen, S. E. (1980) 'Open Plan City', *Architectural Review*, CLXVIII, 1003, September: 141–3.

Rawsthorn, A. (2000) 'Great Court Finally Deserves its Name', *Financial Times*, 27 November: 24.

RIBA Journal (1988) 'Tate Gallery Liverpool', 95, 8, August: 52–5.

Richards, J. M. (1942) *The Bombed Buildings of Britain: A Record of Architectural Casualties 1940–41*, with notes by John Summerson, London: Architectural Press.

Richards, J. M. (1953) *An Introduction to Modern Architecture*, London: Penguin.

Richards, J. M. (1958) *The Functional Tradition in Early Industrial Buildings*, London: Architectural Press.

Richards, J. M. (1980) *Memoirs of an Unjust Fella: An Autobiography*, London: Weidenfeld and Nicholson.

Richardson, C. and Smith, G. (2001) *Britannia Italia Germania: Taste and Travel in the Nineteenth Century*, Edinburgh: VARIE.

Robira, R. Tello i (2002) *Espais Públics: Mirades Multidisciplinàries*, Barcelona: Pòrtic.

Rogers, L. (1995) 'But is it Architecture?', *RIBA Journal*, 102, 11, November: 6–11.

Bibliography

Rogers, R. (1988) *Richard Rogers 1978–1988*, Tokyo: A+U Publishing.

Rogers, R. (1997) *Cities for a Small Planet*, London: Faber & Faber.

Rogers, R. (2001) interview with the author, 8 May.

Rogers, R. and Fisher, M. (1992) *A New London*, London: Penguin.

Rogers, R. with Power, A. (2000) *Cities for a Small Country*, London: Faber & Faber.

Ross, A. (2000) *The Celebration Chronicles: Life, Liberty, and the Pursuit of Property Values in Disney's New Town*, London: Verso.

Rossi, A. (1982) *The Architecture of the City*, trans. Diane Ghirado and Joan Ockman, Cambridge, Mass. and London: MIT Press.

Rowe, C. and Koetter, F. (1978) *Collage City*, Cambridge, Mass. and London: MIT Press.

Rowe, P. G. (1997) *Civic Realism*, Cambridge, Mass.: MIT Press.

Ruskin, J. (1851–3) *The Stones of Venice*, 3 vols., London: Smith, Elder.

Russell, F. (ed.) (1985) *Richard Rogers*, London: Academy Editions.

Rybczynski, W. (1996) *City Life*, New York: Touchstone Books.

Rykwert, J. (2000) *The Seduction of Place*, London: Wiedenfeld & Nicholson.

Said, E. W. (1978) *Orientalism*, London: Routledge.

Salmon, F. (2000) *Building on Ruins: The Rediscovery of Rome and English Architecture*, Aldershot: Ashgate.

Saumarez Smith, C. (2001) interview with the author, 27 September.

Saumarez Smith, C. (2003) Draft of Paul Mellon lecture, February.

Schoon, N. (2001) *The Chosen City*, London: Spon.

Scotsman (2003) 'A Man with Designs on a Better Britain', 17 February.

Scott, A. J. and Soja E. (eds) (1996) *The City: Los Angeles and Urban Theory at the End of the Twentieth Century*, Berkeley, Los Angeles and London: University of California Press.

Scruton, R. (1994) *The Classical Vernacular: Architectural Principles in an Age of Nihilism*, Manchester: Carcanet.

Sebald, W. G. (1996) *The Emigrants*, London: Harvill.

Seldon, A. (ed.) (2001) *The Blair Effect: The Blair Government 1997–2001*, London: Little, Brown.

Self, P. (ed. (1972) *New Towns: The British Experience*, London: Town and Country Planning Association.

Sennett, R. (1977) *The Fall of Public Man*, London: Faber & Faber.

Sennett, R. (1986) *Flesh and Stone*, London: Faber & Faber.

Sharp, D. (1989) 'City as Theatre', *Architectural Review*, CLXXXV, 1108, June: 58–65.

Sherwin-White, A. N. (1939) *The Roman Citizenship*, Oxford: Clarendon Press.

Shostack, L. and Lock, D. (1980) 'Milton Keynes', *New Towns in National Development*, Milton Keynes: IFHP/Open University.

Slessor, C. (1996) 'Social Life', *Architectural Review*, CC, 1193, July: 4–5.

Solkin, D. H. (1993) *Painting for Money: The Visual Arts and the Public Sphere in Eighteenth Century England*, New Haven and London: Yale University Press.

Sontag, S. (1978) *On Photography*, London: Penguin.

Spens, M. (ed.) (1996) *The Recovery of the Modern: Architectural Review 1980–95: Key Text and Critique*, Oxford: Butterworth.

Stallybrass, P. and White, A. (1986) *The Poetics and Politics of Transgression*, London: Routledge.

Stirling, J., Wilford, M. and Associates (1994) *Buildings and Projects with an Introduction by Robert Maxwell*, London: Thames & Hudson.

Street-Porter, J. (2001) 'I'm a Shameless Enthusiast', *The Independent*, 11 February.

Sudjic, D. (1991) *The Guardian*, 2 September: 34.

Sudjic, D. (1992) *The 100-Mile City*, London: Deutsch.

Sudjic, D. (2002) 'War and Pieces', *Observer* (review), 30 June: 10.

Sunday Times (2000) 'At Home or in the Dome it was a Night to Remember', 2 January: 4.

Tafuri, M. (1976) *Architecture and Utopia: Design and Capitalist Development*, Cambridge, Mass.: MIT Press.

Tarn, J. N. (1965) 'Review of Q. Hughes' *Seaport*', *Town Planning Review*, 36, 3, October: 211–12.

Tate Gallery (1986) *The Tate Gallery 1984–6: Illustrated Biennial Report*, London: Tate Gallery.

Tate Gallery (1988) *The Tate Gallery 1986–8: Illustrated Biennial Report*, London: Tate Gallery.

Tello i Robira, R. (ed.) *Espais Publics: Mirades Multidisciplinàries*, Barcelona: Portic.

Theroux, P. (1985) *The Kingdom by the Sea*, London: Penguin.

Thornley, A. (ed.) (1992) *The Crisis of London*, London: Routledge.

The Times (2002) 'The New Manchester', supplement, 6 July.

Town Planning Review (1991) 'The London Docklands Development Corporation (LDDC), 1981–1991', 62, 3, July: 311–30.

Treanor, J. (1999) 'Welcome to America, E14', *The Guardian*, 6 March.

Turnbull, T. (1997) 'In an Ideal World', *Times*, magazine, 2 August: 23–6.

Tyrwhitt, J., Sert, J.-L. and Rogers, E. N. (eds) (1952) *CIAM 8: The Heart of the City – Towards the Humanisation of Urban Life*, London: Lund Humphries.

Vidler, A. (1992) *The Architectural Uncanny*, Cambridge, Mass.: MIT Press.

Vidler, A. (2000) *Warped Space: Art, Architecture and Anxiety in Modern Culture*, Cambridge, Mass. and London: MIT Press.

Walker, D. (1982) *The Architecture and Planning of Milton Keynes*, London: Architectural Press.

Walker, J. (1997) 'Prince Charming?', *Architectural Review*, 202, 1205, July: 68–72.

Wallis, B. (ed.) (1984) *Art After Modernism: Rethinking Representation*, New York and Boston: The New Museum of Contemporary Art in association with David R. Godine.

Walsh, K. (1992) *The Representation of the Past: Museums and Heritage in a Post Modern World*, London: Routledge.

Ward, C. (1993) *New Town Home Town*, London: Gulbenkian Foundation.

Ward, C. (2000) 'High Density Living', *Prospect*, 54, July: 38–41.

Watkin, D. (1977) *Morality and Architecture: The Development of a Theme in Architectural History and Theory from the Gothic Revival to the Modern Movement*, Oxford: Clarendon Press.

Watkin, D. (1982) *The English Vision: The Picturesque in Architecture, Landscape and Garden Design*, London: Murray.

Webber, M. M. (ed.) (1964) *Explorations into Urban Structure*, Philadelphia: University of Pennsylvania Press.

Webber, M. M. (1968) *Beyond the Industrial Age* and *Permissive Planning*, London: CES.

Weston, R. (1988) 'Tate Gallery Liverpool', *Architect's Journal*, 6 July.

White, M. (2000) 'Jools, Her Majesty and a Cast of 10,000', *The Guardian*, 1 January: 3.

Wiener, M. J. (1980) *English Culture and the Decline of the Industrial Spirit 1850–1980*, London: Penguin.

Williams, R. (1961) *Culture and Society 1780–1950*, London: Penguin.

Williams, R. (1973) *The Country and the City*, London: Chatto & Windus.

Williams, R. J. (2000) *After Modern Sculpture*, Manchester: Manchester University Press.

Williams, R. J. (2003) 'Behave', *The Art Book*, 10, 4, September: 21–3.

Wilton, A. and Bignamini, I. (1997) *Grand Tour: The Lure of Italy in the Eighteenth Century*, London: Tate Gallery.

Winter, J. (1980) 'Shopping Centre, Milton Keynes' *Architectural Review*, CLXVIII, 1003, September: 144–56.

Wirth, L. (1938) 'Urbanism as a Way of Life', *American Journal of Sociology*, XLIV, July: 1–24.

Wittkower, R. (1949) 'Architectural Principles in the Age of Humanism', *Studies of the Warburg Institute* XIX.

Wolfe, I. de (1949) 'Townscape', *Architectural Review*, CVI, 636, December: 363–74.

Bibliography

Wolfe, I. de (1971) 'Civilia: The End of Sub Urban Man', special issue, *Architectural Review*, CXLIX.

World Architecture (1992) 'Towering Footing: Cesar Pelli & Associates', 17: 68–9.

Worpole, K. (2001) *Here Comes the Sun: Architecture and Public Space in 20th Century European Culture*, London: Reaktion Books.

Wright, P. (1985) *On Living in an Old Country: The National Past in Contemporary Britain*, London: Verso.

Wright, P. (1993) *A Journey Through Ruins: A Keyhole Portrait of British Postwar Life and Culture*, London: Flamingo.

Young, E. (2002) 'Through the Looking Glass', *RIBA Journal* 109, 7, July: 30–9.

Zweibach, B. (1975) *Civility and Disobedience*, Cambridge: Cambridge University Press.

Zukin, S. (1982) *Loft Living: Culture and Capital in Urban Change*, Baltimore and London: Johns Hopkins University Press.

Zukin, S. (1991) *Landscapes of Power: From Detroit to Disney World*, Berkeley and Los Angeles, Calif.: University of California Press.

Zukin, S. (1992) 'The City as a Landscape of Power: London and New York as Global Finance Capitals', in L. Budd and S. Whimster (eds), *Global Finance and Urban Living: A Study of Metropolitan Change*, London: Routledge.

Index

Page numbers in *italic* indicate illustrations.